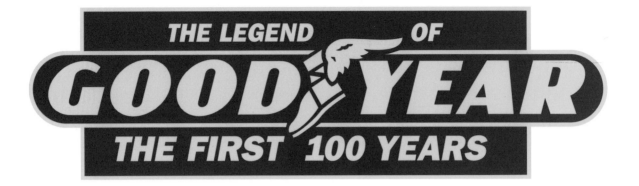

For Becky Tusso,

Best Wishes,

Jeff Rodly 12/97

JEFFREY L. RODENGEN

Also by Jeff Rodengen

The Legend of Chris-Craft

IRON FIST: *The Lives of Carl Kiekhaefer*

Evinrude-Johnson and The Legend of OMC

Serving The Silent Service: The Legend of Electric Boat

The Legend of Dr Pepper/Seven-Up

The Legend of Honeywell

The Legend of Briggs & Stratton

The Legend of Ingersoll-Rand

The Legend of Stanley: 150 Years of The Stanley Works

The MicroAge Way

The Legend of Halliburton

The Legend of York International

The Legend of Nucor Corporation

The Legend of Amdahl

The Legend of AMD

The Legend of Applied Materials

The Legend of Echlin

The Legend of AMP

The Legend of Cessna

The Legend of Pfizer

Publisher's Cataloging in Publication
Prepared by Quality Books Inc.

Rodengen, Jeffrey L.
    The legend of Goodyear /Jeffrey L. Rodengen.
    p. cm.
    Includes bibliographical references and index.
    ISBN 0-945903-35-9

    1. Goodyear Tire and rubber Company 2. Tire industry—United States. 3. Rubber industry and trade—United States. I. Title

HD9161.U54R64 1997   338.7'62782'0973
QBI97-40258

Write Stuff Syndicate, Inc.

1515 Southeast 4th Avenue • Fort Lauderdale, FL 33316
1-800-900-Book (1-800-900-2665) • (954) 462-6657

Library of Congress Catalog Card Number 96-61249
ISBN 0-945903-35-9

Completely produced in the United States of America
10 9 8 7 6 5 4 3 2 1

TABLE OF CONTENTS

FOREWORD

By A.J. Foyt

I T IS AN HONOR to be able to contribute to a book celebrating Goodyear's 100th anniversary, because in my book Goodyear has been a winner both on and off the racetrack. It's hard to imagine racing without the Goodyear name stuck on just about every car, trailer, helmet and driver suit, but it is equally hard to imagine what else would be missing without Goodyear. From radiator hoses to belts, and from automobile and truck tires to landing on the moon, Goodyear has touched — and changed — the world as few companies could.

One area that I can comment on with some authority is racing. My relationship with Goodyear began during the 1963 Indianapolis 500. In those days, Goodyear made tires for stock cars, not for Indy cars. Firestone gave Smokey Yunick a special tire, because the roadster he built was lighter, they said. Mine was just as light, and they wouldn't give me these special tires. I even had titanium brake drums to save every ounce I could. I didn't believe them. I felt it was because Smokey's cars were big in NASCAR and Firestone was battling like hell with Goodyear down there in the Southern stock-car circuit, so they were just playing favorites. Goodyear had just gotten started in racing and they had a pretty good stock-car tire, so they were starting to bother Firestone. Well, I figured if they wanted to screw around with tradition, then I could, too. There wasn't anything in the rules that said you had to run on Firestone tires; it was just expected.

I called Goodyear.

I went straight to my garage and called Tony Webner, who was then director of racing for Goodyear in Akron, and I said, "Listen, we've been runnin' on these skinny, cast-iron tires for so long, and puttin' up with no bite on the track, so why don't you all come on down and have a try at it. I'll run your tires. And, by the way, bring some of those wide stock-car tires with you."

Goodyear brought a supply of their Stock Car Special tires. They were wider than Firestone's, and lower. And slower. It would have made me feel real good if they had come down there and just blown everybody away with the wide tires, but they had been developed for a 3,800-pound stock car and for the high banks of the NASCAR tracks. Indy was a whole other ball game. Goodyear hadn't done any development work on new racing tires for Indianapolis, so I guess I shouldn't have expected them to do any better.

When it comes down to it, I'm as loyal as the next guy. No, I'm a hell of a lot more loyal than the next guy. So when Firestone turned around and gave those other guys special tires, that was too much. It was time for me to switch. I felt personally responsible for bringing Goodyear to the Speedway, and so I made up my mind right there and then that I was going to help them do something about it. I told them that if they would make arrangements to rent the Indy track after that year's 500, I would come and test the tires.

I thrive on controversy. I wore a Goodyear cap every day, and that really got to the Firestone people. But they were so damn cocky. There wasn't a thing in the world anybody could do to shake their hold on the Indianapolis 500. Many had tried over the years, and all of them had failed.

They just hadn't been up against A.J. Foyt before.

Right after the Indy 500 in 1963, Goodyear rented the track for a couple of weeks and we got started on a very tough task. It's tough to push around a company the size of Firestone — unless you've got a very good product.

The one thing we had in our favor was that Goodyear was a lot bigger than Firestone, so they had the money to spend. And it seemed to me, too, that there was more to it than just wanting to win Indianapolis. They kept telling everybody — the press and TV and anybody who would listen — that they were in racing to give their company a "vital" image for the youth market. "They're buying a lot of tires," they said. But I felt it was as much to get to their crosstown rivals, Firestone, as anything. So, what better way to get under their skins than to win racing's greatest prize.

Their first batch of tires wasn't much better than the stock-car tires they had brought down before the race, but we had to start somewhere. I took the roadster out and tested tire after tire, telling them each time what I thought this tire needed and what particular synthetic compound felt best, what stuck better in the turns or broke loose or whatever.

When you start an engine at Indianapolis, there are automatically a couple hundred people in the stands in Turn One. They just sort of materialize. That's how popular the Speedway is. It's open year round for tours, and a lot of people come there just to sit in the stands and pretend that there are race cars on the track. If there happens to be one, people come from all over town the minute they hear an engine running. The word spreads fast.

Among these fans in the stands, we started to notice more and more familiar faces. They wore sunglasses, and hats almost pulled down over their eyes but we knew who they were: Firestone engineers. We went right about our work, and every once in a while somebody would hold up a pit board for me that said "A.J. 158.8" That sent them running like hell right out of the stands. We weren't going that fast, of course, but it was fun to keep them moving around. I'm sure they went to the nearest phone and called Akron: "These bastards are going seven miles an hour faster than the track record!"

That only worked a couple of times, and then they started bringing their own stopwatches. But it was fun while it lasted.

To get a better picture, Goodyear hired a whole bunch of other drivers, including Johnny Rutherford and Don Branson in roadsters and Bobby Marshman in a Lotus Ford. They even tried an English four-wheel-drive Ferguson with Jack Fairman driving, but that didn't work too well, because he couldn't get through the first turn without hitting the wall.

But Goodyear was doing it the right way. If they were going to build improved tires for Indy, they were going to build them for all the cars, not just for a few they picked out. I became sort of the chief tire tester, for a couple of reasons: One, I had gotten there first; two, I could tell a lot better what was happening out on the track.

I get used to the way the suspension feels, too. It's got a sort of pulse that I can feel in my fingertips, and I can tell the instant anything changes. This is why you usually see me in the pits before something breaks, and not upside a wall after it breaks. It's also why I was able to tell Goodyear a lot about their tires. We didn't spend a lot of time patching up my race car or trying to figure out why it was spinning.

All the driving skill in the world couldn't get the extra mile an hour I needed out of the Goodyear tires to get them in the show at Indy in

1964. I tried every combination. I changed weight around on the car. We changed everything. The Goodyears were a mile an hour slower than the Firestones. That might not sound like a lot, but one mile an hour could win just about any 500 if it's coming under the wheels of a top-running car.

Goodyear had a tire in development, however, that could have made the difference. I went to Jim Loulan. "Jim, you've got a tire in Akron that will get Goodyear in the race. Win it, in fact," I said.

"We've been through this before, A.J.," he said. "My engineers say it isn't the tire for Indy. They're afraid of it."

"Listen, Jim," I said. "I'm the one who was out there on it, not the damn engineers. It's a safe tire, and if you don't use it, you're not gonna make the race."

It was no use. They had a tire that was exactly the right compound and tread pattern, and they wouldn't release it. Firestone expected them to run it. They would have run it if they had it.

I even spoke with Goodyear President Vic Holt. "Vic, you gotta tell those guys to let me use that tire," I said. Vic said that he'd have to go by what his development people said. "They're experts," he said. "It's our corporate policy to listen to our engineers. I said, "Okay, there's no other choice. I'm running Firestones."

Even though I thought Goodyear was wrong not to release the tire, it was to their credit that they stuck to their guns. Goodyear doesn't like to play in the gray area. They always want to do the right thing. Safety is everything to them. If one engineer says it might not be safe, Goodyear won't take a chance.

At the last moment, Goodyear released the tire for the race, but it was too late. Even though I had to run Firestones, I wore my Goodyear suit. It wasn't as finely embroidered as the Firestone suits. The winged foot between the "Good" and the "Year" looked more like a carrot than a winged foot. But I wore it. I won the race — my second of four Indianapolis 500's — but I refused to accept Firestone's check.

Not long after I went down to San Angelo, Texas, where Goodyear's test track was. I went down there with my Indy car to break the world's closed-circuit speed record. The record was 183 miles an hour and had been set a couple of years before on Chrysler's test track in Michigan. Like all records, I knew it could be broken.

I went 184 the first lap. A new record. Then I went 194, and finally 200.4 miles an hour. Before I went out, they had said, "Try to get it up to two hundred, A.J.," so I did it.

At one race, I ran a Goodyear Stock Car Special on the right rear and Goodyear Speedway Specials on the other three corners. I set a track record. It gave the car what I called "stagger," and, after that, we tried it often in tire tests if all else failed. We tried everything in tire tests.

Both tire companies were into racing right up to their armpits. Both fought tooth and nail to find more miles an hour, and speeds went up at all tracks.

In 1964, I felt it was time to take on the best in stock-car racing: NASCAR, the National Association for Stock Car Auto Racing. What it really means is balls-out racing from wire to wire in a big American sedan that they call a stock car, which is, of course, about as far from stock as I am from a chess champion.

The guys who drive in NASCAR are legends, too. In those days, many of them got their start running moonshine on some back Southern road at night, with a carload of cops chasing them flat out. They always sounded like my kind of race drivers.

When I got to Daytona, which is the Indianapolis of stock-car racing, I found out that everything I had heard was true. They were harder charging than most of the Indianapolis drivers. More than that, they raced every weekend, and that's tough. They all knew each other's driving style like they knew their own.

I knew it was going to be tough competing against the southern drivers who raced every week. They knew the tracks and they knew each other. And they weren't the slightest bit impressed with the fact that I was two-time Indianapolis winner and the first four-time USAC champion. Their champion was Richard Petty, and they had USAC drivers come down before to take over. It hadn't worked.

The track record at Indy was 158 miles an hour. In 1965 Darel Dieringer sat on the pole at Daytona's Firecracker 400 with a speed of 172. Man, that's motoring. Dieringer's Mercury was the only Ford product that had a chance.

Dieringer got an early lead, but he couldn't hold off the Mopars. Petty took over at about the fortieth lap, and Bobby Isaac and I were right behind him. The battle between Isaac and Petty and me went on for lap after lap, until Richard blew his engine. After that it was back and forth, Isaac one lap and me the next. Until there was only one lap left.

Isaac was leading and I was right on him. Right on him. A couple of times I was so close you couldn't tell if I was tapping his bumper or not. The papers said I was, But I really wasn't. You try not to hit somebody at 200 miles an hour, and we were running pretty close to that in the straightaways.

Isaac was right in the middle of the groove. He expected me to pass coming out of Four, but as we came out of Two, headed for the back straightaway, I made my move — earlier than most of them would have done it. If I got by in Two, I could hold him off. I knew it.

I drove up high on the bank and started past Isaac on the outside. The force of breaking the draft, plus the speed from coming down off the high bank, shot me right square in the path of Isaac's front bumper. I felt my car get a little light, like it was up on its tiptoes, but I kept my foot to the floor. Isaac had two choices: Hit me square in the side, which would have meant crashing both cars at 175 miles an hour, or back off. He drove down low on the apron and backed off.

I won Daytona. No driver had ever won at both Indianapolis and Daytona before. And I did it in the same year.

Some days you eat the bear, and some days the bear eats you. I went to Riverside to run a Holman and Moody Ford on the road course. The course wasn't built for stock cars, but, then the stock cars weren't built for a road course, so I figured that about evened things out.

That day at Riverside had turned into the longest day of my career. I started out like a house on fire, but about halfway through the race, I lost my brakes. I mean, they were gone. But I was following Junior Johnson and Marvin Panch, and I had confidence in their ability, so I was running as hard as they were. but the guy in front of them got in trouble and they had to brake. All three of us braked, in fact. Two of us slowed down. I kept pumping, but nothing happened. You always keep hoping. Hell, I've been upside down and still pounding on the brakes.

Now I had two choices: Hit Junior full bore and probably hurt him bad or swing right and drive off the course. There was about a 30-foot drop off the track to the right, so that didn't make that alternative too attractive, but it was the one that I chose. When the car left the track, at about 150 miles an hour, the wheel dropped down into a hole in the dirt and the right-front part of the bumper dug in; it catapulted the car about fifty feet in the air. It felt like I had been shot out of a cannon.

A lot of drivers have said that when they crash, it all happens so fast they don't remember anything. They sort of blank out. Well, maybe they want to blank out, because I remember every second of it. While I'm waiting to hit, I always anticipate the pain. It hurts in every joint, even if you don't break anything. Hell, it even hurts your fingernails.

The car came down right square on its top. Everything got real quiet. The only thing I could hear was a strange wheezing. Then I realized it was me gasping for air. That's all I remember until I woke up in the hospital the next day.

I had a broken back and a fractured heel and several other broken bones and a punctured lung. It was the first time I had really been hurt bad in a race car. I had been bruised and banged up before, but nothing like this. You're always bruised. You can see black-and-blue areas where the shoulder harness was, and you ache all over. But this time I couldn't even breathe without pain running all over my body.

The newspaper articles said I would probably never race again. After seven weeks I got back into a race car. I had almost perfected my walking to the point where people couldn't see the limp. But every time I slid in through the window of the race car at the Atlanta track, I thought I was going to pass out.

During the race I ran hard, although there were times when the pain caused my vision to blur. I went past Marvin Panch and into Turn Three, and when I lifted, the car didn't slow down. The throttle was stuck wide open. I thought, "Oh, no, not Riverside again."

I went past Panch and spun the car toward the wall. It was better than hitting the concrete head on.

The pain shot through me like I had been hit by an elephant rifle when the car crashed sideways into the wall. And everything was quiet again. I could hear a race car go by from time to time, but I just wanted to sit there for a minute. When I pulled myself out the window of the car, I thought for sure I was going to pass out, but I told myself, "No way, buddy boy. You're not gonna pass out here in front of 60,000 people."

I waved to the crowd before I got into the ambulance to go the infield hospital for a checkup. I lay down inside. But I didn't pass out. In fact, I was back in the pits in time to see Panch come in, suffering from heat exhaustion. Leonard Wood ran up to me and grabbed me by the arm. "Can you take over, A.J.?" he asked.

I didn't have time to think about it. "Hell, yes," I said. And I got in the car.

Panch was in first place when he came in, and I kept the car there for the last third of the race. Later, in victory circle, I said, "If you can't beat 'em, join 'em."

The string of injuries carried over to the next year. I was roaring down the front straightaway at Milwaukee in the Indy car when the suspension broke. I knew I was going to crash. It was the third time in as many weeks that something had broken on the car. And I crashed every time.

The start of the 1967 season was the worst of any for me. I've never said it before, but I made myself come back. I could have retired at that point and lived very comfortably for the rest of my life. But I wanted to race. The only thing was that I was scared every time I got in the car. By pushing myself even harder than I had before, I did start winning again; and that's the greatest ther-apy in the world. It was at about this point that I realized that I was as much afraid of losing as I was of getting hurt.

By the time I got to Indianapolis, I was riding high again.

Carroll Shelby's engineer had called before the season started and asked me if I wanted to drive the Turbocar. I told him, "Hell, no, turbines are for airplanes." After watching Parnelli Jones put it on the pole at Indy, I wondered if I had made a mistake. But I figured the car would break and we wouldn't have to worry. I was hiding my head in the sand, because it was clearly faster than anything out there, including my two cars.

I followed Parnelli lap after lap, driving harder than I had ever driven. with four laps to go I felt it was all over, but I kept pushing Parnelli. I can never say if that was the reason or not — the car may have broken anyway — but on the next lap Parnelli slowed down. By the time I went past him, he was coasting. I was about to move into a very select circle of three-time Indianapolis winners.

I was already counting the money on the white-flag lap. All I had was the main straight-away to go and the race was mine. But Bobby Grim spun coming out of Four and hit the wall in the main straight. Chuck Hulse spun into Carl Williams, and there were cars spinning every-where. There was smoke all over and I couldn't see where to go. I figured that whatever I hit I was going to take to the finish line with me. I wasn't going to be denied that victory.

When I came out of the smoke and saw a clear racetrack, I couldn't believe it. I had missed everything. Pat Vidan waved the checkered flag as I drove past him, and then he brought out the red flag to stop the race. I was the only car to finish the full 200 laps, because the track was com-pletely blocked.

It was a momentous occasion for both Goodyear and myself. I became the first Goodyear driver since Howdy Wilcox in 1919 to win the Indy 500. I feel a great sense of pride for the role that I was able to play in Goodyear his-tory, as one who rallied them into the fray, as a tire tester and as a driver.

After the mid-seventies, Firestone wasn't around anymore. Within ten years, Goodyear had run them off the racetrack. They came to the Speedway loaded for bear and they flat got run out. And it wasn't all just dollars. Sure, Goodyear spent millions; but they had better engineers and better products. Goodyear stayed right there, and corrected every problem as it came along.

I would go on within weeks to win the grand-daddy of all sports-car races, the 24 Hours of LeMans, along with my co-driver Dan Gurney. Ford had put together a really professional racing team. Their Mark II cars were as sleek-looking as any Ferrari ever made. I was mighty glad to have Goodyear on the pavement when the long straight-away allowed you to push it over 210 miles an hour.

Everybody always assumed I would retire if I ever won Indy four times. After all, people must have figured, there's never been a four-time winner before, and Foyt is 42 years old, so ...

Late in the 1977 race, when I was out front, what people had been saying went through my mind. They were right, of course; it was time to quit. I had been to the winner's circle three times already, and here I was headed there for a record fourth time. Once again, on Goodyear tires.

It had been one of those races where I felt I was going to win from the start. I mean, really felt it. I felt it with my steak and eggs that morning and I felt it as my challengers fell off, one by one.

By the time they waved the checkered flag at me, I had completely changed my mind. It was a very short retirement. The sight of the black and white waving just for me was something that I wasn't anyways near ready to walk away from. Or the cheering crowd. I wouldn't have quit for anything. There were a lot of surprised people in the winner's circle when I said, "See you next year."

I've had my ups and downs, but I've had a lot of fun in life, and I've made a good living doing something I love to do. I really couldn't have had a better life, but I've worked hard at being number one. I told my family years ago, "You should never settle for second, that's wrong."

I've never learned to settle for second. And neither has Goodyear.

Portions of this foreword have been excerpted from *A.J. Foyt*, by A.J. Foyt and William Neely.

A.J. Foyt is still driving. In 1996, he participated in the NASCAR truck series in Phoenix and Las Vegas.

As team owner he won the 1996 inaugural Indy Racing League Championship. As of this printing, a Foyt-owned car has finished in the top-six in seven of the first eight races of the 1997 season. Two of his four children, Jerry, 35, and Larry, 20, were rookies in the USAC Formula Ford 2000 Series in 1997. And grandson A.J. IV, 13, is competing in both go-karts and junior dragsters in Texas, having won several track championships since he began racing in 1994.

INTRODUCTION

FEW COMPANIES have left tracks intertwined so closely with American history as The Goodyear Tire & Rubber Company. Founded at the dawn of the motor age, Goodyear took to the skies and eventually traveled to the moon. The company's innovations, such as its pioneering work in airships during World War I and synthetic rubber during World War II, contributed to America's military prowess in times of national emergency.

Today, the Goodyear blimp is an intrinsic part of major sporting events, while Goodyear tires have revolutionized handling, safety and performance on the highway and on the racetrack. The company itself, a multibillion-dollar global enterprise, is the nation's number one tire manufacturer, well on its way to becoming number one in the world.

Goodyear's pioneering spirit began in 1898, when Frank Seiberling founded the company with his brother Charles because the two wanted to participate in an enterprise "that affords opportunity for invention."

Frank Seiberling chose the name "Goodyear" to honor Charles Goodyear, the man who invented the process of rubber-curing, which he called vulcanization. Exactly how Charles Goodyear made his revolutionary discovery remains open to debate. The most delightful version has it that

Goodyear, fearing his wife's reaction to the mess he created in her kitchen (after he promised to find a paying job), threw a concoction of raw rubber mixture in the oven to hide it, then out the window into the snow.

Goodyear's discovery resulted in a workable, resilient material, and turned the rubber industry into a prosperous enterprise, crucial to the world's development. The inventor tackled the problems of rubber with religious fervor, paying little attention to such mundane issues as earning a living. His wife and children suffered privation, while he sank deep into debt. In 1860, Goodyear died penniless.

Fortunately, the Seiberling brothers and their successors were more pragmatic. Charles Seiberling believed that a company should be like a family: paternalistic to its employees and a good neighbor within its community.

Starting with carriage and bicycle tires and soon progressing to automobile tires, Goodyear's success translated into a safer and more comfortable lifestyle for its customers and its workers.

By 1916, the company had become the largest tire manufacturer in the world. Innovations such as the State-Seiberling Tire-Building Machine and the Straight Side tire, plus some brilliant marketing techniques, helped the company overwhelm its rivals.

Company leaders such as P.W. Litchfield weren't content to succeed only on the ground; he and other Goodyearites wanted to conquer the air. True to its inventive nature, Goodyear produced its first airship in 1911. By the time America joined World War I in 1917, Goodyear was an important supplier of airships and observation balloons, which offered critical advantages on the battlefield.

Like other American companies, Goodyear prospered during the twenties and then struggled through the Great Depression. The tire business, linked so closely with automobile sales, was hit hard by the economic crisis. However, the company's strong financial foundation allowed it to ride out the difficulties and even cautiously expand.

In 1940, with war already underway in Europe, Goodyear constructed the nation's first synthetic rubber factory. Since natural rubber was in short supply, this innovation proved critical. By October 1945, 89 percent of the rubber used in the United States was synthetic, contributing to such important supplies as gas masks, fighters and bombers, military and civilian vehicles, life jackets, rubber boats, blimps and self-sealing fuel tanks, capable of absorbing enemy fire without exploding.

Perhaps the company's most important contribution to Allied victory was its foray into aeronautics. The Goodyear Aircraft Company, incorporated in 1939, produced wheels, brakes, tires, fuselages and other critical components for a wide variety of aircraft. GAC also produced the FG-1 Corsair for the Navy.

The years following the war were marked by innovative products and rapid global expansion. In the fifties, the company took a leading role in the nation's atomic energy program, and in the sixties, it was instrumental in landing a man on the moon. The company entered the radial market in 1972 with the Custom Steelguard.

Like many companies, Goodyear was the target of a hostile takeover during the eighties. Although the company triumphed, it emerged from the decade burdened with debt. Stan Gault, the former Rubbermaid CEO who became chairman in 1991, engineered a remarkable turnaround.

In 1996, Samir Gibara became chairman and CEO of the company that played such an important role in American history. Under Gibara, Goodyear, the nation's number one tire maker, is positioned to become number one in the world.

ACKNOWLEDGMENTS

A GREAT MANY individuals and institutions assisted in the research, preparation and publication of *The Legend of Goodyear: The First 100 Years.* The principal archival research, including the development of historical timelines, was accomplished by my extraordinarily talented and resourceful research assistant, Lisa Allen. Her tireless and enthusiastic investigation turned up fascinating facts and anecdotes from Goodyear's earliest days.

Without the generous assistance of scores of Goodyear executives, employees and retirees, this book would have been impossible to produce. Principal among these are Samir Gibara, chairman, chief executive officer and president; Chuck Sinclair, manager of North American Tires Public Relations; John Perduyn, vice president of Public Affairs; Linda Fleisher, executive assistant to John Perduyn; Christopher Aked, director of Public Affairs; and P.F. "Doc" Pingree, manager of Special Projects.

Several former top executives greatly enriched the book by discussing their experiences at the helm of the company. The author extends particular gratitude to these men for their candid recollections and anecdotes: Charles Pilliod, former CEO and chairman, who also served as the

United States Ambassador to Mexico; Stanley Gault, former CEO and chairman; Robert Mercer, former CEO and chairman; Tom Barrett, former president, CEO and chairman; and Hoyt Wells, former vice chairman, president and COO.

Also providing valuable insights were: Richard Adante, vice president of Materials Management; James Boyazis, vice president and secretary; Randy Browning, director of Global Exports; Mike Burns, vice president of Human Resources and Total Quality Culture; Nissim Calderon, vice president of Research; Eugene Culler, executive vice president of North America Tires; Walter Curtiss, director of the Goodyear Technical Center; Dennis Dick, vice president and general manager of the Chemical Division; Lee Fiedler, vice president of Goodyear and president of Kelly-Springfield; John Fiedler, former executive vice president of the North American tire division; Joe Gingo, vice president for the Asia Region; Jerry Jenkins, public relations manager of the airship *Stars & Stripes;* Bill Massey, manager director of Goodyear-Argentina; Gary Miller, vice president of Purchasing; Clay Orme, vice president of Product Supply; John Polhemus, vice president of the Latin American Region; Tom Riley, manager of Global Airship Operations; Mike Roney, manager director of Goodyear-Brazil; William Sharp, president of Global Support Operations; Fred Steel, manager,

Goodyear's tire manufacturing plant in Topeka, Kansas; Richard Steichen, vice president, Worldwide Tire Technology; George Strickler, vice president of finance for North America Tires; Sylvain Valensi, vice president of Europe-SBU; Jim Weaks, Indianapolis tire service technician; James Whiteley, vice president, Government Compliance and Product Quality; and Jesse Williams, vice president of Human Resources and Employment Practices.

I would especially like to thank Larry Chambers, chief pilot-in-charge of the airship *Stars & Stripes,* which I piloted under his supervision.

Retirees who shared memories of the company include James W. Barnett, former vice president of Original Equipment Sales Worldwide; Scott Buzby, former president of Goodyear Canada; George Hargreaves, former president of Celeron Corporation and Robert Hehir, former vice president of Environmental Safety and Health Assurance Programs.

For the racing section, particular gratitude is extended to Stuart Grant, general manager of Worldwide Racing, and Leo Mehl, former director of Global Racing Operations for Goodyear, as well as current executive director, Indy Racing League, and vice president, Indianapolis Motor Speedway. Race car drivers who took time from their busy schedules to provide insights about Goodyear include Mario Andretti, Derek Bell, Sir Jack Brabham, Robert Dyson, A.J. Foyt, Don Garlits, Jeff Gordon, Dave Marcis, Rick Mears, Benny Parsons, Don Prudhomme, Bobby Rahal, Al Unser, Jr., and Darrell Waltrip.

Further assistance for the racing section was providing by Cory Watkins, Keith Waltz, Scott Reicz, Chris Mears, Patty Reed, Tommy Lamance, Lisa Guth and Kelly Malone.

Archivist John Miller also provided valuable help, as did Aaron Vandersommers of Goodyear's Audio-Visual Department. Special thanks goes to *Air Force Magazine*, which thoughtfully provided several images.

Special mention goes to Fred Kovac, who passed away shortly after he was interviewed. It was a true pleasure to spend time with Kovac, the former vice president of Technology-Business Planning. He will be missed.

As always, the author extends a particular word of thanks to the dedicated staff of Write Stuff Syndicate. Proofreader Bryan Henry and transcriptionist Mary Aaron worked quickly and efficiently. Particular thanks goes to Alex Lieber, associate editor; Karen Nitkin, executive editor; Art Directors Sandy Cruz, Kyle Newton and Jill Apolinario; Fred Moll, production manager; Jill Thomas, assistant to the author; Marianne Roberts, office manager; Christopher Frosch, marketing and sales manager; Rafael Santiago, logistics specialist; and Karine Rodengen, product coordinator.

1800 — Charles Goodyear was born in
New Haven, Connecticut.

1860 — Charles Goodyear dies a pauper.

1839 — Goodyear accidentally brings
rubber into contact with a hot stove,
inadvertently discovering vulcanization.

1898 — Sensing opportunity, Seiberling
buys an old strawboard plant for
$13,500. The Goodyear Tire & Rubber
Company is born.

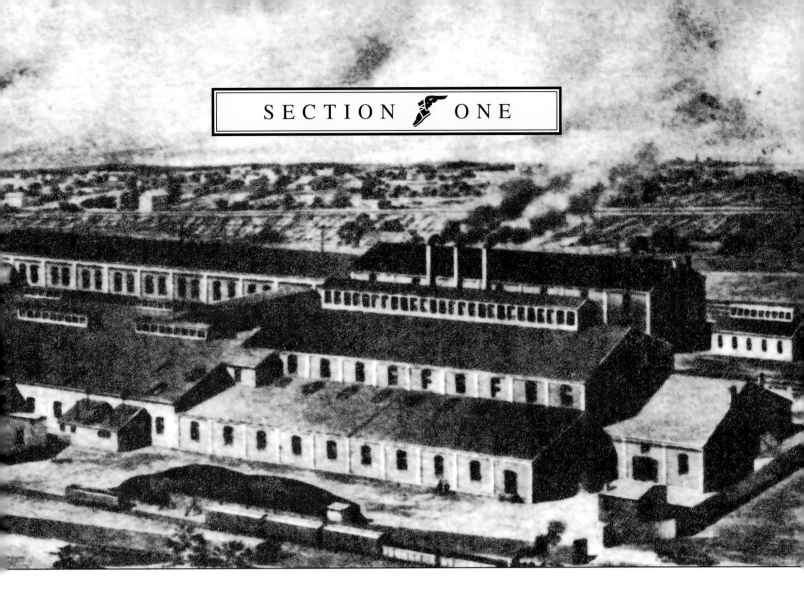

SECTION ✈ ONE

1900 — P.W. Litchfield, who would become the "brain" of Goodyear, is hired as factory superintendent.

1908 — Henry Ford's affordable Model T is a sensation with middle-class consumers, and car registrations skyrocket.

1916 — Goodyear becomes the world's largest tire company.

1905 — Designed two years earlier, Goodyear heavily markets the Straight Side tire.

1909 — Goodyear tire sales jump 400 percent from the previous year.

An artist's rendering of the "Happy Accident," which led to the discovery of vulcanization. Several conflicting stories of the accident exist.

CHAPTER ONE

CHARLES GOODYEAR & THE FORTUNATE ACCIDENT

1834–1860

"The temperament of Mr. Goodyear is a combination of the mental and vital, or Nervous-Sanguine. Warmth, zeal, sprightliness, and restless energy seem to be the leading characteristics. ... Hope, Firmness and Combativeness are also large in his head."

— 1856 issue of *American Phrenological Journal*[1]

N THE SPRING of 1898, Frank Seiberling of Akron, Ohio, ran into a business acquaintance in the lobby of a Chicago hotel. A short while later, he walked out of the building holding the deed to an abandoned strawboard factory in east Akron, with little idea of what to do with it.[2] By August, he and his brother Charles had decided to go into the rubber business. With an initial capital stock of $100,000, The Goodyear Tire & Rubber Company was born.[3]

On November 21, 1898, a carriage tire became the first product of the company that 18 years later would become the largest tire manufacturer in the world.[4] In its hundred-year history, Goodyear would enjoy rapid growth and immense success as it became intertwined with the development of the automobile and the airship, and as it served a vital role in military campaigns and space exploration.

But the story of The Goodyear Tire & Rubber Company really begins in a New England town far from Akron, with a man who would never meet Frank Seiberling nor envision the global company that would bear his name. Indeed, Charles Goodyear would die a pauper because he was too proud to profit from his efforts.

In the winter of 1839, in a house in Woburn, Massachusetts, the often-mocked but indefatigable inventor Charles Goodyear dropped a mixture of rubber and sulfur on a hot pot-bellied stove. This moment of clumsiness was the culmination of years of trying to turn raw rubber, which suffered problems of temperature sensitivity and tackiness, into a workable, resilient material. Accidentally, Charles Goodyear discovered the process of vulcanization.

Charles Goodyear

Charles Goodyear was born in 1800 in New Haven, Connecticut, and died in 1860. During his lifetime, he witnessed innovations such as the cotton gin, the McCormick reaper, Robert Fulton's steamboat and the iron smelting process.[5] A product of the Yankee spirit of invention, Goodyear's family tree included Stephen Goodyear, a London merchant who helped found the New Haven colony and had once served as its governor.[6] Charles' father, Amasa Goodyear, was himself an inventor. He manufactured the first pearl buttons to be seen in the United States, as well as the metal buttons worn by soldiers during the War of 1812.[7]

A bust of Charles Goodyear. He wanted to become a minister but was dissuaded by his mother. Instead, Goodyear's religious fervor was focused on rubber.

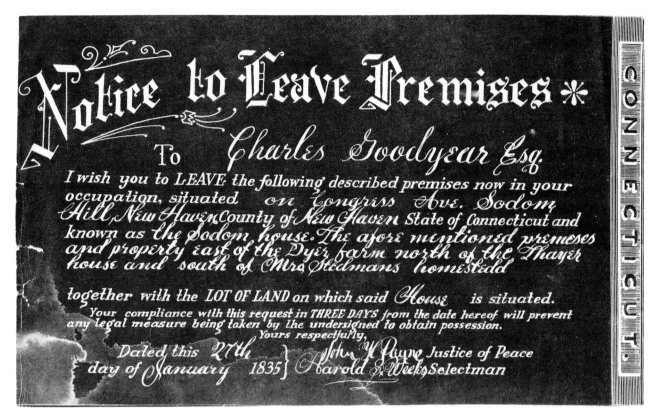

Goodyear's single-minded pursuit to turn rubber into a viable commodity had a disastrous effect on his family life and his finances, as this 1835 eviction notice shows.

At age 16, Charles was an energetic and serious young man, interested in joining the ministry. Amasa steered his son away from the religious life, but Charles would continue to harbor a belief that his life served a higher purpose.[8] Charles and his new bride, Clarissa, moved to Philadelphia, where he opened the nation's first hardware store.[9] Specializing in his father's products, Goodyear grew prosperous, and he and Clarissa had five children during the first 10 years of their marriage.[10]

But the devastating economic panic of 1827 forced Goodyear to close the store, leaving him deeply in debt. Unlike his business partners, he refused to declare bankruptcy and was sent to debtors' prison in 1830, the first of several such imprisonments.[11]

The Problems with Rubber

In 1834, Goodyear stumbled upon the problems that had plagued the rubber industry from its beginning and kept it from becoming a useful product. While visiting New York City, he looked into a shop window of the Roxbury Rubber Company and noticed a life preserver with a poorly designed inflation valve.[12] He believed he could design a better one, and he returned to the store several days later with an improved version. Talking with the store's owner, E.M. Chafee, Goodyear was told that "what the company really needed was a way to stop rubber from melting, sticking and decaying in hot weather, and cracking in cold weather."[13] Goodyear took Chafee's words as a personal challenge.

Rubber had been used for centuries by the natives of South America, who pierced the trunks of rubber trees to catch the milky liquid that flowed, drying it over fires or in the sun, and then shaping the goo into thin shoes or toys.[14] Shortly after discovering America, Christopher Columbus had noted in his diary that Haitian children played with an interesting elastic ball made from this substance. But from Columbus' time to the day Charles Goodyear made it a workable and valuable commodity, rubber was viewed by Europeans and

Americans mainly as a curiosity. The first specimen of rubber sent to Europe arrived in 1736 with French explorers. It saw little use except as an oddity displayed by wealthy Europeans or as a pencil eraser — hence the term rub-ber — until Charles McIntosh created a rubberized raincoat in 1823.[15] The McIntosh became popular in Scotland, a country that rarely experiences extremes in temperature, but other rubberized products were less successful. Impressed with the material's waterproofing abilities, Europeans sent thousands of pairs of shoes to South America, where natives would dip the footwear in liquid rubber.[16] But the rubber was temperature-sensitive and the rubberized shoes tended to crack in winter and become sticky messes in summer. Besides, few people could afford shoes that were sent halfway around the world to be dipped in what the South Americans called the "caoutchouc," after the sound rubber made when it was stretched.[17]

The First Rubber Company

The Roxbury Rubber Company was the world's first incorporated rubber shoe manufacturer, and had been in business only a short time when Charles Goodyear paused to peer in its window. In 1833, E.M. Chafee, of Roxbury, Massachusetts, made patent leather shoes by dissolving rubber in turpentine and spreading the mixture over cloth, adding lamp-black for color.[18] Believing this was the breakthrough, Chafee went into business with $35,000. His enterprise quickly grew as more than $2 million in investments poured in. But by the summer, goods manufactured in the cool months of the previous autumn, winter and spring were returned to Chafee's factory; rubber shoes and coats were melting in the summer heat, resulting in foul-smelling,

In 1937, Goodyear unveiled a statue of Charles Goodyear, honoring the man who made the rubber industry possible.

black, sticky messes.[19] The partners of the Roxbury factory met one summer night to bury $20,000 worth of ruined goods, attempting to hide both the smell and the evidence from uneasy investors.[20] The mysteries of rubber had not been solved.

Charles Goodyear believed that rubber could be improved through a "tanning" or "curing" process similar to that done to animal hides.[21] Forsaking other interests, he worked tirelessly with rubber, adding various elements to try to cause a lasting chemical change. At home, he turned his wife's kitchen into a laboratory. During the periods he was jailed for non-payment of debt he asked for a marble slab, a rolling pin, and pieces of rubber and chemicals.[22] The enthusiasm which might have served him well in the ministry was instead directed to invention.[23]

In 1838 he met Nathanael Hayward, who had discovered that subjecting a mixture of sulfur and rubber to sunlight greatly reduced stickiness.[24] Excited, Goodyear wrote a patent application for the illiterate Hayward, purchased the patent for $200, and put Hayward to work for him.[25] Then Goodyear discovered that washing rubber in a bath of nitric acid produced similar results. He thought this was the curing process he had been seeking.[26] Goodyear believed that his acid bath produced a chemical change throughout the entire sheet of rubber, and not merely on the surface as earlier processes had done.

With the backing of a brother-in-law, Goodyear went into business in Woburn, Massachusetts. He rented a house at 280 Montvale Avenue for his family, and a nearby factory for the production of rubber shoes and fabrics.

At first, business was good. In 1838, Goodyear was awarded a patent for his acid process and began a one-man public-relations campaign on the virtues of rubber. He manufactured rubber toys and clothing, thin overshoes and umbrellas. He wore a rubber suit. He sent letters printed on rubber to Henry Clay, John Calhoun and President Andrew Jackson.[27] People began to notice, and soon his line of shirred goods — made by adding thin layers of rubber to fabric — was selling briskly. For the first time since the early days of his hardware store, Charles Goodyear was a success.

But once again, prosperity was short-lived. Goodyear won a government contract to produce 150 mailbags as well as life-preservers, a pet project since the day he had passed the one in the Roxbury store.[28] The finished mailbags were hung in the Woburn factory until the date of delivery. One night, upon returning from a business trip to New York, Goodyear walked into the factory and found 150 fabric neck straps hanging from

hooks, with a rolling black mass on the floor beneath them. The rubber had not withstood the summer heat. Soon, the familiar complaints began as customers returned products. The factory closed shortly thereafter.

The "Happy Accident"

Like his successes, Goodyear's defeat was short-lived. The "happy accident" of 1839 has become the stuff of legend, and various sources relate differing details of Goodyear's discovery of vulcanization. Perhaps the most interesting is found in *Charles Goodyear: An Intimate Biographical Sketch*, in which author Hugh Allen tells of Clarissa Goodyear's possible involvement. Her husband's tireless experimenting had left the family so poor that it was dependent on neighbors for food, and she begged Charles to give up rubber, or at least promise to concentrate his energies on making money. But one winter day in 1839,

Charles Goodyear's house, 280 Montvale Avenue, in Woburn, Massachusetts, where Goodyear is said to have discovered the vulcanization process. The house was destroyed in 1972 after attempts to turn it into a museum failed.

Above: The Vulcanite Court, Charles Goodyear's exhibit at the 1851 World's Fair, held in London. The entire display was made of rubber.

Below: Artifacts made of rubber that belonged to Charles Goodyear, which included a cane and even a pocketknife, located in the center of the picture. This photo appeared in *National Geographic* in 1970.

after Clarissa had gone to the store, he hurriedly mixed some rubber with sulfur. Upon hearing his wife's return, he threw the rubber into the stove, retrieved it before it could begin to smell, and tossed it out the window into a bank of snow.[29]

Goodyear's own account, told in his 1854 book *Gum-Elastic*, moves the action from his house at 280 Montvale Avenue to a nearby Woburn store. Goodyear wrote of himself in the third person:

"At the dwelling where he stopped whenever he visited the manufactory at Woburn, the inventor made some experiments to ascertain the effect of heat upon the same compound that had decomposed in the mail-bags and other articles. He was surprised to find that the specimen, being carelessly brought in contact with a hot stove, charred like leather. He endeavored to call the attention of his brother, as well as some other individuals who were present, and who were acquainted with

the manufacturing of gum-elastic, to this effect, as remarkable and unlike any before known, since gum-elastic always melted when exposed to a high degree of heat. The occurrence did not at the time appear to them to be worthy of notice; it was considered as one of the frequent appeals that he was in the habit of making, in behalf of some new experiment."[30]

In both accounts, Goodyear did not apply a rubber compound to high heat since he knew that rubber melted so easily. The accident was lucky because it showed Goodyear that when rubber is mixed with sulfur, and then subjected to the right amount of heat for the right length of time, a durable material could be produced. The rubber had "charred" because the chemical change worked not merely on the surface but throughout the material.

The discovery that would mean so much to the rubber industry — and eventually the world — was not a happy one for Goodyear's family. Spurred by his discovery, Goodyear ignored the practical demands of living. Throughout that winter and the next, the family was destitute; at one point, Goodyear sold his wife's linens and even his children's schoolbooks for money to continue his experimenting.[31]

Goodyear was actually contacted by a company that wanted to buy rights for his acid-curing process. Goodyear went so far as to return money to the company, along with a note telling company officials that he had recently found a better method and would let them know when he had perfected it.[32]

By now Goodyear's behavior bordered on the obsessive. He exhibited the energy

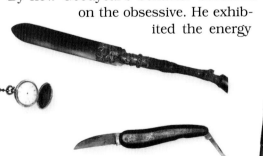

and purpose of a zealot, believing himself responsible for perfecting rubber and offering its uses to mankind.[33] He was scorned by his neighbors, who "thought he was a shiftless, lazy man, cracked on rubber" and became irritated at the "smell of burning rubber [that] was always around the house."[34] People pitied his wife and children. The family was so poor that upon the death of one of his sons, Goodyear, lacking money for a funeral, walked the child's body to the cemetery and dug the grave himself.[35]

A Man Obsessed

Goodyear named his heating process vulcanization, for Vulcan, the Roman god of fire. He experimented with different ratios of rubber to sulfur at various temperatures and times, seeking the optimum conditions to produce rubber that could be easily molded and hardened into a durable and flexible material. Intent on his research, he failed to patent the process for four years, a decision that would come to haunt him.

In 1841, in Springfield, Massachusetts, Goodyear produced a few yards of rubber sheeting in a heated cast-iron trough, the first successful application of the vulcanization process.[36] By 1850, several companies had licensed Goodyear's vulcanization process, and by 1856 the United States was importing more than 2 million pounds of rubber from Brazil and 340,000 from Java, an island of Indonesia.[37] With his brothers and a brother-in-law, Goodyear opened a small factory to make rubber shoes and other products, but he

Above: The famous orator, lawyer and statesman, Daniel Webster, who represented Goodyear during his patent infringement lawsuit in 1852. Goodyear won the suit.

Below: Charles Goodyear's own book, of the history of rubber, *Gum-Elastic*, appropriately made out of rubber material.

soon lost interest and returned to his experiments, making lists of various uses for rubber and then trying them out.

Goodyear's zeal — or fanaticism — was studied even while he was still alive and experimenting. An 1856 issue of *American Phrenological Journal* analyzed the size and shape of Goodyear's cranium to explain his behavior.

"The temperament of Mr. Goodyear is a combination of the mental and vital, or Nervous-Sanguine. Warmth, zeal, sprightliness, and restless energy seem to be the leading characteristics.

... The reader will observe a slight swelling-out of the upper part of the organ of Constructiveness, where it joins Ideality, at the temple, which indicates the tendency for invention, experiment and discovery. ... Hope, Firmness and Combativeness are also large in his head.[38]

What the phrenologists did not find in Goodyear's skull was a good deal of practical business sense, something his long-suffering family could attest to. Apparently uninterested in the economic potential of rubber products, Goodyear did not seek the vulcanization patent until 1844. Although it was awarded to him on June 15 of that year, his delay and subsequent licensing out of his process cost him dearly. Two weeks before Goodyear received his American patent, England granted one to Thomas Hancock for the identical process, preventing Goodyear from receiving the British rights.[39] Hancock would later admit he didn't try the process until after he had seen a vulcanized sample that Goodyear had sent to England through an agent, but the patent was not overturned.[40]

Worse would follow. On the same day, Goodyear was awarded the United States patent, a man named Horace Day was rejected for the same claim. As a result, Day would become Goodyear's nemesis.

The feud between the two men lasted for years. Day had agreed to purchase patent rights from Goodyear, but then refused to pay the inventor and began to manufacture goods without a license. The culmination of the fight occurred with the celebrated "Great India Rubber Suit" of 1852. The famed Daniel, then U.S. Secretary of State, represented Charles Goodyear.[41] Goodyear won the suit but Webster's fee was $25,000 — more than Goodyear ever made from his discovery of vulcanization, and a sum he could not repay.[42]

Charles Goodyear received little fortune for his efforts but much fame. In 1851, Goodyear was invited to the first World's Fair, "The Exhibition of the Works of All Nations," held in Hyde Park, London.[43] There, he displayed "The Vulcanite Court," a $30,000 exhibit in the Crystal Palace made wholly of rubber. He featured rubber furniture, rubber clothing, rubber globes and art objects, rubber gloves and buttons, rubber umbrellas and walking sticks, even rubber eyeglass frames and rubber rings inlaid with jewels. The exhibit was well-received, and Goodyear was invited to France for an even larger show, for which he was granted the prestigious French Cross of the Legion of Honor.[44] Goodyear's second wife, Fanny, brought the medal to him as he sat in jail for debts that his backer had failed to pay.[45]

On July 1, 1860, Goodyear died penniless, more than $200,000 in arrears.[46] He had never been interested in the potential profit that his incredible innovation could have reaped, and he considered the battles over patents and profits distasteful. He wrote in *Gum-Elastic*: "It is repulsive to the feelings, that improvements relating to science and the arts, and especially those of a philanthropic nature, should have been made subject of money-making and litigation by being patented."[47]

Though he died poor, Goodyear was honored for his efforts, even in jail. Daniel Webster, summing up his legal argument during the 1852 patent case, predicted that Goodyear would "go down to posterity in the history of the arts in this country, in that great class of inventors, at the head of which stands Robert Fulton ... in which class will stand ... the humble name of Charles Goodyear."[48]

But 38 years would pass before the company that made Goodyear's name a household word would come into existence. That story begins with Frank Seiberling in 1898.

The original strawboard factory, purchased in 1898 by Frank Seiberling for $13,500.

CHAPTER TWO

THE FOUNDING OF GOODYEAR

1898–1904

"I thought, 'The rubber business started here in Akron; there is rubber labor here. I can marshal some experience. More than all that, it is a business that affords opportunity for invention.' ... At six o'clock in the morning I landed — I was a rubber man."

— Frank Seiberling, undated speech[1]

FRANK SEIBERLING, founder of The Goodyear Tire & Rubber Company, was born in 1859, not long before the death of Charles Goodyear, on a farm outside of Akron, Ohio. Seiberling, his brother Charles and their seven sisters moved to Akron a few years later.

Frank grew up in an environment that celebrated initiative and achievement. His father, John Seiberling, was an inventor who made and lost several small fortunes in the course of his lifetime. Besides owning 40 patents on farm machinery, he dabbled in cereals, railways, banking and entertainment.[2]

After spending two years at Heidelberg College in Tiffin, Ohio, Frank followed his father's example by opening a twine and cordage company, and worked in milling and the streetcar business as well.[3] After more than 20 years, Frank Seiberling accumulated managerial experience in manufacturing, sales, finance and management.[4] But the wealth he had accumulated evaporated when the United States experienced one of the most devastating business panics up to that time. A panic on Wall Street, triggered by the failure of the Philadelphia and Reading Railroad, resulted in widespread unemployment and labor unrest. By 1898, the year of the Spanish-American War, 38-year-old Frank Seiberling found himself "a good many thousand dollars poorer than nothing."[5]

Seiberling traveled to Chicago to liquidate some family property when he stumbled upon a business opportunity. In the lobby of the Fremont Hotel, Seiberling ran into H.C. Nellis, a business acquaintance from the F. Gray Company of Piqua, Ohio.[6] As the men chatted, Seiberling learned that the site of a strawboard plant once owned by his father was currently vacant. The property had come to the F. Gray Company when the Akron Woolen & Felt Company failed, and Nellis wanted to sell it quickly. He quoted a price of $40,000 for the two buildings and mill that sat on 12 acres in east Akron.

Seiberling knew the strawboard plant well. When he was 16 years old, he had done the bookkeeping for his father.[7] He remarked that it would be difficult to find a buyer at that price, and Nellis admitted he would accept $25,000. Lacking both financing and an idea of what to do with the factory, Seiberling offered to buy it if Nellis halved his second price. In less than five minutes of negotiating, Seiberling agreed to purchase the property for $13,500.[8]

Seiberling may have whittled down the price but he was still broke. He negotiated a schedule

---

Before rubber tires, wooden wheels made hauling equipment, like this fire wagon, a chore, especially after rains turned roads into mud pits.

that required a down payment of $3,500, borrowed from a brother-in-law, and four yearly payments of $2,500.[9] It was a good deal, but that night, on the train back to Ohio, Seiberling couldn't help but wonder if he had made a mistake. First of all, he had no capital to invest in a new venture, and secondly, he had no idea what form the venture would take. But Seiberling was never one to pass up an opportunity. His family was prominent in Akron — his father was famous for having installed the first bathtub in the area — and he had brothers-in-law who would surely help him.[10] The question remained: what to do with his new purchase.

Seiberling first considered starting a paper mill, since the buildings bordered the Little Cuyahoga River, which would provide water, and paper was a steady business. But he felt uneasy imagining himself a paper magnate. Seiberling recalled his thoughts during that nighttime train ride in an undated speech given years later.

"As the matter kept revolving in my mind during the night, the thought kept growing on me: how can I have any pleasure in making one article, one thing, one motion. Just like putting bricks through a ... mill, one brick, one brick, one brick; one yard of paper, one yard of paper. The business seemed to me to be of deadly

monotony. It wasn't suited to my type of mind or my activities."[11]

The Rubber Business

Seiberling wanted a business to provide both success and pleasure, the former measured by economics and the latter by challenge and change. Looking out the train window and mulling what pursuit could offer financial prosperity as well as plenty of activity for his restless mind, he finally hit upon rubber.

"I thought, 'The rubber business started here in Akron; there is rubber labor here. I can marshal some experience. More than all that, it is a business that affords opportunity for invention.' ... At six o'clock in the morning I landed — I was a rubber man."[12]

The plant's location made rubber an ideal choice. It was near both the river and a B&O Railroad line, providing easy transportation for goods and materials. Furthermore, Akron was a booming industrial town, home to 50,000 people and dozens of recently established manufacturing plants, including B.F. Goodrich and the Diamond Rubber Company.[13] Akron's population was full of skilled workers, 2,000 of whom had lost jobs during the economic turmoil of the 1890s.[14] Seiberling knew that many of these workers were still seeking steady, decent-paying jobs by 1898.

Moreover, Frank and his brother Charles had seen some of the new "horseless carriages" built in Akron. These early automobiles were little

---

Top left: John Franklin Seiberling, father of Frank and Charles, was himself an innovator and entrepreneur. He owned more than 40 patents at the time of his death.

Middle left: Frank Seiberling, who founded The Goodyear Tire & Rubber Company, at age seven.

Left: The future wife of Frank Seiberling, at age seven. She was one of the first stockholders, along with Charles' wife and an assortment of in-laws.

more than novelties, and not practical for serious travel in a nation that still lacked a comprehensive road system. But Seiberling believed that if the horseless carriage caught on, the demand for rubber would increase dramatically.

The Seiberling brothers had gained some experience in the rubber industry through their father's involvement with the Akron India Rubber Company, so it took little effort for Frank to persuade Charles to join the new venture.

The brothers' first task — securing financing — was little trouble for men with deep ties in the community, and by August 1898, they had sold 900 shares of common stock at $100 per share, with $43,500 paid in.[15] Original stockholders included the Seiberling brothers and their wives; brothers-in-law H.B. Manton, L.C. Miles, and R.C. Penfield; David and George Hill, owners of the Hill Sewer Pipe Company; and Charles Dick, head of an Akron law firm and a future Ohio state senator.[16] At the first shareholders' meeting, David Hill — who had purchased $30,000 in

Charles (right) joined his brother Frank Seiberling (below) to start The Goodyear Tire & Rubber Company. "Charley" would be known by employees as a man who never neglected a friend or a poker game.

stock[17] — was named president; his son George, vice president; Henry Manton, treasurer; and Frank Seiberling, general manager and secretary.[18] Later that year, Charles Seiberling assumed the role of secretary.

The Seiberling's second task was to renovate the dilapidated mill. The first "capital investment" of the young company amounted to $217.86, paid to workers who fixed the sagging floors, leaky roof and rusted machines.[19] Frank purchased second-hand rubber machinery: mills for mixing, fabric, vulcanizers, tube machines and a boiler.[20] It was during this period that Frank Seiberling decided to name the new company after Charles Goodyear to honor invention, risk and perseverance. On November 21, 1898, with a payroll of 13 employees, The Goodyear Tire & Rubber Company began producing carriage tires, bicycle tires, horseshoe pads and rubber sundries.[21]

Patent Warfare

The company's first sale, recorded December 1, was $25.80 for a number of small tubes and hoses, known as sundries, for use in pharmaceutical bottles.[22] By the end of the first month, Frank Seiberling recorded $8,246 in sales.[23] In spite of this promising start, the company was soon embroiled in patent disputes, the same misfortune that had plagued Charles Goodyear decades earlier.

The nation was in the midst of a bicycle craze, so the company's earliest bread-and-butter products were carriage and bike tires, both of which were protected under patents. The carriage tire patent was held by the Rubber Tire Wheel Company, headed by Edwin S. Kelly of Springfield, Ohio, while the Tillinghast bicycle tire patent was held by The Single Tube Automobile and Bicycle Tire Company.[24] Goodyear had been granted a license to use the Tillinghast patent.[25] But both patents would cause Seiberling to seethe, and would even ignite a feud between Seiberling and Kelly that would simmer for years.

Until 1890, carriage tires often slipped their wheels when going over bumps. The problem was alleviated with the introduction of a tire-fastening device, which, by 1898, had become an industry standard.[26] Kelly had purchased the patent, and was fighting The American Tire Company over patent infringement just as Goodyear began manufacturing its first products. Although the rubber industry hoped the courts would rule for American, thus opening the market, a Brooklyn court ruled for Kelly on December 23, 1898. This was a severe blow to Goodyear, which had been in business a mere month and two days.

Seiberling knew he needed to get a license from Kelly, but, according to Seiberling's personal account, he was never given the chance. In late December, he contacted Kelly, who agreed to visit the Goodyear plant a few days later. When he didn't arrive, Seiberling learned that upon stopping at B.F. Goodrich, Kelly was advised not to grant a license to the young company, which was sure to "last only a few months."[27] To Seiberling's growing irritation, Kelly even tried to hire away one of his salesman, Joe Burrows. In

early 1899, Seiberling decided to manufacture carriage tires without a license, irrespective of the risk. He was sure that the Kelly decision would be reversed on appeal. And he was simply mad at Kelly.

Not surprisingly, Kelly sued under the name of a syndicate company called Consolidated Tire. Kelly had sold the patent to Consolidated Tire, which subcontracted rubber companies to actually perform the manufacturing.[28] While the battle was being fought in courts, Seiberling decided to wage his offensive in the marketplace, and had his men figure cost factors to the penny to price the tires well below any others on the market, as he explained in a speech.

"I made up my mind that the only way we could ever cope with the situation was to fight them commercially and beat them to their knees. ... Within four months we sold $143,000 worth of solid carriage tires, or pretty nearly half as much as the entire Kelly business."[29]

The strategy worked. Wanting to capitalize on Goodyear's rapid success, Consolidated offered to drop the lawsuit if Goodyear would stop the cutthroat price war. Furthermore, Consolidated would agree to buy tires from Goodyear. Kelly initially offered $50,000 in guaranteed annual business, which Seiberling promptly turned down since it was a fraction of his current sales. After several months of talking, the parties agreed on a figure of $600,000. Sweet as the deal sounded, The Goodyear Tire Company would find itself in court again; this time as both plaintiff and defendant.

Consolidated continually refused to accept Goodyear tires, claiming they were of inferior quality. After months of rejections and unpaid invoices, Seiberling sued for $57,000 in unpaid bills. In response, Consolidated reinstated the patent suit.[30]

Seiberling's reaction was swift. He announced in the newspapers that his company was independent of Consolidated and had a new, improved tire — the Burrows' Wing tire. The company also contacted leading clients of Consolidated, who switched to Goodyear's less-expensive product.[31]

Bicycle Tires

The carriage tire business soared. Seiberling's strategy originally was to scare Kelly into retreat, but business was so good that Seiberling decided to continue it. By 1900, sales were booming but, ironically, the company was strapped for cash. Since the patent suit with Consolidated was pending, Goodyear's carriage tire earnings were put into escrow under a bond of $250,000, posted by R.C. Penfield, who became the company's president when David Hill resigned in 1899.[32] The company had to rely on its other principal product — bicycle tires — to stay afloat until the court decision was handed down.

If the Kelly incident showed the brash spirit of Goodyear, the bicycle tire taught its executives another key lesson. Salesman Joe Burrows was committed to the quality of the carriage tire line he oversaw, but Goodyear's bicycle tire was another story. The company needed to sell prod-

Akron was home to thousands of skilled workers. The tire industry required both brain and brawn, particularly in its early years.

ucts quickly to make up for the profits held in escrow and so it underpriced the bicycle tires, an infringement of the Tillinghast patent's price control. The patent license was withdrawn, a move which might have shut down the entire department and probably the company. Goodyear had to find a way around the patent.

The company soon found the answer by creating a two-ply tire, using thin strips of muslin to separate the plies of rubber, until vulcanization.[33] To keep costs down, the muslin was soon replaced with tissue paper — often toilet paper bought by the roll from the M. O'Neil Company, a department store in downtown Akron.[34] The two-ply tires, called Tip Tops, cost 48 cents apiece to make, and the rubber was cured in only three and a half minutes to provide high-volume production. However, the quality was less than ideal, as Seiberling himself admitted. "When you cure rubber in three and a half minutes, you haven't much of a cure. ... And of course a tire that could be made for 48 cents didn't contain too much rubber and was mostly a compound, and it wasn't worth a whoop."[35] Such mass-production hurt the company's reputation, which was practically non-existent anyway.

Goodyear churned out an average of 3,000 of its Tip Top carriage tires per day, twice as many as any of its competitors. As Seiberling said, "That would be all right if you knew that they would stay on the rim and carry the fellow around the corner, but most of them [didn't] and the chickens commenced to come home. All over the country we heard about those 'rotten Goodyear tires.'"[36] The reputation of the company began to suffer in all areas, and Seiberling and his officers decided that making a fast buck was less important than earning respect with quality.

Meanwhile, carriage tire sales were rolling, helping Goodyear's sales to double from $508,597 in 1899 to $1,035,921 in 1900.[37] By 1900, the company featured six manufacturing departments: bicycle tires, bicycle sundries, the press room (horseshoe pads), solid and cushion tires, pneumatic and carriage tires, and drum tires.[38] It had begun exporting to Canada, England and France, and would soon open sales branches in New York, Chicago, Kansas City, Cincinnati, Boston and St. Louis.[39] The most significant event of 1900, however, came when Goodyear hired P.W. Litchfield.

P.W. Litchfield

Litchfield became Goodyear's factory superintendent on July 15, 1900. He took the job, he later explained, because he was 25 and thought he could "afford to gamble a couple of years."[40] A graduate of the Massachusetts Institute of Technology, Litchfield had worked for three differ-

The Kelly-Springfield group around 1900. Frank's business nemesis, Edwin Kelly, is sitting in the center. Goodyear bought its rival in 1935.

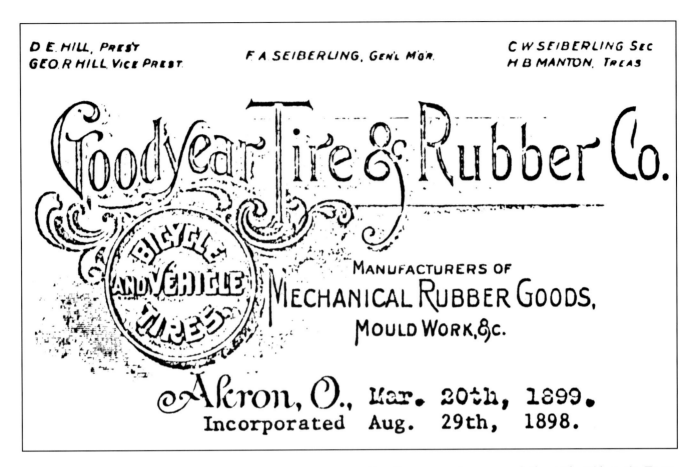

D E. HILL, PRES'T
GEO. R HILL, VICE PRES'T.

F A SEIBERLING, GEN'L M'G'R.

C W SEIBERLING SEC
H B MANTON, TREAS

Goodyear Tire & Rubber Co.

MANUFACTURERS OF
MECHANICAL RUBBER GOODS,
MOULD WORK, &c.

BICYCLE AND VEHICLE TIRES

Akron, O., Mar. 20th, 1899.
Incorporated Aug. 29th, 1898.

Goodyear's original letterhead logo.

ent tire companies in the east. As such, he was Goodyear's first technically trained tire engineer.[41] From 1900 to 1902, despite financial straits, Litchfield set up a "primitive development department."[42] By 1904, Frank Seiberling had been granted 16 patents in vehicle tires, manufacturing process and rubber machinery, and Joe Burrows had been granted four.[43]

With his commitment to quality and passion for innovation, Litchfield was a perfect complement to the Seiberling brothers, themselves complements to each other. Frank was the "hand" of Goodyear, the dynamic force of motion, part organizer, part salesman, part cheerleader. He was a decision-maker and a risk-taker, qualities that later earned him the nickname "the Little Napoleon of the rubber industry."[44] Charles Seiberling was Goodyear's "heart," the unofficial head of Human Relations. A compassionate,

attentive man, he earned the title "Akron's First Citizen" for his belief in business's duty to give to its community, which involved Goodyear in civic improvements.[45] Paul Litchfield — who would serve three decades as chief executive officer — was Goodyear's "brain," designing better products just ahead of the competition and insisting on high standards of quality for both products and human behavior. Litchfield replaced the bottle of whiskey that was ever-present in the company's medicine cabinet with a bottle of ammonia, and upon touring the factory and spying employees playing poker in a dark corner, he politely told them it was their last poker game on company time. For several years thereafter, the game was played weekly at his house.[46]

In 1901, the patent suit was still pending, the profits from carriage tires in escrow, but the company forged ahead, constructing a new office building on Akron's Market Street and hiring George Stadelman as sales manager. In 20 years at Goodyear, Stadelman never made a speech, making him a seemingly odd candidate to be a

Great men of rubber. Standing with Frank (in front, with hat and mustache) and Charles Seiberling (second row on the left, with a hand on his shoulder) is P.W. Litchfield (center, with flower). Other leaders of the rubber industry in the group include Harvey Firestone, and William O'Neil, president of the General Tire and Rubber Company.

salesman. Shy, intellectual and kind, he shared Litchfield's zeal for quality as well as his integrity, which inspired trust in customers and would soon figure largely in positioning Goodyear with automobile manufacturers.[47]

By 1902, despite its rapid sales growth, the company had yet to pay dividends to stockholders, instead putting its slim profits into development and scientific research of the automobile tire, in order to be ready when the automobile industry began to grow — as the Seiberlings and Litchfield were certain it would.[48]

On May 6, 1902, the patent case was settled when the appeals court ruled against the Consolidated-Grant patent. Had the decision gone the other way, Goodyear would have been bankrupt. Instead, three years of carriage sales earnings were released from escrow, and at the plant on the banks of the Little Cuyahoga, a celebration roared. One employee climbed to the roof of a building and nailed a new broom to the top of the flag pole, signifying a new, clean start for The Goodyear Tire & Rubber Company.[49]

The court decision paved the way for true prosperity, but soon Goodyear was to be dealt another blow. Frank Seiberling was surprised to realize the untenable financial situation of his company. The Consolidated patent litigation had been costly, and Goodyear was living on loans. During the litigation, Seiberling had not wanted to be caught napping because of the patent dispute — in which he felt himself assuredly in the right — and so had continued capital improvements and product innovations, increasing sales personnel and expanding product line to include golf balls and horseshoe pads.[50]

In 1903, the company paid out $66,035 in interest charges, much of it to R.C. Penfield, Seiberling's brother-in-law and onetime Goodyear president who was a frequent endorser.[51] That year, three of Goodyear's biggest customers, E.G. Eager & Company, Toledo, and Straus Tire Company of New York, went out of business, and Goodyear found itself overstocked with inventory and accumulating bad debt.[52]

"As of August 31, 1903, Bills Payable to banks, suppliers and others totaled $825,800 and ordinary accounts payable $12,362. There was only $17,456 cash on hand and in banks. Accounts and Bills receivable totaled $593,143 against which a bad debt reserve of $103,524 had been set up. ... While margin of profit before expenses had been good, the charge-off of bad debts and other losses which had been accumulating resulted in a loss for the fiscal year 1902-1903 of $187,668.14."[53]

The Rich Man's Panic of 1903 caused a general decline of business, and as Goodyear's sales fell, creditors demanded quick payment. When R.C. Penfield's finances collapsed and he fled the country, the company faced disaster. Frank Seiberling struggled to get credit extensions, but failed. Finally, facing bankruptcy, he contacted Rubber Goods Manufacturing Company to negotiate the sale of Goodyear. His original intentions are unclear, but the terms of the proposed sale were so good, he used them to persuade creditors that the company could thrive if given time.[54] A financial reorganization ensued. Preferred stock was issued, loans were rewritten, and at the end of it, Seiberling had saved his company.

Expenses were slashed. Goodyear reduced its sales branches from 12 in 1902 to five by 1904, cutting salaried employees from 37 in 1903 to 15 one year later. The number of factory employees shrank from 637 to 281.[55] There were days when Frank Seiberling had to borrow money from friends to make payroll. Charles Seiberling once laughed about guarding the office in case the sheriff arrived to close the plant while Frank was out foraging for funds. It was bitter humor.[56]

Goodyear's decline was only temporary. Even as the company faced imminent doom, it created its own salvation by pursuing two innovations that stand as the most crucial developments in the first decade of The Goodyear Tire & Rubber Company. The first was the Goodyear Detachable Automobile Tire and Universal Rim, the tire that made possible the rapid growth of the auto industry. It was also the Tire that Made Goodyear. The second was the Tire Building Machine, which would revolutionize the manufacturing process and dramatically improve production within the industry.

Ingenious innovations in 1909 would make tire-building less arduous but some work, like making beads, still required a skilled hand.

CHAPTER THREE

WINGED VICTORY

1905–1916

"Mother asked Father what emblem he was going to have — what would he have to honor this happening? Father looked up and saw the Wingfoot statue. Father told Mother he was going to have the Wingfoot Mercury because it will help carry our tire around the world — some day Goodyear will be circling the earth."

— Frank Seiberling's daughter, Irene Harrison[1]

GOODYEAR EMERGED from its first financial crisis battered but optimistic. By 1905, the company had a plant containing 200,000 square feet of floor space, a workforce of 300 and branches in several major cities.[2] That year, it became the industry leader in the manufacture and sale of carriage tires.[3]

Unfortunately, the usefulness of the carriage was about to decline as the popularity of the automobile rose, and Goodyear was but a minor player in the new automobile market. In 1905, the company's automobile tire sales accounted for just 1¾ percent of the nation's total. By contrast, U.S. Rubber topped $30 million in sales and Akron competitor B.F. Goodrich reached nearly $9 million. Those two companies alone captured 90 percent of the market.[4]

Frank Seiberling, P.W. Litchfield, and sales director George Stadelman were keenly aware of the potential of the motorized carriage, despite its uneven growth. Two things seemed to guarantee its success: the need to transport materials to manufacturers and goods to consumers, and the public's growing desire to travel more freely. Industrialization and Western expansion had increased both production capacity and consumer demand, but as John Bell Rae wrote in *The American Automobile Industry* in the early part of this century, "The cost of moving goods 30 miles inland by road in the United States was as great as the cost of carrying the same goods across the Atlantic."[5] J.F. Starley's 1885 invention of the modern bicycle, with its two evenly sized wheels, enticed individuals in both urban and rural areas with its ease of movement. Hiram Percy Maxim, a pioneer of the auto industry, noted that the bicycle "directed men's minds to the possibilities of independent long-distance travel."[6]

The Advent of the Automobile

In 1905, the American automobile industry was in its infancy, buzzing with energy and purpose but lacking a firm sense of direction. Only 12 years had passed since the Duryea brothers of Springfield, Massachusetts, built the first working gasoline-powered automobile in the U.S.[7] In 1898, Cleveland's prosperous bicycle manufacturer, Alexander Winton, had sold his first gas-powered car and begun a brief reign as the nation's original leader in automobile sales.[8] Other automobile manufacturers soon followed, and by 1905, some 183 new companies had

The statue of the Winged Mercury that inspired Frank Seiberling to use the Wingfoot as Goodyear's trademark.

begun to manufacture cars. Many other companies, such as bicycle and carriage manufacturers and producers of farm machinery, locomotives and even household appliances, added automobiles to their product lines.[9] Between 1900 and 1910, an average of one automobile company went into operation every week.[10]

Not everyone was a fan of the automobile, but everyone was talking about it. Magazines and newspapers debated whether horseless carriages should be banned from public parks because of their noise and tendency to frighten horses.[11] *The New York Times* lamented the prevalence of "incompetent drivers" who made the auto both a nuisance and a danger.[12] The common refrain shouted to early automobile owners was, "Get a horse!"[13] Thomas Edison had predicted in 1895 that it was only a matter of time before carriages in every major city were motor-driven, but that same year, *Scientific American* assured readers that the "horse would never be dethroned."[14]

The first automobiles were flimsy contraptions, offering passengers no protection from the weather and little guarantee of safety. Philip Hillyer Smith, in *Wheels Within Wheels: A Short*

History of American Motor Car Manufacturing, wrote that "this age produced pioneer motorists as well as pioneer manufacturers." In his book, Smith recalled an anecdote about his family doctor, who owned a Model A Ford.

"On descending a hill one day, the brakes failed to have any retarding effect and the good doctor prepared to jump rather than crash into a stone wall at the bottom of the hill. But a moment before he jumped a car wheel fell off and the car dragged to a stop. Did this brush with death lead to an abandonment of the motorcar? It did not. The doctor bought a Mitchell."[15]

Car engines were powered by steam, electricity, or gasoline, and there was much public discussion regarding the pros and cons of each method of propulsion. Steam cars, such as the famous Stanley Steamers, were quiet and relatively fast, but required the driver to stop often to fill the tank with water. Electric motors were also quiet, but the cars were slow-moving,

Though it took a few years before cars became practical, an automobile craze was soon sweeping the nation.

and the batteries had short life spans. Gasoline-powered cars were annoying, with their raucous noise, hard-to-turn crank starters, and sour-smelling exhaust.[16]

Adding to the automobile owner's dilemma was the condition of the roads. At the turn of the century, there were less than 200 miles of hard-surfaced highway in the United States outside the major cities, so that a simple day's outing could subject a driver to conditions reserved today for off-road races.[17]

Bicycle owners had begun to clamor for better roads in the late 1800s, and the fight was taken up by auto enthusiasts. It wasn't until 1916, with car registrations topping 1.5 million nationwide,[18] that the Federal Aid Road Act appropriated $75 million for the construction of rural post roads. According to a 1921 Chamber of Commerce report, the money was used to "connect practically every city and town of 5,000 or more inhabitants in the United States" so that "practically 90 percent of the nation's population will live within 10 miles of a Federal Aid road.' "[19] By the late 1920s, more than half a million miles of surfaced road covered the United States.[20]

Even on paved roads, the first auto tires made driving a tricky business. They were essentially overgrown bike tires, smooth-tread pneumatics that skidded often and lasted only about 2,500 miles.[21] The industry standard was the Clincher tire, which featured a rubber bead — the part that holds the tire to the rim — that required a crowbar "and a bit of profanity" to stretch for mounting and demounting.[22]

Because the tires wore out so quickly, car owners grew frustrated with the time and effort required to change them. Horse-lovers and naysayers claimed this major inconvenience would destroy the automobile's success. A better tire was needed, and the three big companies — U.S. Rubber, B.F. Goodrich and Diamond — concentrated on perfecting the Clincher's basic design, confident that it would remain standard for the foreseeable future.[23] According to W. D.

Shilts, who joined Goodyear in 1905 and compiled an unpublished company history, the "over-confidence" of the other rubber companies "was one of Goodyear's hidden assets."[24]

Goodyear's First Innovative Tire

Seiberling and Litchfield had learned an important lesson from the disputes over the Kelly and Tillinghast patents: innovation was the only way an upstart company could compete with the established corporations. Goodyear's management, which included the Seiberling brothers, Litchfield, Stadelman, head mechanic William State and plant superintendent William Stephens, had never liked the Clincher tire and began working on a different design as early as 1900, when auto registrations totaled only

A 1911 ad from *Life* magazine hailed the success of the No-Rim-Cut tires, which made the aggravating Clincher tire obsolete.

Equipped with wagon-wheel style tires from Goodyear, this early passenger bus went into operation in 1910 in Pennsylvania.

4,192.[25] Goodyear's first innovation involved adding a braided piano wire to the tire's bead, the idea of a Cadiz, Ohio, inventor named "Nip" Scott.[26] The wire was cured into the bead, which held the tire onto the rim with a complicated set of locks. Since the tire didn't curve in to fit the rim, as the Clincher did, it could hold 10 percent more compressed air, providing a more comfortable ride.[27]

The tire was named the Straight Side, and in 1901 Goodyear adopted the Wingfoot trademark to advertise its new product, first using it in an advertisement in *The Saturday Evening Post*.[28] The trademark was Frank Seiberling's idea. Irene Harrison, Seiberling's daughter, recalled how he was inspired by a statue of the Winged Mercury sitting at the bottom of the stairs in their home.

"At that time Father would come and go at noon by trolley to eat lunch. One noon he came in and said to Mother, 'At long last, we've gotten to the point that we've developed our pneumatic tire for the automobile.' ... Mother asked Father what emblem he was going to have — what would he have to honor this happening? Father looked up and saw the Wingfoot statue. Father told Mother he was going to have the Wingfoot Mercury because it will help carry our tire around the world — some day Goodyear will be circling the earth."[29]

But Mercury, the Roman god of transportation, flew more slowly than Seiberling hoped. An exporting company, Davis & Allen, marketed the Straight Sides in England, securing the Prince of Wales and Sir Thomas Lipton among its customers, but the performance of the tires was less than noble.

"A story is told of how Lord Salisbury, while riding at Brighton one day on Goodyear tires, had a

puncture. His resourceful chauffeur filled the casing with hay from a nearby field and started on home. ... Soon there was an imperious command from his Lordship in the back seat to stop the car. The friction in the hay had set fire to the car."[30]

The tires performed no better in a 1902 London road race, blowing out in the heat of competition. Litchfield, who paid his own way across the Atlantic on a cattle boat to attend the race, sailed home frustrated but determined.[31] By late 1903, he had written out the specifications for the Quick Detachable Tire, a straight-side tire with improved resiliency designed to prevent blowouts.[32] The new tire featured an open-weave rivet fabric between the tread and tire carcass, which would "rivet" these components together during vulcanization by allowing rubber to flow through.[33] The tire was held by a metal locking device requiring a new kind of rim, designed once again by Nip Scott. The rim could fit either a clincher or the new lock-on straight side. With this innovation, the Universal Rim was born.[34]

The Quick Detachable Tire

Goodyear staked its future on this tire. The additional air pressure of the Straight Side provided a more cushioned ride, and the resilient rivet fabric absorbed road shocks and eliminated the problem of tearing at the rim, advertised with the slogan, "No Rim Cuts."[35] Furthermore, the tire was much easier to lock on and remove. The company had a truly superior product and wanted the world to know. In late 1905, splashy ads for

A 1970 photo of Henry Ford's Model T. This reasonably priced car would start an automotive revolution, one which Goodyear rolled with.

Above: A Goodyear tire is fitted on an early Buick.
Inset: Goodyear distributed free booklets to the public that explained the construction of tires, and how to choose the best tire.

the new "Quick, Detachable, 10% Oversize, No Rim Cut, Straight Side Tire" ran in *The Saturday Evening Post* and other national magazines.[36] Stadelman's salesmen "went out like inspired prophets of a new religion."[37] Because the tire required a new rim, Goodyear would have to capture the original equipment market, selling directly to the auto manufacturers. The industry remained skeptical, owing to Goodyear's earlier reputation for manufacturing poor-quality bicycle tires.[38]

By 1907, the company's sales to automobile manufacturers barely topped 3,000 units, and its customers were primarily small and relatively unknown companies, not the big names of the day like Winton, Packard, or Pierce-Arrow.[39] But the auto industry itself had yet to hit its stride. As Frank Seiberling wrote in 1920, the Goodyear management team "believed in the future of the automobile and for six years ... carried on the development and sale of pneumatic automobile tires at a financial loss just so that we might be ready to supply these tires when the boom which we felt sure would come actually got under way."[40] Seiberling, the de facto leader of Goodyear, became head of the company by title in 1906, when he was elected president.

In 1907, auto registrations hit 43,000, nearly double the figure of just three years previously, and by 1909, the number again tripled to 123,990.[41] At that time the automobile was still considered a "rich man's toy," and companies like Cadillac, Oldsmobile (which had been purchased by General Motors a year earlier) and Packard worked hard to attract wealthy consumers.[42] But Henry Ford envisioned mass market potential, and his determination to produce a "car for the multitude" was realized when in 1908 the Model T "Tin Lizzie" debuted.[43]

Ford's Model T offered reasonable performance at a middle-class price. The spectacular success of this automobile represented a turning point for the automobile industry. In one year, from 1907 to 1908, the average wholesale price of a car fell from $2,100 to $1,288.[44] In 1908, 1,200 Model Ts rolled off the line on Goodyear tires — a number below the sales of Goodrich and U.S. Rubber, but a landmark order for Goodyear.[45]

However, the transition from the clincher to the detachable tire was still taking longer than Goodyear's management had hoped. In late 1907, Stadelman announced that the company would sell the Universal rim directly to auto manufacturers who did not want Goodyear tires.[46] This was a brilliant strategy because, although car companies

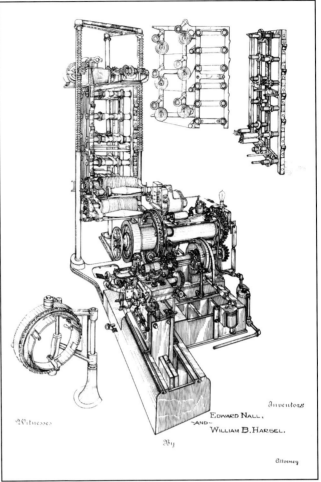

Right: The schematic of the State-Seiberling tire-building machine.

Below: The tire machine reduced some of the most grueling tasks, such as stretching tough, stiff fabric to form the tire carcass.

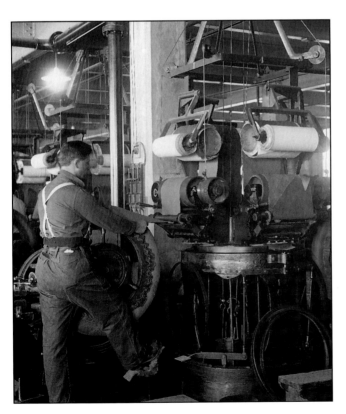

shunned the detachable tire, they used the rim. This allowed the consumer to choose either the detachable or the clincher tire.

In a second shrewd move, Goodyear's board of directors voted to license companies to make the detachable tires and rims. Michelin, for example, with its superior reputation and firm contracts, took out a license, and sales began to pour in.[47] As more new automobiles featured the Universal rims, Goodyear's business on renewal tire sales jumped. Customers saw for themselves the difference in the ways the tires were mounted and heard about the tires' reliability and comfort. They began to choose the straight side tires, and the clincher tire started a swift decline.

Lacking capital to set up a network of stores, Goodyear sold its products through service stations and automobile accessory shops. Goodyear management believed that informed consumers would naturally choose its Detachable Straight Side Tire, so the company's marketing was aimed at educating the public. To accomplish this, the company began to sell through dealers rather than directly to consumers. Dealers were carefully selected and trained to help discerning consumers pick the right brand.[48] Stadelman wrote out detailed sales pitches for the dealers to use, and in return, he and Frank Seiberling offered dealers a higher profit margin on Goodyear tires.[49]

The company also issued free booklets titled "How to Select an Auto Tire." Advertisements invited the public to pick up copies from local Goodyear dealers.[50] In a 1909 *New York Times* article, George Stadelman warned consumers to "master the elemental points of tires and tire construction" in order to save money, and an advertisement from the same year emphasized Goodyear's quality.[51] An advertisement from the same year proclaimed in bold letters, "15,000 Miles from One Auto Tire," and the opening line promised that "Goodyear Detachable Auto Tires have done this and better — scores of times." The advertisement stated that the secret was the tire's superior construction, which combined the best of the moulding and wrapping methods of other brands but eliminated their "hidden defects."[52] Some ads acknowledged the higher price of the detachable tire as compared to the clincher, but assured the public that "an oversize tire, with added air capacity, is worth more than a tire without it."[53]

The State-Seiberling Tire-Building Machine

By 1908, Goodyear's strategy and aggressive media campaign were paying off. Tire production increased from 12,626 in 1905 to 23,712 in

Above: A cross-section of cord tire.

Below: With orders rolling in, Goodyear's tire room was always in motion.

1908, while factory employment rose to 579 during the same period.[54] Daily production of the detachable straight side tire, which in 1905 stood at 90, had jumped to 900 by 1908.[55] Total sales doubled from $2 million in 1907 to $4 million the following year.[56] The factory never stopped, with workers alternating on three eight-hour shifts.[57] Nearly 12,000 sets of tires were sold to car manufacturers by August 31, 1909, the end of Goodyear's fiscal year — a 400-percent increase over the previous year. By 1912, the number of tire sets sold to car manufacturers would exceed 120,690.[58] Ads began bragging that 30 percent of all new cars rode on Goodyears. In 1911, the exact figure was 36 percent.[59] The days of borrowing money to meet the payroll from friends and brothers-in-law were over.

The company's new challenge was to meet the growing demand. From 1909 to 1913, Goodyear undertook a major construction and renovation project, investing more than $1.5 million in 1912 alone.[60] The factory grew from 15 acres to 45, and the size of the machine shop was doubled. Two stories were added to the office building on Market Street, and the first two of three tall smokestacks on Plant 1 were erected.[61] Still, the plant was small compared to the volume of business rolling in. The company could meet its orders only because of another important innovation: the State-Seiberling Tire-Building Machine.

In February 1909, *The New York Times* reported that Goodyear had recently put into operation four machines that improved both tire quality and manufacturing capacity.[62] Workers who previously manufactured tires by hand had to carry up to 250 pounds of iron core and alternating layers of fabric and rubber on their bruised shoulders. The *Times* reported that these workers could now rely on machines to do much of the work, speeding up the process and providing uniform quality.[63]

"All chance of weakness in any spot is now declared done away with by the machine's unvarying strength. ... To give the greatest mileage, the fabric must be stretched to an absolutely even tension over each portion of the tire, and each alternative layer of fabric must be given the same tension of those previously put

To gather latex from Hevea trees, used to make rubber, workers cut V-shaped gashes in the bark and caught the dripping latex in cups.

on. This evenness of tension can never be given where human hands are depended upon, as tires made in the morning when a man is fresh will be stretched more tightly than later in the day, when his muscles are weary."[64]

The Tire-Building Machine was invented in 1904 by Goodyear's superintendent William Stephens. It was later perfected by head shop mechanic William State in 1907.[65] Its success soon grabbed the attention of other manufacturers. The machine maximized space, a blessing since Goodyear's unit tire production went up 30 times from 1908 to 1912 but floor space expanded only four times. Two men working on each machine could turn out an average of 37 tires per eight-hour shift.[66] Frank Seiberling, who owned the machine's patent, boasted of Goodyear's output and demonstrated the machine to other manufacturing concerns. By 1909, 50 companies had licensed the device.[67] During the life of the patent, Goodyear took in more than $2 million in royalties.[68]

Expanding Interests

Although the automobile tire was Goodyear's core of profitability, it was not the company's only line. Under President Seiberling, Goodyear expanded dramatically, opening its first international plant in Ontario, Canada, in 1910.[69] In addition to tires, the plant, located in the town of Bowmanville, made industrial products such as hose and belting, sold through branches opened in several Canadian cities. In 1912, with its eyes on the European market, Goodyear started a sales branch in London,[70] and the next year announced plans to open a $1.8- million rubber factory in Rio de Janeiro, the first in South America.[71]

As part of the company's industrial relations which began in 1912, the Goodyear Heights housing project was Frank Seiberling's pet project aimed to attract family men to Goodyear.

In 1909, realizing the importance of the Wright brothers' accomplishments with early aircraft, Goodyear engineers produced a pneumatic tire especially for airplanes, replacing the sled runners and bike tires some fledgling aviators employed.[72] The tires, called Goodyear Wing Aeroplane Cord Tires, were used in the first transcontinental flight, completed by Calbraith Rogers in 1911. In a trip lasting 49 days, Rogers flew from Pasadena, California, to Sheepshead Bay, New York, in a Burgess-Wright biplane. Goodyear's participation in this historic flight foreshadowed the company's important role in the future of aeronautics and space exploration.[73] The next year, Goodyear's engineers came up with a fabric for lighter-than-air aircraft, and the company began planning its first blimp.[74]

As Goodyear was capturing the automobile tire market in the United States, the Diamond Rubber Company, soon to be absorbed by B.F. Goodrich, acquired the American rights for a new cord tire developed by the Palmer Tire Company in England.[75] Called the Silvertown, this tire used woven cords bound by thin cross-hairs to reduce the tearing of standard square-woven fabric.[76] In response, Goodyear's engineers developed a fabric with cords slightly thicker than the square-weave, but held together by cross threads so fine they were broken under vulcanization, thus eliminating the chafing that weakened the tire.[77] In 1913, Seiberling convinced race car driver Ralph de Palma to use the new multiple-cord tires in the Indianapolis 500. Both the public and other drivers were impressed.[78] The following year, every car in the race was equipped with Goodyear cord tires.[79]

What had begun as Frank Seiberling's impulse purchase was fast becoming a major company. Suddenly, the management was no longer familiar with every employee. To maintain a sense of unity, the employee newspaper, the *Wingfoot Clan*, was established in 1912 to "promote in a large organization that close understanding, goodwill and justice between the employees and the Management which exist in small factories," as Paul Litchfield wrote.[80] The company was ahead of its time in many areas, and developed a uniquely paternalistic relationship with its employees. The company offered classes in English and citizenship for foreign-born employees;[81] established one of the

Goodyear workers who emigrated to the United States could take "Americanization" classes to learn the language and customs of their adopted country. In turn, Goodyear got a better-educated employee.

nation's first industrial hospitals;[82] installed water fountains in the factory; opened a cafeteria for workers; and started the Goodyear Relief Association, a mutual benefit plan to provide financial aid for ill workers.[83]

Furthermore, ground was broken on the Goodyear Heights housing project, an elevated tract of land 10 minutes walking distance from the factory.[84] Employees could choose from three basic building plans and finance with 20-year mortgages that let them buy the houses at cost-plus-interest if they remained Goodyear employees.[85] In an address to stockholders, Frank Seiberling explained that the housing project would link Goodyear's fortunes to the American Dream. With Goodyear Heights, the company hoped to attract:

"Men of character — sound in body, sound in mind, sound in citizen thinking. Taking the broad view into the future, it believes that it can only get those conditions, not out of the tenant, but out of the homeowner, and therefore it is promoting the development on Goodyear Heights. ... We believe that the workingmen on the Heights will always be the great balance wheel in this plant, the force that will keep it steady and going forward."[86]

In January 1916, Goodyear again moved forward internationally, opening branches in South Africa, Australia and Argentina.[87] It was operating a cotton mill in Connecticut to make fabric for its multiple-cord tires and would purchase land in Sumatra and Arizona for plantations to produce rubber and cotton and build its second tire factory in Akron.[88] Goodyear's total tire production would nearly double from 1915 to 1916, hitting 4,118,399 to make it the world's largest tire company and kick off the slogan, "More People Ride On Goodyear Tires than on Any Other Kind."[89]

1917 — To prove the durability of the pneumatic cord tires, Goodyear launches the Wingfoot Express truck line.

1920 — An economic downturn catches Goodyear severely overextended, and threatened with bankruptcy.

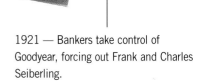

1917 — Goodyear begins producing airships and observation balloons for the military.

1921 — Bankers take control of Goodyear, forcing out Frank and Charles Seiberling.

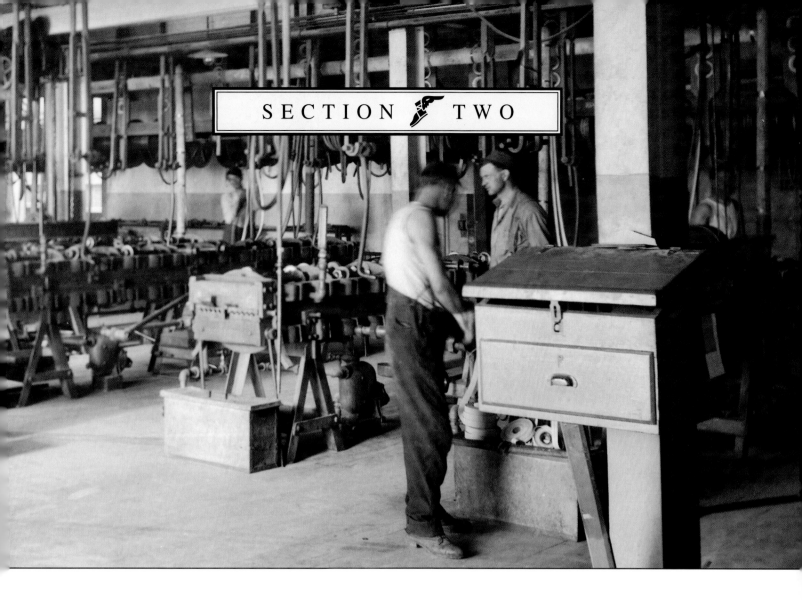

1921 — Morale plummets as Goodyear lays off workers and staff. Tired of the miasma of fear, P.W. Litchfield reignites enthusiasm during a management meeting.

1929 — Company stock returns to dividend-paying basis, six months prior to Black Monday.

1926 — As Goodyear resumes prosperous growth, P.W. Litchfield is named company president.

Victorious "doughboys" march past cheering Goodyearites on Market Street. Goodyear supplied vital products ranging from gas masks to airships.

CHAPTER FOUR

THE WINDS OF CHANGE

1916–1921

"They built a mighty industry, far flung and worldwide; one that bulked big among the giants of business, but they never lost the human touch. They were our friends, friends to us of the shop."

— Tribute to the Seiberling brothers, 1921[1]

BY 1916, Frank Seiberling's prediction that the Wingfoot trademark would encircle the globe was coming true. Buoyant at having become the world's largest tire manufacturer, Goodyear's management set its sights even higher. Executives vowed to surpass U.S. Rubber to stand as the largest rubber company in the world. With sales orders being written faster than the factories could fill them, Seiberling believed such achievement was inevitable, and his optimism was infectious. A 1917 article in the *Wingfoot Clan* enthusiastically described the history of Goodyear as cause for "gratitude and thanksgiving."[2]

The company certainly had reason to celebrate. In 1917, sales topped $100 million for the first time.[3] Upon the celebration of its 20th anniversary in 1918, Goodyear listed more than 20,000 names on its growing payroll.[4] By 1919, Goodyear maintained 124 branches in all major American cities.[5] The company distributed tires through more than 20,000 dealers nationwide and listed more than 25,000 stockholders.[6]

Growth in An Uncertain World

The "war to end all wars," which had begun in 1914, brought with it years of global struggle and privation. Even before the United States entered the war, business conditions had grown erratic, posing new problems in exporting goods and importing raw materials in and around war zones. Germany's unrestricted submarine campaign added to the problems.

In spite of the uneasy circumstances overseas, Goodyear added another innovative product to its string of successes — the pneumatic cord truck tire. The design was drawn in 1912, but the tire wasn't introduced until 1916.[7] The first of its kind, the pneumatic tire contained an inner tube of air that provided a softer ride.

The tire eventually became standard on automobiles, but acceptance was gradual. Most people within the auto industry, as well as in the general public, were convinced that solid tires were necessary to support the heavy loads carried by trucks.[8] But Litchfield and his development team, noting the slowness of solid-tired motor trucks, believed pneumatic tires could increase speeds and usefulness. The tire's air cushion would better absorb treacherous road conditions, they reasoned, and its traction and nonskid properties would make it easier to climb up and down steep hills.[9]

By 1916, Frank Seiberling's prediction that the Wingfoot symbol would "carry our tire around the world" had come true.

Seiberling and Litchfield reasoned that pneumatic tires could make trucks more valuable than railways for hauling goods, opening a vast market for tire sales.

The Wingfoot Express

The new tire was met with skepticism, and once again Goodyear undertook a public relations campaign to promote its product. On April 9, 1917, the Wingfoot Express was launched when a five-ton Packard truck fitted with 38-by-7-inch front and 44-by-10-inch rear cord tires rolled out of Akron bound for Boston.[10] That first trip was

---

Goodyear built several of its own trucks in 1920 to demonstrate the value of tandem rear wheels.

Below: To show the dependability of newly developed pneumatic tires, Goodyear's truck line transported goods across the nation. Truck crews faced bad roads and often had to build their own bridges.

bumpy, due to bad roads and worse weather, and the truck took 19 days to deposit its load of tires at Goodyear's Boston branch. The return trip, thanks to improved weather and a lighter load of fabrics, took only five days.[11] Soon, amid much marketing fanfare, the Wingfoot Express fleet was regularly making the round trip in only five days, faster than travel by train.[12]

In a 1919 memo, G. M. Stadelman wrote of the sales potential of the pneumatic truck tire. "There are 7 million farms which already use close to 75,000 trucks, 425,000 tractors, and other motor equipment in almost unbelievable amounts. Here alone is a present market for hundreds and hundreds of thousands of tires, and for miles and miles of belting and hose."[13] With this enormous potential in mind, Goodyear expanded its publicity campaign. Trucks equipped with the new tires were shown at county fairs and auto shows, contributing to a nationwide movement to motorize the farm.[14] In July

1918, the company sponsored a 3,000-mile trip to the Eastern states for 50 Boy Scouts, who traveled in five cord-tire-equipped trucks, one bearing a makeshift kitchen.[15] The boys rode and slept in three of the trucks, with a fourth carrying camping gear, and visited Gettysburg, Philadelphia, Boston and Washington, where they were entertained in the East Room by President Woodrow Wilson.[16]

The scouts were Goodyear's own troops, part of a tradition that started after P.W. Litchfield met some Canadian scouts while traveling by ship from Quebec. Impressed with the organization's emphasis on personal character, Litchfield brought the idea back to Goodyear, and a scout lodge was built in Goodyear Heights.[17] The Goodyearite in charge of supervising the trip was Edwin J. Thomas, who had joined the company two years before, served as the assistant to Litchfield's secretary, and was hardly older than some of the scouts. In 1940, he would become the company's eighth president.[18] Under Thomas' direction, the journey was completed without a single tire blowout, a fact Goodyear emphasized to the public.[19]

The following year, Goodyear launched the first transcontinental trucking line in the nation. On September 1, 1918, two large trucks left Boston with loads of fabric and an accompanying pilot car, stopping to unload the fabric at the Akron plant and reload with airplane tires, and arriving in San Francisco on September 22.[20] Each truck had two drivers. While one drove, the other slept, uncomfortably cramped behind the

Goodyear trucks embark on the summer of 1918 Boy Scout adventure, a tour that covered 3,000 miles in nine days.

driver's seat. The actual road time for the 3,700-mile trip was 289 hours, slowed by poor trails over the mountains and rotted bridges, some of which had to be hastily rebuilt to get the trucks across rushing streams.[21] More than 70 percent of the roads traveled were unpaved, and Goodyear earned favorable reviews for the tires' performance under trying conditions.[22]

By 1926, the production of pneumatics would overtake solids, and by 1930, would beat them 10 to 1.[23] In a speech before the United States Chamber of Commerce, Frank Seiberling confidently announced that "the introduction of the motor truck into our commercial life sounds the death knell of the short-line railroad."[24]

Goodyear's First Plantation: "The Place Where Women Wash Their Hair"

Meanwhile, the bloody conflict in Europe disrupted rubber supplies and caused the price of imported rubber to fluctuate. As early as 1910, Goodyear's management began to explore the feasibility of developing its own overseas rubber plantation.[25] Although an expensive proposition, rubber plantations had been successfully created by other companies. Thousands of acres in the Middle East, for example, had been converted, with promising results.[26] Stock in the plantations soared, for rubber produced under controlled conditions was a purer, more cost-effective product than that gathered by bands of workers cutting their way through jungle.[27]

Still, it was a risky proposition, Litchfield would later recall. "This would be our largest outside investment. It was something we could not direct personally. ... However, we felt that over the long swing it was a good business risk. The world would continue to use more and more rubber."[28]

Goodyear was visited by representatives of a Dutch syndicate looking to sell land in Sumatra, Indonesia.[29] In the spring of 1916, Goodyear's Singapore buyer, Jack Blandin, inspected the land, and on his recommendation the company purchased 20,000 acres in Sumatra, less than one-tenth of which had been cleared and planted with cocoa and tea.[30] The rest was dense jungle.

Accustomed to Ohio's rolling farmland and temperate climate, Goodyear's management had little idea of how to set up a plantation in a rain forest. Initially, Blandin tried to hire a company in Sumatra to clear the land, plant rubber trees and oversee workers. However, the available companies required exorbitant fees and percentages as well as complete control over daily management, and none would agree to work more than 2,500 acres a year.[31] Upon hearing how much bidders wanted, along with such limiting clauses, Litchfield reportedly "hit the ceiling" and told Seiberling the company should take care of the plantation itself.[32]

Before joining Goodyear in 1912, Blandin had limited experience growing rubber in Mexico for a New York syndicate,[33] so he and L.G. Odell, the manager of the Akron plants' crude rubber department who had made the six-week journey to Sumatra, were told to develop the land in whatever way they saw fit.[34] Also sent to Sumatra were E. L. Demmon, a college senior whose experience studying Michigan forestry had been primarily with hard pines and oaks, but who at least understood plant pathology; and John Ingle, a graduate of Massachusetts Tech.[35]

More than 7,000 workers from the nearby island of Java were hired, and they immediately set about felling trees and pulling out the 12-foot high stumps with steel cables. Within a year, 5,000 acres had been cleared; within four years, all 20,000 acres were ready for planting.[36] The plantation was given the name Dolok Merangir, using the language of the local Batak tribe to describe "the place where women wash their hair."[37]

Hevea trees, the principal source of industrial rubber, were planted in orderly rows. A few years later they were ready for tapping, a process similar to gathering sap from maple trees. Using a special knife, workers would make a shallow gash in the bark and attach collection cups into which the latex would flow.[38] The latex was taken to collection stations on the plantation where it was strained into large tanks and mixed with acid to hasten coagulation. At this point, the rubber formed into "a doughy white mass, while the liquid part of the latex [was] drained off in much the same manner as the curd separates from whey as milk turns sour."[39] Rollers were used to squeeze the substance flat, and the sheets were dried and smoked, then pressed into bales for shipment to the factories.[40]

Even when it was in full operation, the plantation could not fulfill the company's voracious need for raw rubber — and the management did not want it to. In a 1920 article from *System* magazine, Frank Seiberling explained his reason to enter the raw materials market.

"In the first place, if we endeavored to supply everything that we need, not only should we be unable to check our own costs with the market

A worker on the Dolok Merangir plantation collects latex as it drips from V-shaped cuts in the tree.

costs and thus lose the invaluable stimulus of the competition, but also if for any reason our own markets failed us, we should have no other prepared markets to turn to. We would rather control only enough of the supply to keep check on the market and if necessary to stimulate it. If market prices grow out of reason because of outside demand, we are able from our own sources to provide a minimum supply which will prevent our national organization from shutting down and disintegrating."[41]

Goodyear's Cotton Plantation

Later in 1916, the company opened a cotton plantation in southern Arizona. Strong-fiber cotton was crucial to the success of the cord truck tire, with its increased stress of heavy loads and long distances. But before the invention of rayon and nylon, the only usable cotton was the long-staple variety produced in Egypt's Nile Valley and on the Sea Islands off the coasts of Georgia and the Carolinas.[42]

World War I had virtually stopped imports from Egypt, and the Sea Island supply was being devastated by the boll weevil insect.[43] Litchfield learned that the United States Department of

Agriculture had conducted successful experiments growing a similar cotton in the Salt River Valley of Arizona, and in 1916, with tire sales climbing, Litchfield traveled to the Southwest for the purpose of enticing ranchers to convert the land to cotton fields.[44] He found no takers even after guaranteeing that Goodyear would buy at above-market prices. Once again, the company took charge. Land was purchased and The Southwest Cotton Company was formed as a subsidiary to operate the plantation.[45] In his autobiography, *Industrial Voyage*, Litchfield described the process of cultivating the arid land.

"Almost overnight an army of men started moving in, hundreds of Mexicans who threw up brushwood and adobe shelters, and a still larger force of adventurers, drawn from all over the West by the lure of good pay, men who went from one big construction job to the next. We soon had 2,000 men on the job — and 1,200 mules at the peak, more than half the mule population of the state.

"Big caterpillar tractors rumbled in from the Coast, were hooked up in tandem with a length of railroad steel between them, set off across the desert. Other gangs were drilling wells, putting in

In 1916, the desert was made to "blossom like a garden" with cotton, which was used to build cord truck tires. Goodyear turned to growing cotton because the war interrupted cotton supplies.

pumps, building power lines, laying out a network of concrete canals and irrigation ditches, building highways, town sites, even a railroad.

"The property was so large and the roads so bad that we had to buy an airplane to get over it."[46]

In December 1917, Seiberling wrote to his stockholders that the men had made the desert "blossom like a garden" to the extent that more than 4,000 acres of cotton had been produced.[47] From 1918 to 1919, more than 6.7 million pounds of cotton were picked on a 10,000-acre tract.[48]

World War I

On April 6, 1917, with Great Britain on the verge of collapse, the United States finally abandoned its position of neutrality and entered World War I. Traditional ties to Britain, combined with Germany's unrestricted submarine campaign prompted America to enter the conflict. Although the war would cost many American lives, it would also open new opportunities for American businesses, including Goodyear.

By the time war was declared, Goodyear was second in the nation in sales of tires, with revenues exceeding $103.5 million. The company was still behind U.S. Rubber, which reported revenues of more than $171 million.[49] Many smaller companies, such as Fisk, Lee, and Kelly-Springfield, competed for the remaining business, mostly in the replacement tire market.[50]

With its manufacturing facilities and emphasis on research and development, Goodyear was uniquely positioned to aid the war effort in what was the first mechanized conflict. For the first time, airplanes dueled over battlefields, adding a new dimension to warfare. At the war's onset, enemy pilots merely waved as they passed each other to observe troop movements. By 1918, however, large numbers of pilots engaged in wild dogfights. As a result, the United States Army wanted an airplane fuel tank that could self-seal when hit and wouldn't collapse if the plane crashed. Of the several designs submitted, Goodyear's was chosen.[51]

Although the company supplied a number of rubber-related products, such as gas masks, to the war effort, Goodyear's biggest contribution was in the field of aeronautics. The company's first wartime order came in February 1917, when the Navy contracted Goodyear to construct nine of 16 airships to be designed after Germany's Zeppelins, which had caught the Allies off guard.[52] Although a few smaller B-Limp airships — nonrigid lighter-than-air — had been produced,[53] the United States had no rigid airships and gained knowledge of their peculiar construction from inspecting fragments of downed German Zeppelins.[54] At that time, Goodyear had the only Aeronautics Department in the rubber business and thus was the only factory in the country able to begin work immediately. The company had been making successful balloon envelopes since 1913, some for the Army as observation tools and others for racing; a Goodyear balloon had won the national contest of 1914.[55]

Seiberling viewed the airship project as a "patriotic duty."[56] Under the direction of Bill State, 720 acres of land bordering Fritch's Lake, renamed Wingfoot Lake and lying about 12 miles from the

---

Goodyear competes in an early balloon race. The company was successful in international racing, winning its first contest in 1913, a floating dash from Paris to England.

The B-15, a Goodyear-built Navy airship, stationed at Pensacola, Florida. During World War I, the company built about 100 airships.

Akron plants, became the site of a powerhouse, a hydrogen plant and a 400-foot-by-100-foot-by-100-foot hangar, the largest in the country.[57] The first Navy blimps were classified as F-ships, containing a gas capacity of 77,000 cubic feet. From the envelope a fabric-covered airplane fuselage was suspended, used for the crew and a front-mounted single engine.[58] Goodyear completed the ship by the end of May, some six weeks earlier than the Navy had requested, while the Wingfoot Lake hangar was still under construction.[59] The ship was assembled in a large shed at a Chicago amusement park and flown to Akron for an unofficial test run.[60] The airship completed all but 20 miles of its scheduled flight, landing in a field just west of Medina, Ohio, because the engine was low on oil.[61] Still, the 400-mile flight was the longest of its time, and the Navy was jubilant.[62] With a few fresh quarts of oil, the blimp took off again and landed near Wingfoot Lake, and Naval officers announced the blimp fleet would be operating by mid-August to help hunt submarines, supplementing the operations of submarine chasers and reserve destroyers.[63]

The U.S. Army called on Goodyear for its traditional product line as well, ordering solid truck tires in huge volumes. Though Goodyear retained no records of the exact figures, some 100,000 tires were left in France alone after the Armistice was signed in 1918. The French government then offered them for resale in the United States at a discounted price.[64]

In 1918, government business accounted for 15 percent of Goodyear's total sales.[65] During the war, the completed Wingfoot Lake hangar was used by the Navy as a training base for balloon and blimp pilots.[66] On the production line, James Cooper was made foreman of the "balloon room" and developed a process to eliminate bulges and wrinkles from the finished envelopes. During World War II, an armed cargo ship bore his name, a posthumous honor for his contributions to aeronautics.[67] At its peak, the Aeronautics

Department employed 2,000 men and women.[68] By the end of the war, Goodyear produced 822 observation balloons and 39 blimps, as well as the majority of tires for 11,000 military planes.[69]

As the war dragged on, the rubber industry faced a supply shortage.[70] Operating under rules set down by the War Industries Board, companies could have all the rubber necessary to fill direct government orders, including supplies for the railroads and the Red Cross, but other civilian orders were restricted.[71] The worst crunch came in the summer of 1918. Supplies grew so restricted that Goodyear stopped making bicycle and carriage tires as well as rubber bands.[72] A coal shortage prompted the government to shut down rubber companies every Monday, a demand Goodyear got around by agreeing to make only war products on those days and then by purchasing its own coal mine in Adena, Ohio, and contracting with the Wheeling Township Coal Mining Company to run it.[73] Other industries that required rubber began to feel the effects of the war. Automobile production, for example, fell to half what it had been the previous summer.[74]

Goodyear was also hit hard by the loss of labor. About 6,200 of its men volunteered or were drafted into service.[75] To alleviate the labor short-

Above: Women workers build tires during World War I. Though traditionally a man's job, women were needed to accomplish many non-traditional roles during the war.

Below: The Wheeling Township coal mine was purchased by Goodyear in 1918 during a coal shortage. The company operated the mine until 1949.

age, more than 3,000 women were hired to do what had traditionally been considered men's work. Goodyear also started a program to train deaf-mutes for factory work, employing about 200 during the war and as many as 600 afterward.[76] With workers in high demand, wages rose. The average hourly rate in January 1917 was 46 cents an hour for a laborer, increasing to 68 cents by November 1918, when overtime pay was established at time-and-a-half for hours in excess of a 48-hour week. Double overtime was established for Sundays and holidays.[77] To maintain morale, the company undertook several programs, using the *Wingfoot Clan* to encourage workers' contributions to war efforts. Based on these pleas, 11,000 employees bought First Liberty Loan bonds, and more than 18,000 employees contributed an average of $29 to the War Chest.[78] Using shame as a way to encourage maximum effort, the *Wingfoot Clan* defined the term "slacker" as a man who stays safely at home

but fails to give his best on the production line to support his brothers overseas.[79]

Turning Toward Peace

At the time of the Armistice in November 1918, Goodyear had 7,200 workers devoted to war products and looked forward to the return of 6,000 soldiers.[80] Approximately half of the women who had been hired during the war wanted to remain working, and Seiberling assigned William Stephens to develop a plan to "convert to peacetime operation with minimum disruption of employee morale."[81] Men who came back found jobs waiting for them, and more than 6,000 workers, including 1,500 women, were converted to peacetime production.[82] Goodyear quickly increased its domestic sales force to 1,000 field representatives working out of 66 branches.[83] Salesmen wooed dealers with new fervor, since during the war the company had lost fully one-third of its licensed dealers to product and labor shortage.[84]

Goodyear also set its sights more keenly on the export market. Prior to the war, Goodyear's main European competitors were Germany's Continental, France's Michelin, England's Dunlop, and Italy's Pirelli. The war eliminated Continental's export business and severely distracted the others, so the timing was right to challenge their market share. By 1916, Goodyear had established subsidiaries in such cities as Birmingham and Manchester, England; Glasgow, Scotland; Belfast and Dublin, Ireland. Other branches or representative agencies were started in Barcelona and Madrid, Spain; Sydney, Australia; Java, Indonesia; Buenos Aires, Argentina; and Rio de Janeiro, Brazil; Mexico City, Mexico; and Havana, Cuba.[85] By 1919, Goodyear's export business reached $8.5 million, an impressive increase from only $500,000 six years before.[86]

In September 1919, *Financial World* expressed astonishment at the rapid growth of the company, but was confident that Goodyear's success would continue. However, analyst Park Mathewson warned Goodyear to "be well prepared" for wide swings in common stock and the price of raw materials.

A plaque was put up in the lobby of Goodyear's headquarters to honor the company's World War I casualties.

"With this probable success in manufacturing and marketing conditions, it is only necessary for the company to consider with equal care the administrative and finance division, which become more complicated and arduous as the organization grows, and its various functions and activities embrace into the manufacturing of other lines and even the production of raw material."[87]

The words would seem prophetic just a few years later.

The years following World War I were Akron's "Silk Shirt Era," so-called because many rubber workers sported silk shirts and felt hats as markers of prosperity.[88] The city's Chamber of Commerce proudly displayed the slogan, "Akron, the City of Opportunity," on a large billboard, and employment in the rubber industry swelled from 22,000 in 1913 to 70,000 in 1920.[89] For the financial year ending October 31, 1919, Goodyear reported a sales increase of $37.5 million, reaching an all-time high of almost $169 million.[90] Vice President of Sales Bill Stadelman noted that sales would have been even higher if the factories had been able to make products as fast as the salesmen could write orders.[91]

In 1921, expansion projects that had been started before the war were finally completed at the Akron plants, the Canadian factory and the

Connecticut cotton mill.[92] A 158-acre tire plant and cotton mill were built in Los Angeles in 1919. Advertised as The Goodyear Tire & Rubber Company of California, this was the first West Coast factory established by a major rubber company.[93]

To finance the expansion, $50 million worth of common and preferred stock, split evenly, were sold during the war.[94] Seiberling preferred to sell stock directly to current holders, customers and employees because he distrusted Wall Street bankers.[95] In October 1919, Seiberling sent a letter to stockholders announcing the company's intention to again double its authorized capital to $200 million, split evenly between common and preferred stock.

> *"One year ago, due to the restrictions of the government and conditions growing out of the war, we were employing approximately 14,000 men, making at the low point in our production (November) less than 11,000 tires per day, with a volume of business approximating $8 million per month.*
>
> *"Since the close of the war, with restrictions and control removed, we have rapidly rebuilt our organization until now we are employing 25,000 men, making in excess of 29,000 tires per day and our business for this month will approximate $20 million in volume.*
>
> *"Notwithstanding this large increase in volume, we have not been able to produce product in excess of 70 percent of our sales requirements."*[96]

The "two-and-one" campaign offered two shares of preferred stock with one of common, with a 150-percent common stock dividend.[97] Few stockholders took the offer, but the campaign to sell to employees paid off. Both the *Wingfoot Clan* and *Goodyear: A Family Newspaper* ran articles announcing the sale of stock and recounting Goodyear's glorious history. One article read, "In the proceeds of this rarely paralleled business development and expansion, the Goodyear Company is not unmindful of its employees who have had so large a part in this work and calls their attention first to the significance and the opportunity."[98] Employees could purchase stock through payroll deductions, and many secured bank loans to take more than they could comfortably afford.[99] The directors set an example by purchasing $546,000 of stock themselves.[100]

The amount of stock sold, however, was insufficient. The company's finances were weakening even as sales continued to climb due to its rapid expansion.

The year 1920 appeared more promising, however. Goodyear's business in its third quarter exceeded that of the previous year by 59.3 percent.[101] Throughout the spring, sales averaged nearly $1 million per day, and the plants processed 8 million pounds of rubber and 3 million pounds of fabric each month.[102] Even with its own plantations, Goodyear purchased the majority of its raw materials from outside sources and had to order several months in advance to guard against shortages and allow time for shipping. In another appeal to the stockholders on May 27, 1920, Seiberling wrote:

The 158-acre tire plant and cotton mill, built in Los Angeles in 1919, was the first West Coast factory to be established by a major rubber company.

"By reason of general business conditions the company has been compelled to carry a very much larger supply of materials of all kinds than under normal conditions, our current assets now standing at $11,232,496.88 and your directors feel that it is in the interests of the company and its stockholders that the capital investment of the company should be increased by the sale of additional preferred and common stock."[103]

Seiberling offered $30 million of additional stock, two-thirds of it preferred, but it was too late.

From Prosperity to Desperation

Economic depression hit the country that summer. Automobile production in January 1921 was half of what it had been in January 1920. Rubber prices and demand dropped, leaving Goodyear with a huge supply plummeting in value with outstanding — and noncancellable — orders for more as interest rates rose.[104] By November, the rubber inventory had depreciated by millions of dollars.[105]

Goodyear was caught severely overextended, and the signs of its prosperity — the plantations and plant expansions, the large sales force and extravagant ad campaigns, the new branches and subsidiaries — now seemed expensive liabilities. The company could not finance its success. From March to December 1920, what had been a single month's supply of fabric became a nine-month supply. A three-month inventory of rubber lasted three years.[106] The Akron plants that had used 4.3 million pounds of fabric in March were using just 500,000 pounds in December. A single firm, Taylor, Armitage & Eagles, Inc., had Goodyear committed to more than $11 million in fabric, with substantial contracts also signed with other fabric and rubber suppliers.[107]

As Litchfield observed, "Once the thing started it built like a snowball rolling downhill, carrying everything with it."[108]

Goodyearites line up to buy company stock as part of Frank Seiberling's attempt to shore up capital reserves.

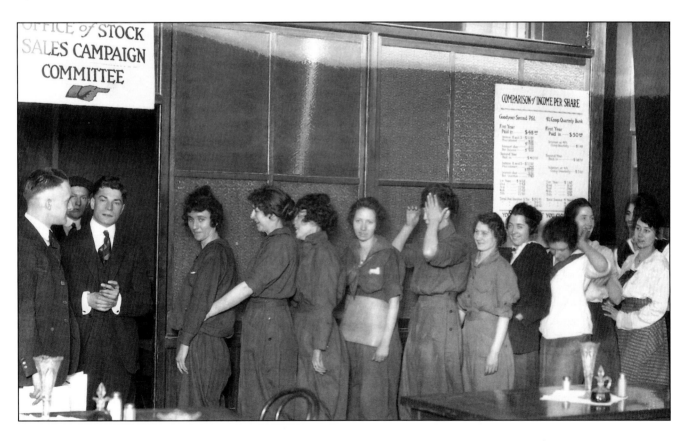

The depression of 1920-21 hit the automobile industry hard, and "the stout hearted Seiberling was buffeted from banker to banker as he sought money to tide [the company] over."[109] A temporary arrangement was reached with Goldman, Sachs, a prestigious New York banking house, but Litchfield later admitted that "the business had grown so fast ... no one knew just how much we did owe in contracts and commitments, and it would take the accountants, lawyers and financial men months to find out."[110] Goldman, Sachs demanded an audit by Price, Waterhouse & Company; the audit found that the amount needed to refinance Goodyear was upwards of $85 million, instead of the $50 million that had been estimated.[111]

As Litchfield recalled, "around Christmas Day" the bankers recommended more permanent arrangements, a suggestion that "sounded like receivership," the last thing Goodyear's management wanted. Aside from wresting control from the men who had nurtured and grown the business, the bankers' plan "might drag down banks and industries to whom [the company] owed money."[112] To stave off receivership, the directors negotiated with four committees formed to protect varying interests: bank creditors, merchandise creditors, preferred stockholders and common stockholders.[113]

Negotiations ensued. Goodyearites who had borrowed to buy stock were solicited for more collateral. A $500,000 life insurance policy on Frank Seiberling was canceled and the money paid into the company's treasury. Management salaries were cut by 40 percent.[114] Rumors flew through Akron that Goodyear had set up a lookout by the B&O Railroad to spy any "potential bearers of bankruptcy papers and race back with the news."[115]

On May 11, 1921, the Plan and Agreement of Readjustment of Debt of Capitalization was adopted unanimously by a board that lacked any other option.[116] The Authorized Capital Structure, as per balance sheet dated February 1, 1921, adjusted to show the effect of the new financing, consisted of:

> "$30,000,000 — first mortgage bonds
> $27,500,000 — debentures
> $30,342,000 — prior preference stock
> $65,532,000 — 7 percent preferred
> stock (old)
> $10,000 — management stock
> $1,000,000 — common stock.
> "To avoid showing a deficit the asset side of
> the balance sheet carried an item of $12,500,000
> 'Special account, patents, and good will.'"[117]

The bonds and debentures were bought at 90 percent of par by syndicates, with one share of

As prices and demand for tires dropped, rubber and fabric inventories grew and depreciated.

common stock given with each $100 debenture, for a total of 275,000 shares. The bonds were redeemable at 120 and the debentures at 110, and both carried interest rates of 8 percent.[118] Prior preference stock was offered to merchandise creditors at 125 percent of their claims.[119] Three management stock trustees — Clarence Dillon of Dillon, Read; Cleveland banker John Sherwin; and Owen D. Young, chairman of General Electric — were authorized to appoint a new board of directors.[120]

Resignations were demanded of all present officers.[121] Clyde Schetter, in his unpublished company history, wrote, "It has always been believed that Frank Seiberling was confident that he would be included in the new organization," but on May 12, as Litchfield and Stadelman were being informed of their continuing roles with the company, Clarence Dillon advised both Frank and Charles Seiberling that their resignations would be accepted along with that of Treasurer Edward Palmer.[122]

On May 13, 1921, Frank Seiberling presided over the last meeting of the old board. When his resignation was accepted and seconded, he rose from his chair and left the room quietly, leaving the company he had founded in the hands of 38-year-old E.G. Wilmer, its new president.[123] Worker Hugh Allen paid tribute to the Seiberling brothers in the May 17 *Wingfoot Clan*:

"They built a mighty industry, far flung and worldwide; one that bulked big among the giants of business, but they never lost the human touch. They were our friends, friends to us of the shop.

"So today, while we can rejoice that Goodyear is to go ahead, that Litch and Stad are to stay with us and sincerely extend to the new executive good wishes to success in his big responsibility, we'd be unworthy of the fellowship of the Clan of Goodyear if we did not pay tribute of honor and respect to our late leaders and let them know we were not unappreciative of their long friendship. God bless them."[124]

E.G. Wilmer took control of Goodyear in 1921, after the Seiberlings were forced out.

The "Little Napoleon of the Rubber Industry" would long be praised for his expansive courage, his energy and his willingness to take risks. But his departure left many shaking their heads and saying Frank Seiberling "followed his dreams and ambitions without keeping his financial feet on the ground."[125] After six months, Seiberling began anew, founding with Charles the Seiberling Rubber Company in Barberton, Ohio, right in Akron's backyard.[126] Although it would never rival Goodyear, the company grew to be the eighth-largest rubber producer in the country.[127] Frank Seiberling stayed at the helm until his 80th year. On August 11, 1955, he died at the age of 95, and employees at both companies mourned his passing.[128]

A sea of Goodyearites washes over Market Street, marking the change in shifts.

CHAPTER FIVE

ROLLING WITH THE PUNCHES

1921–1929

"The friendly Seiberling atmosphere was gone now. There were strange faces everywhere, auditors, accountants, lawyers all over the place, men asking questions, checking things, calling for records, skeptical of everything we had done in 20 years, and unsympathetic to the program which had become so much a part of my life."

— P.W. Litchfield, 1954[1]

DURING THE NINE months leading up to the May 1921 announcement of Goodyear's financial reorganization, P.W. Litchfield's hair turned white.[2] The company's sales force and branch staffs were cut in half, and more than 1,700 salaried and office workers lost their jobs.[3] Construction of Akron's Plant 3 had been halted, and the companies in Canada and California reduced to bare-bones organizations.[4] The Seiberlings were out, the bankers were in, and employee morale was at an all-time low. Workers donated money to put up bronze plaques in honor of the Seiberling brothers.[5]

The only managers to retain their positions were Litchfield as vice president of production, G.M. Stadelman as vice president of sales, and W.D. Shilts as assistant secretary.[6] The new president, E.G. Wilmer, told Litchfield that the impression on Wall Street was that the company had grown "fat and soft with easy prosperity" and would have to be "rebuilt from the bottom."[7] Wilmer had some experience with the manufacturing of steel, gas, and chemicals, but not rubber.[8] He was primarily a financial man, a graduate of George Washington Law School, whose number-crunching skills had been noticed by Clarence Dillon of Dillon, Read.[9]

Wilmer did not immediately set about building Goodyear up from the bottom. First of all, he was occupied with the details of the reorganization, renegotiations with creditors and convincing stockholders to exchange old certificates for new voting stock.[10] Secondly, as he admitted to Litchfield and Stadelman, he knew nothing about rubber and Goodyear, although a mess financially, was strong in production and sales.[11]

The months following reorganization were a time of adjustment, described by Shilts as a "period of fear" during which employees came to work uncertain whether they still had jobs.[12] The new management, men provided by Leonard Kennedy & Company, were charged with reviewing every department in order to increase efficiency.[13] In his autobiography, Litchfield recalled the incredible change in the company that he had helped create.

"The friendly Seiberling atmosphere was gone now. There were strange faces everywhere, auditors, accountants, lawyers all over the place, men asking questions, checking things, calling for records, skeptical of everything we had done in 20 years, and unsympathetic to the program which had become so much a part of my life."[14]

The All-Weather balloon tire, which first appeared in 1923. Goodyear was the first to establish the wide stance and oversize feature.

Order from Chaos

Even Stadelman and Litchfield, who had been assured of their future with Goodyear, began to suspect they were training their own replacements when Wilmer assigned men to their offices to check on what they were doing.[15] Dissatisfied with the cuts the company had made prior to the reorganization, management ordered new layoffs, with laborers and office staff being reviewed on an individual basis.[16] Departments were

forced to cut costs wherever possible. Between 1920 and 1921, the average supervisor-to-worker ratio increased from 1:11 to 1:20.[17] New financial controls were implemented that required departments to obtain executive approval before committing funds in excess of $25,000.[18] Beginning in September 1921, the Law Department, organized under C.F. Stone, authorized all new contracts except small routine sales and purchases.[19] G.A. Einbecker was brought in for a few months to set up a new accounting system, and in the fall, Charles Brook took over as the company's first comptroller.[20] Unprofitable products, including solid clincher tires, baby carriage and wheelchair tires, hoof pads and certain mechanical goods, were phased out.[21]

Litchfield admitted that the budgetary controls were needed, but said he and Stadelman, who had enjoyed so much freedom under Seiberling's leadership, felt like "racehorses hitched to a plow."[22]

New management looked skeptically at what it called Litchfield's welfare programs: the employee relations plan that had been a pet project for several years.[23] Litchfield's attitude — echoed by Frank and Charles Seiberling and George Stadelman — was that "good men are not an expense any more than good tools or quality materials," and that providing employees with recreation, education and

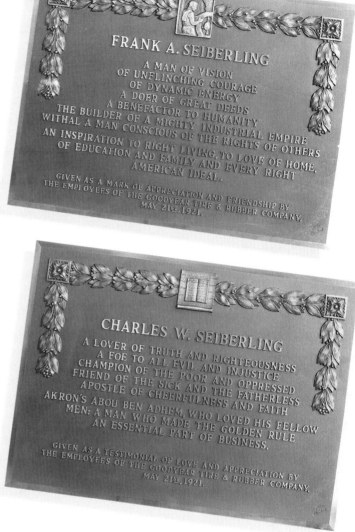

Above: Employees purchased bronze plaques to honor the Seiberlings following their resignations in 1921.

Above left: G.M. Stadelman was one of the few to survive the change in management.

Left: P.W. Litchfield believed strongly in keeping worker morale high by providing many amenities. This paternalistic attitude toward employees would become a hallmark of Goodyear.

labor representation increased their loyalty to the company, thus their job performance.[24]

The showplace of this conviction was Goodyear Hall, a $2 million investment in worker satisfaction and community relations.[25]

Completed in April 1920, the facility featured the largest gymnasium in the state of Ohio; a 1,785-seat auditorium; classrooms and laboratories for Goodyear Industrial University; an entire floor for women complete with lockers, showers and meeting rooms; chambers for the employee representation group; bowling lanes, a billiards room and a rifle range; a cafeteria; and a branch of the Ohio Savings & Loan Bank.[26] To the new management, this seemed wasteful. Nothing could be done about an expensive building already standing, but Wilmer questioned the validity of carrying out programs such as the Industrial University, the Industrial Assembly and company-sponsored athletics during a time of financial crisis.

Litchfield vehemently defended the programs. The classes, said Litchfield, trained better

The stage in Goodyear Hall, the six-story recreation and meeting center, completed in 1920.

employees, and sports programs created a sense of community, cooperation, and "team spirit."[27] In its first two years, more than 20,000 employees had attended classes at the university in subjects such as bookkeeping, typing and personnel relations, as well as high school curricula for those who had not earned a high school diploma.[28]

Even closer to his heart was the Industrial Assembly, an employee-representation plan modeled after the United States Congress. Designed to invest laborers with a "voice in management,"[29] the assembly was composed of two branches, a house and senate, with 40 representatives and 20 senators (the latter usually employees of long service) elected by a vote of "Industrians," workers 18 years of age and older who were American citizens, could understand English, and had six months of continuous company service or one year total service.[30] The Assembly could legislate on any area of industrial relations, including wages, with the stockholders' interests protected by the factory manager's retained veto power.[31] In the first four months

The Controversial Views of P.W. Litchfield

IN 1946, P. W. LITCHFIELD'S 1919 booklet, *The Industrial Republic*, was republished as part of a four-book volume of the same name. In his foreword, Litchfield wrote that his goal was to seek "more equitable distribution" of the benefits of capital.[1] Such language, as he said in his autobiography, caused some people to label him a socialist at a time when fears of communism were gaining momentum in the United States.[2]

The comparison some people made between Litchfield and Karl Marx was absolutely unfounded, for Litchfield believed that production was the fruit of a joint venture of capital and labor, rather than belonging exclusively to the laborer. As he wrote in *Industrial Voyage*, since capital supplies the tools to make labor efficient, and the laborer supplies the energy to make the product, both should reap the rewards.[3] *The Industrial Republic* discussed what he saw as a counterproductive relationship between those controlling the capital and those performing the labor. A few excerpts from the book clarify his views.

On the division of capital and labor as a result of industrialization:

"The result of this evolution has been to create a class of capitalists who do not work, and a class of laboring men who do not save and who have no capital. It must be perfectly evident to anyone that there can be no community of interest whatsoever between these two classes, and the division of a population into two classes of this nature results in endless friction and continual collective bargaining, neither side being satisfied with the ever-varying results.

"Thence follows strikes, lockouts and loss of product, as the capitalist who does not work always desires to have as much reward as the

Above: The interior of the Goodyear Hall gymnasium, the largest in the state of Ohio.

Left: Litchfield emphasized teamwork. Intramural sports such as basketball, baseball and hockey were encouraged.

capitalist who does work, and the laboring man who saves nothing always desires to live as well and be as well taken care of in the future as the man who saves a part of the results of his labor for a rainy day. Neither of these desires is right, but both are merely special privileges which can only be granted by injustice to others.

"Increased production and the ability of the earth to support an increasing population depends entirely upon both Labor and Capital working together."[4]

On providing workers with a voice in management:

"The world does not owe every man a living, but it does owe every man the opportunity to earn a living, and each industry as a duty should do its share in affording men the opportunity to earn that

after its inception in July 1919, the Assembly had established permanent work shifts, a better overtime pay schedule, half-holidays for Saturdays, and settled a walkout of machinists.[32] It was unpopular among other business leaders, who considered such labor representation radical and

leftist, but Litchfield convinced Wilmer that in a time of declining morale, its existence was crucial. Swayed by Litchfield's impassioned pleas, Wilmer allowed the program to continue.[33] Some 40 years later, company historian Clyde Schetter reflected on the legacy of the Industrial Assembly system.

---

living up to its ability to do so. ... Management can then grant to those who qualify by age, length of employment and, possibly, understanding a common language, the rights of industrial citizenship on the basis of equality for the purpose of selecting representatives by a direct vote with power to legislate on all matters, to ensure justice to the working men as a whole, and to represent them in dealing with the other partners, Capital and management, for the mutual advantage of all."[5]

Litchfield believed that after capital received its share of interest, and laborers their share of wages, any profits left that was not reinvested in the business should be divided between the two groups.[6]

"The main cause of industrial unrest is the ill will of the laboring force. We have spent relatively too large an effort in the past to obtain the good will of the customer, and those who furnish the capital, and too little to obtain the good will of Labor. The time has come for a serious consider-

Ahead of its time, Goodyear instituted gym classes for women as well as men.

ation and some definite action toward the solution of this problem. Realizing the problem, the possible solutions will be many. Any real solution, however, must obtain the good will and confidence of Labor, and this can only be done by direct representation of Labor in Management."[7]

It was perhaps not surprising that Litchfield's views received scorn from both the right and left. Many in management saw his vision of industrial democracy as impractical at best and socialist at worst, while the more radical factions of labor believed it did not go far enough.

In a 1925 article that appeared in *The Industrial Pioneer: An Illustrated Labor Magazine*, put out by the Industrial Workers of the World, an anonymous Goodyear employee told his story of "Rubber Slavery in Akron." The writer mocked the Industrial Assembly as a placebo to workers' egos, saying it had no real power and was controlled by the management.[8] The Goodyear Heights housing project, rather than offering workers a chance at home ownership, was intended to mire workers in debt in order to keep their "noses on the stone," the author contended.[9]

Special venom was aimed at the "Flying Squadron," another of Litchfield's projects, which provided management training to selected employees through a combination of classes and experience in every area of the company. (E.J. Thomas, who would succeed Litchfield as the company's president, was its most notable alumnus.) Calling the Industrial University Goodyear's "private head-fixing institution," the anonymous writer identified the aim of the Flying Squadron as creating "a body of loyal workers trained to break a strike in any department should one occur."[10]

There is no company record of it, but one can imagine P.W. Litchfield's sigh.

"While it was no Utopian panacea for either labor or management, it is a fact that Goodyear and its personnel enjoyed a harmonious coexistence without strike or strife for 17 years under the Industrial Assembly plan with both management and labor working together to advance the company's interest."[34]

Above: The interior of a Goodyear dealer, selling both tires and industrial products.

Below: The All-Weather traction tire was constructed with Supertwist cord, which allowed tires to handle greater speeds without quickly wearing out.

Litchfield would later credit Wilmer for understanding that "an industry could not judge everything on the basis of an immediate return, must think of long-range results as well." But the reconciliation of "financial and industrial thinking" took time.[35] Under the new cautious atmosphere, Litchfield watched morale plummet. Employees were resentful of the new rules and terrified of being fired. Late in 1921, Litchfield's secretary, E.J. Thomas, handed him some notes with the reminder that he had a morning meeting with the branch managers, Wilmer, and other executives. By now, Litchfield was tired of the miasma of fear around him. As related in *Industrial Voyage*, Litchfield

stuffed the notes into his pocket, walked into the meeting, and "blew his top."[36]

"'Up to now this company has been retreating,' I said. 'That was necessary. But we've reached the point now ... where we've got to quit retreating and start fighting. We've got to stop thinking about saving money and start thinking about making money. We can't pay off our debts by cutting expenses. We can only do that by going after business and getting it. We've lost a lot of money, but that isn't important as long as we haven't lost the fighting spirit that built this company.

"'We have plenty of weapons to fight with. ... The public is with us. They have found out that year after year Goodyear has given them the best damned tire in the world.

"'This company was not built by ordinary men using ordinary methods,' I concluded. 'It was built by thoroughbreds who outstripped their competitors in sales, production, development, engineering, and everything else. We can do it again. It will take hard work, courage, drive, determination. But no one is ever licked until he admits he is. You men are still thoroughbreds. Let's start fighting.'"[37]

After 30 minutes of venting on this theme, Litchfield finished his speech with the dawning awareness that perhaps he had just lost his job. Instead, Wilmer was the first to shake his hand, and the men in the room cheered.[38] In later years, many of those present attributed this talk with rousing the spirit that would, by 1926, make Goodyear the largest rubber company in the world.[39]

Goodyear emphasized developing and training dealers who would work exclusively with Goodyear tires. One program suggested dealers try direct customer contact to boost sales, using form letters like the one on the right.

The Price of Success

During the 1920-21 depression, small tire manufacturers who were not saddled with large inventories were able to increase market share through aggressive discounting.[40] Tire prices dropped an average of 15 percent in May 1921, then an additional 15 percent in November. Between March 1920 and November 1921, the average consumer price on 10 sizes of tires fell from $48.05 to $28.35.[41] The nationwide depression made economy a central concern in consumer choice, and in 1922, Goodyear decided to produce second- and third-line tires for the lower-end market.[42] The result was the second-line Wingfoot and the lowest-priced Pathfinder. A retail price list from October 18, 1923, shows the price comparison of the three lines:

"TIRE (Trade Name)	TYPE	PRICE
All-Weather Heavy Tread	Premium	$18.25
All-Weather Clincher Cord	1st line	14.00
All-Weather Clincher Fabric	1st line	12.35
Wingfoot Clincher Cord	2nd line	11.85
Wingfoot Clincher Fabric	2nd line	10.35
Pathfinder Clincher Cord	3rd line	9.65
Pathfinder Clincher Fabric	3rd line	8.00[43]

Goodyear also changed its attitude toward dealers. By October 1920, replacement sales were conducted through 32,000 automobile tire and 7,000 truck tire service stations, the result of Stadelman's "Sell All The Dealers" campaign.[44] However, 85 percent of these also carried other brands, which became a problem during times of tough price competition when dealers sold off existing stock of all brands before ordering more from Goodyear.[45] Wilmer decided the company needed dealers who would be loyal to its products, and Goodyear began securing dealers who would work exclusively with Goodyear tires.

The depression of 1920-21 was relatively short-lived, and tire production, which had hit a low of 5,152,503 in 1921, increased by 50 percent the next year and continued to climb.[46] Efficiency had been increased due to the mass-production principles implemented under Cliff Slusser, with the result that by 1925 the general output ratio of one tire per day per employee had risen to two tires per day per employee.[47] Also in 1925, company sales passed the $200 million mark for the first time.[48]

In 1923, Wilmer was elected chairman of the board and opened an office at 120 Broadway in New York City, and Stadelman began a brief term as president.[49] That year, the company introduced the Supertwist tire cord.[50] The name was coined by Arthur Kudner, the copywriter who originated the slogan, "More People Ride On Goodyear Tires Than on Any Other Kind."[51] Supertwist was developed in response to technological improvements in truck design, which allowed trucks to reach speeds between 25 and 35 miles per hour.[52] Regular pneumatic tires wore quickly at those speeds, and Goodyear sent Sam Steere, superintendent of the California textile mill, to the mill in Killingly, Connecticut, to

Inset: A *Saturday Evening Post* ad promoting the new Pneumatic cushion tires, which offered long-suffering commercial truck drivers an easier ride and greater reliability.

Left: The economic downturn that cost the Seiberling brothers their company was short-lived. By 1923, Goodyear was once again looking to hire workers in an industry with high turnover.

work on improving the fabric.[53] Steere found that increasing the twist in the yarn enhanced both resiliency and strength. In 1923, the new fabric was used in the Wingfoot truck tire, with excellent results.[54] The following year, Supertwist was used for all pneumatic truck and balloon tires.[55]

The balloon tire also debuted in 1923. Several companies developed a similar low-pressure tire around this time, but the balloon was based on the oversize principle to which Goodyear had claim.[56] With an increased air volume and thinner sidewall construction, the balloon featured lower air pressure and a wider ride, thus increasing passenger comfort.[57] In late 1923, Dodge was the first to try them as original equipment, and soon the tire had "swept the market."[58] In June 1925, *The New York Times* reported that practically every car manufacturer had adopted the balloon tire as standard equipment.[59]

A less successful product of the period was the Neolin shoe sole, developed in 1915 and dropped in 1924 after a massive advertising campaign that, according to Stadelman, tried to force an unwanted product on the consumer.[60] Neolin

soles were sturdy but difficult to attach to the shoe, and despite improvements in design, consumers did not accept them. Goodyear had better luck with rubber shoe heels, and in 1925 became the world's leading manufacturer of this product, able to make the claim that "More People Walk On Goodyear Heels Than On Any Other Kind."[61]

Renewed Prosperity and a New President

The year 1926 unofficially marked the end of the difficult period of adjustment during which the company rose from near bankruptcy to a new pinnacle of success. The year began with the untimely death of George Stadelman at age 53 on January 22, after a brief illness exacerbated by the stress of having been robbed at gunpoint in his home.[62] He died nine days after celebrating his 24th anniversary with Goodyear.[63] Shortly after Stadelman's death, Litchfield was summoned to New York and told by Clarence Dillon and Wilmer that he was to become the next president, although the decision would not be announced until the annual board meeting in March.[64] He was not to tell anyone, not even his wife.

Litchfield kept the secret, watching with amusement the "maneuvering for position among some of the men in the Wilmer group" who believed

A sample display of the new tires, the Pathfinder and the Balloon, in the mid-1920s.

the management was unlikely to pick another Goodyearite to follow Stadelman.[65] On March 29, 1926, "Litch," as he was still called by many on the factory floor, was elected president.[66] C.F. Stone, Cliff Slusser and Charles Stillman became vice presidents.[67] Wilmer exited the company altogether, resigning his chairmanship to become president of the Dodge Brothers automobile company, which had been purchased by Dillon, Read.[68] Goodyear operated without a board chairman until 1930, when Litchfield assumed the role.[69]

As president, Litchfield's first project was to settle the legal disputes that had raged since 1922, when the Seiberlings, whose fortune was tied to Goodyear stock, led a fight to return control of the company to shareholders.[70] The various legal wranglings were known collectively as the Weiss suits, after Mrs. Laura Weiss, who penned a letter to the board attacking the legality of the reorganization.[71] Especially at issue was the contract with the Leonard Kennedy management group, which was controlled by Schlesinger and Dillon, Read. Under the contract, Kennedy was to be paid a flat fee of $250,000 per year for five years, with an additional 5 percent of profits in excess of $10 million, up to $20 million.[72] In the first year of the contract, the contingency fee arrangement paid Kennedy $308,000, and was discontinued because of stockholders' protests.[73]

Litchfield "took a neutral position," but he understood the stockholders' frustration. Goodyear was again making impressive profits, which were being eaten up by the provisions of the reorganization plan.[74]

"We were obligated to retire portions of the 1921 bonds and securities each year, and it was to our advantage to do this as fast as we could since they paid 8 percent interest. It was to our interest as well to call in the prior preference stock because of the high dividend rate.

"In the five years we had paid out some $33 million in interest and redemption charges. Dividends on Goodyear preferred were already in arrears, and would have to be cleared up before common stock could get anything. The $10,000 management stock carried with it control of the company, and would until the last of the twenty-year bonds were paid off."[75]

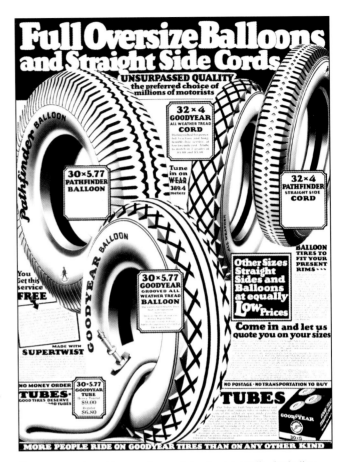

The company bought space in a variety of print media, including farm trade publications such as *Hoard's Dairyman*, as well as national publications.

Owen Young, chairman of General Electric, was appointed mediator. In 1927, an agreement was reached that provided for the issuance of $60 million in new five-percent bonds, the retiring of all the 1921 securities, and authorization of new preferred stock, allowing the exchange of old stock for new at a ratio of one-and-one-quarter shares for one.[76] At a July 11 meeting, Litchfield's presidency was extended for three years and he was made a director, the only Goodyear officer on the board.[77] As part of the agreement, the lawsuits were dropped.[78]

In April 1929, after a nine-year lapse, common stock returned to a dividend-paying basis. However, this sign of financial health was short-lived.[79] October 29, 1929 — Black Monday — was just six months away.

1911 — Goodyear builds its first airship
envelope, but the craft explodes during flight.

1928 — Construction of the airdock
begins in Akron.

1924 — The Goodyear-Zeppelin
Corporation is incorporated to build airships for the U.S. military.

1929 — Goodyear struggles through the
Depression, but is positioned well to survive the crisis.

1933 — The *Akron* crashes into the Atlantic during a thunderstorm.

1936 — The company and the union sign a new contract in March, ending the five-week strike.

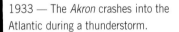

1936 — Goodyear workers walk off the job in February, beginning "The Great Strike of 1936."

1936 — The German *Hindenburg* bursts into flames, effectively ending the future of airships as passenger liners.

The *Akron* was launched in 1931, after its christening by First Lady Lou Hoover. Two years later, the airship would plummet into the ocean.

CHAPTER SIX

YACHTS IN THE SKY

1911–1941

"I will always believe that if ... airships had had anything like the attention given to airplanes, fleets of both types would be patrolling world air routes today."

— P.W. Litchfield, in his 1954 autobiography[1]

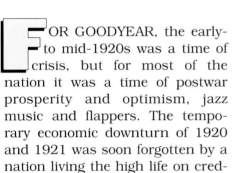

FOR GOODYEAR, the early-to mid-1920s was a time of crisis, but for most of the nation it was a time of postwar prosperity and optimism, jazz music and flappers. The temporary economic downturn of 1920 and 1921 was soon forgotten by a nation living the high life on credit. Cracks in that prosperity were already evident, however. Farmers experienced loss after loss, and consumer debt skyrocketed while savings diminished. In some areas of the country, such as parts of Missouri and Texas, the Great Depression had become a fact before the stock market crashed in October 1929.

In the three years following Black Monday, 100,000 workers lost their jobs each week.[2] Bread lines stretched for blocks. Farmers who lost their land to banks loaded their possessions in wagons or cars, hoping to find work on the West Coast. Homeless people in cities sang biting songs about President Herbert Hoover and called their cardboard-and-scrap-metal villages "Hoovervilles." The public voted in a new president — Franklin D. Roosevelt — in 1932. A man of action, Roosevelt enacted program after program in his New Deal, but by the mid-1930s, Depression had become a way of life.

Ironically, the downturn of the early twenties, which had almost erased Goodyear from the industrial map, positioned it well to survive the greater economic hardship of the thirties. In the spring of 1932, President Litchfield assured 300 factory and sales executives that although "general conditions were worse now than in 1921, the company's own position was better, since it had learned its lesson then and had strengthened its finances till they were now the soundest perhaps of any company in the rubber industry."[3]

Goodyear was able to hold steady throughout the Depression, and even open new factories in places such as Brazil, Argentina and Sweden.[4] New products introduced included Pliofilm, a moisture-proof packaging material; the first pneumatic tractor tire in 1932; Airfoam, a cushioning material; and the first American-made synthetic rubber.[5] Despite these innovations, the company had to endure falling production and profits. Between 1929 and 1930, tire production fell from 23 million to 17 million, and net sales dropped from $256 million to $204 million.[6] In 1932, Goodyear operated in the red for the first time since 1921, recording a net loss of $850,394.[7]

Goodyear balloons were used for both war and whimsy. These figure balloons flew in the Macy's Thanksgiving Day Parade in 1931.

The Airship Program

During this challenging decade, Goodyear developed what would grow to be its greatest public relations strength. The Goodyear story of the 1930s is one of labor strife, economic tightening, and product expansion. But it is also the story of the airship.

Goodyear's leadership in aeronautics during the thirties was solidified by its building of two giant airships, the *Akron* and *Macon*, as well as its operation of a fleet of blimps for public relations purposes. Goodyear's explorations in the air would have far-reaching impact, positioning it for later involvement in the U.S. space program. "Throughout the early thirties Akron was a focal point of world aviation interest," wrote company historian Clyde Schetter in his unpublished manuscript.[8]

From the start, Goodyear's interest in airships was split between three aims: providing technology for the military; furthering public interest and confidence in the name Goodyear; and arousing popular and governmental support for a transoceanic passenger airship fleet.

The company's involvement in aeronautics could be traced to the summer of 1909, when Frank Seiberling and his sons witnessed an early flight of the Wright brothers.[9] Seiberling was so impressed that the company built its first airplane tire by the end of the year to replace the sled runners and bicycle tires that were used at the time.[10]

In 1910, P.W. Litchfield attended two air meets in Europe and saw his first airship, which he preferred to planes because it depended on lifting gas to keep it aloft rather than on an unre-

During the Civil War, balloons were used to observe enemy troops. They would be used for defensive purposes in both world wars.

liable engine.[11] Litchfield secured the patent rights from a company in Edinburgh for a machine to spread dissolved rubber on wing fabric. He then hired two graduates from the Massachusetts Institute of Technology, and put them in charge of developing aeronautics.

Goodyear made its first airship envelope, or bag, in 1911 for Melvin Vaniman, whose plan to fly across the Atlantic ended in tragedy when a spark from the engine set fire to the hydrogen-filled bag. The flaming airship plummeted into water off the New Jersey coast, killing Vaniman and several crew members.[12] Seiberling was distraught, as his letter to a friend attests.

"The fateful end has taken all the heart out of me for the development of aeronautics, and yet I cannot but have the feeling that someone will push on where Vaniman has left the work, and that the toll of death will contrive to be paid as the science advances, just as has been done in all the previous developments of this character."[13]

The *Wingfoot Clan* told employees that "Man will doubtless someday navigate the air in safety; we are now only paying the heavy price."[14] Disheartened but committed, Goodyear workers

continued to make envelopes for racing balloons. In 1913, a Goodyear balloon won the James Gordon Bennett race across the English Channel.[15]

This experience positioned Goodyear for important military contracts during World War I, when it rushed to make 1,000 balloons and approximately 100 airships to be used in war patrols.[16] The contracts continued after the war.

Before and after photos of Melvin Vaniman's ill-fated flight of Goodyear's *Spirit of Akron*. Below: Vaniman attempted to fly across the Atlantic in 1911, but was killed when the airship caught fire and crashed.

The Goodyear Blimp: A Continuing Tradition

O N APRIL 4, 1960, Goodyear delivered its last blimp to the United States Navy. Two years later, the Navy announced it was retiring its fleet of 17 airships. The blimps had been rendered obsolete by the use of helicopters and radar for anti-submarine defense.[1] As early as the fifties, there had been some executive grumbling at Goodyear about the cost of maintaining blimps that appeared to have no practical purpose. But when Robert Lane was hired as Goodyear's director of public relations he used the *Mayflower*, *Columbia* and *America*, as "ambassadors in the sky."[2] Lane immediately dispatched *Mayflower* on a six-month tour of the eastern seaboard.[3] As he pointed out to management, "Nobody else has a blimp. It's like having the only ad in *Life* magazine, the only sign in Times Square, the only billboard along the Los Angeles Freeway."[4]

The blimps promoted the Goodyear name in a way unmatched by other forms of public relations. The Goodyear blimp flew over the Rose Bowl and Orange Bowl football games. It drifted above the World's Fair, the Indianapolis 500 and other auto races, and the America's Cup yacht races.[5]

When wintering in Florida, the *Mayflower* took tourists on half-hour cruises along the beach for just $5 per person.[6] During the 1965 drought, it reminded New Yorkers to conserve water, for which Goodyear received commendations from city newspapers and Mayor John Lindsay.[7] In 1966 the ship was fitted with a 105-foot-by-14.5-

foot "Skytacular" sign featuring 1,540 light bulbs to illuminate night messages. In 1969, the "Super Skytacular" sign measured 189 feet by 25 feet and featured 3,780 lamps connected by 80 miles of wiring.[8]

Tom Riley, manager of Global Airship Operations, arrived at Goodyear in 1963, when Lane was redefining the blimp's role. He started his career as part of the blimp's crew, traveling either on the ground in a truck or in the blimp. He sometimes drove across the country at speeds rarely exceeding 45 miles an hour. He said that although the technology has improved, the basic operation of the blimp hasn't changed.

"The crew has to travel ahead of the blimp and stay in radio contact, get to the airport, drill stakes into the ground, lay out the cables, lay out the mooring mast. The blimp attaches by the nose to the mooring mast. You really have to have a feel for the thing, even with all of the equipment today. You can't rely on instruments when you're just a few feet from the ground. My proudest moment was when I first landed that devil. The guys on the ground crew grab the ropes and the pilot puts the power into reverse and slows down. If the

During World War II, Goodyear envisioned a more aggressive role for the airship as an aerial aircraft carrier. This interesting design was never put into production, although the concept had been tested years earlier.

crew tugs on the rope a little too hard, you look sloppy. Then one person stays behind to watch the blimp, while everyone else then goes to the hotel and has dinner together."[9]

The *Columbia* has since been replaced with the *Eagle.* All Goodyear blimps are built to military specifications, just as they were for the Navy, a standard that other corporate blimps don't often match. "Our fabric is very, very heavy. The impregnation process is really old but it is something that we know how to do, and it's pretty much what we stuck with. The newer blimps, so to speak, don't really last as many years."[10]

A public opinion poll taken in the sixties revealed that one out of every five Americans remembered having seen the blimp, although the craft had only flown over certain parts of the country. In areas where the ship actually flew, 41 percent recalled it and said they were favorably impressed with Goodyear.[11] "The Blimp" meant a Goodyear blimp, and it had become an American icon, living as much in imagination as in the sky. "A lot of people think we're behind every blimp that's out there," Riley added.[12]

The Goodyear blimp would fulfill a role a thousand times more important than public relations after Hurricane Andrew devastated South Florida in 1992. The *Stars & Stripes*, based in Pompano Beach, Florida, was on its way to cover the season-

opening Dallas Cowboy game, in Dallas, when Goodyear's corporate office began receiving calls from the White House and from Florida Governor Lawton Chiles, recalled Jerry Jenkins, public relations manager.

"They wanted to know if we could send the blimp down there. Well, we had to work out what our role would be. In communicating with the emergency management folks, they had come up with a list of addresses, telephone numbers and information they wanted us to display on the electronic message board. We knew that wouldn't work, because it would take three hours to read. When we finally got home, it was determined that the simplest, most efficient way that we could be part of the solution was to provide very short, very concise messages. One of the problems the Red Cross people were having was that aid stations had been established throughout the area, many times around the block from people, but they didn't know it and were reluctant to leave their homes, or what was left of their homes. The aid stations were divided by color: White stood for information, blue for goods and services and red for medical aid. So it became very simplified. The text ran within a matter of moments, and anyone that cared to look up and see it, there it was."[13]

Jenkins said the blimp flew over the area for 12 nights, between noon and midnight. At an altitude of 1,000 feet, the blimp's message was visible from a mile away. "That was probably one of the most interesting and unique situations I've ever been put into in my career."[14]

As seen over the Golden Gate Bridge, by 1966, Goodyear was able to dispatch night-time billboards using over 1,500 light bulbs to blaze a 105-foot-long message in the evening sky.

The company delivered 21 blimps between 1922 and 1925, along with one semirigid airship, the RS-1.[17] Perhaps more importantly, the company manufactured blimps for its own purposes.

The Wingfoot Express and Pony Blimps

World War I was the first conflict involving aircraft, and the feats of fliers like Eddie Rickenbacker, the famous air ace who downed 26 German aircraft in four months, had stirred the public imagination for the romance of flight. After the war, Goodyear sought to capitalize on this interest by manufacturing small blimps to be used for public relations. In 1919, the *Wingfoot Express* and a smaller class of blimp, called the Pony, made their debuts.

Again, disaster struck. The *Wingfoot Express*, named for the company's old trucking line, had been assembled in the same Chicago building used as a hangar during World War I, and it met a dramatic end on July 21, 1919.[18] Piloted by Jack Boettner, one of Goodyear's most experienced aviators, the blimp was flying over Chicago's business district, known as the Loop, when the hydrogen-filled bag suddenly caught fire and the ship plunged 1,500 feet to the ground. Boettner and his mechanic, Henry Wacker, fitted the three passengers with parachutes, but in the air, all three were set afire by falling bits of the bag. They burned before reaching the ground. Boettner parachuted safely to the roof of a building and Wacker landed on a busy Chicago street, but the flaming blimp crashed into a bank, killing 10

Two balloon racers stand before their ship. On the right is Ward T. Van Orman, one of Goodyear's first successful balloon racers.

Above: The skylight of the Illinois Savings and Trust, where pieces of the *Wingfoot Air Express*, flown by pilot Jack Boettner (below), fell through. Ten people inside the bank were killed, but Boettner survived. Before the accident, he had a perfect safety record.

people. The company paid more than $250,000 in wrongful death claims.[19]

Goodyear was discouraged but continued to push forward with the Pony blimp, which proved a huge success. Pony blimps were named for their small size. Each had a capacity of 35,300 cubic feet and was powered with a single four-cylinder gas engine that could reach a maximum speed of 40 miles per hour.[20]

The first Pony blimp enjoyed its initial flight at the 1919 Chicago Aero Show and was later sold to Commercial Airship Syndicate of Kansas City, marking the company's first sale of a commercial airship.[21] Other Ponys were built in 1920, with one operating to much fanfare throughout California. In 1921, Goodyear California set up the Pony

Blimp Passenger Service, which made regular flights between Los Angeles and Catalina Island, a 39-mile trip. The company's plans to start a similar service from Akron to Detroit were suspended during the 1921 refinancing and reorganization.[22]

The California-based blimps were popular with the public, engaging in stunts captured on newsreel and shown to the nation's new crop of filmgoers. Demonstration flights were provided at $10 to the public. A blimp was used to demonstrate deep-sea fishing in the water off Portuguese Bend; another was sold to film producer Marshall Neilan to shoot aerial scenes for a movie about George Armstrong Custer. In a stunt that twice highlighted the Goodyear name, a blimp landed on the front lawn of the estate of Douglas Fairbanks and Mary Pickford to deliver a set of tires. When a bill for the tires was inadvertently sent to Fairbanks, he responded that the publicity Goodyear had received should be payment enough.[23]

In 1925, Litchfield's wife, Florence, christened the *Pilgrim*, the first helium-inflated commercial

Above: A 1921 picture of the Pony blimp, used here to catch fish.

Inset: The Pony blimp was a public relations coup for Goodyear.

airship, and the first with the control car and passenger cabin enclosed and streamlined with the gas bag.[24] By 1929, the fleet included five more ships, all in operation simultaneously: the *Puritan*, the *Volunteer*, the *Mayflower*, the *Vigilant* and the *Defender*.[25] All were named after winners of the America's Cup, honoring Litchfield's vision of the airship as a flying yacht.[26] These were used for cross-country flights, and air docks were built at Los Angeles and Gadsden, Alabama, and leased in such cities as Miami and St. Petersburg, Florida.[27] The publicity value of the blimp fleet was immeasurable. Between 1925 and 1932, Goodyear blimps flew more than 1 million miles, safely carrying 92,874 passengers.[28] Blimps flew signs and made appearances at public gatherings. In one event, actor and former Olympic swimmer Johnny Weismuller was towed on an aquaplane by a Goodyear blimp at the Cleveland Great Lakes Exposition.[29] Other celebrities who enjoyed blimp flights included Charles Lindbergh, Will Rogers, Eddie Rickenbacker and Jimmy Doolittle, who led the daring air raid over Tokyo in 1942.[30]

The *Defender* was christened at the National Air Races in Cleveland on August 30, 1929, by

Amelia Earhart.[31] With its capacity of 178,000 cubic feet, the airship was the largest in the fleet. The following year, flying above Long Key, Florida, it dropped a letter to a vacationing President Herbert Hoover wishing him an enjoyable stay.[32]

The Goodyear-Zeppelin Corporation

Even more impressive to the public mind was the rigid airship, or Zeppelin, which enjoyed its heyday in the 1930s. While both were categorized as dirigibles — defined as any lighter-than-air craft which is engine-driven and steerable — blimps and Zeppelins differed in terms of internal structure.[33] Blimps held their shape with internal gas pressure, whereas Zeppelins were made "rigid" by internal metal support frames. Lieutenant A.D. Cunningham of the Royal Navy Air Service gave the blimp its name. While inspecting his air station, he flipped his thumb over the gas bag of a nonrigid dirigible and imitated the sound it made: "Blimp."[34]

The Zeppelin was named for its inventor, Germany's Count Ferdinand von Zeppelin, a retired cavalry officer who developed the first practical rigid airship in 1900.[35] In the ensuing 18 years, he and his crew made 115 rigid airships, many used by the German government. The Zeppelin gained the world's attention when it was employed in bombing raids on London during World War I.[36]

After the war, the United States military expressed interest in the rigid airship, and in 1922, the Navy began talking with Goodyear about building a Zeppelin.[37] The company enthusiastically agreed. Litchfield and Wilmer visited Germany to see about acquiring patent rights, and in 1924 the Goodyear-Zeppelin Corporation was incorporated.[38] In lieu of money, the deal traded a one-third interest in profits for the Germans' technology.[39]

By 1924, the company had drafted a proposal to build an airship that would be used for training, research and development, and promotion.[40]

The ship was to be powered by three 600-horsepower Packard motors. It would feature streamlined cars, crew quarters and a glass-

Wingfoot Lake at the time it was a Naval Air Station. Pictured are members of a Navy training session.

Above: The giant Airdock after construction.

Right and Below: The first and second rings being raised inside the Airdock. The rings would eventually become part of the *Akron*.

In 1926, Congress approved the five-year plan for Zeppelin research and construction. When the funds were appropriated in 1928, the cities of Akron and Cleveland both lobbied Goodyear, asking to be the site of the proposed airship hangar. Akron, which had offered to purchase 600 acres of land to establish an airdock and a city airport, was chosen. In 1928, construction of the great Airdock was begun.[43]

It was an auspicious decision for the city. With turns of a silver shovel by Litchfield, Akron Mayor G. Lloyd Weil, and J.B. Huber, chairman of the Akron Chamber of Commerce, ground was broken on November 14, 1928.[44] Designed by Wilbur Watson and Associates, with construction supervised by Goodyear's veteran engineer Bill

enclosed control car with 360-degree visibility.[41] Litchfield persuaded Dr. Karl Arnstein, one of Germany's key aeronautical engineers, to come to Akron with a dozen associates. The group arrived in 1925 and was greeted by E.J. Thomas, then Litchfield's assistant, who helped to locate adequate housing and introduced them to the features of the company and the city of Akron.[42]

State, the Airdock was the largest freestanding structure of its day, measuring 1,175 feet in length, 325 in width, and 211 feet high.[45] More than 1 million cubic yards of earth were moved, 1,300 25-foot piles were driven into the ground for the foundation, and some 8,000 cubic yards of concrete were poured to create the 364,000 square feet of floor space.[46] Eleven parabolic arches formed the basic structure.[47]

The Airdock was a tourist draw, attracting crowds as large as 50,000 on pleasant summer weekends.[48] At a time when Americans had little good news to cheer them, the airship seemed a technological marvel, something to restore confidence in the country's ability to recover from

Above: The U.S.S. *Akron*, moving out from the Airdock.

Below: The crew of the *Akron* enjoyed amenities such as a Tappan stove and a kitchen, which fed the 76-man crew in shifts.

the worst depression in its history. Throughout the spring of 1931, onlookers gathered outside department store windows, which displayed the 110-pound aluminum Tappan stove that would be a feature of the "Flying Kitchen," where meals for the crew of the *Akron* would be prepared.[49]

Finally, on August 8, 1931, the ship was christened. As it hovered in the Airdock above the crowd, First Lady Lou Hoover said, "I name thee *Akron*" and pulled a cord to release 48 white pigeons representing the states of the Union.[50] The ship was raised slightly, then pulled back to its lower position as a nod of honor to Mrs. Hoover. More than 150,000 in attendance cheered, while millions more listened to the ceremony on the radio or saw it later on newsreel footage. The *Akron*, and its hometown, were sources of national pride.

After several test flights, the *Akron* made its first official voyage in September 1931, carrying 111 passengers,[51] and was delivered to the Navy base at Lakehurst, New Jersey, in October.[52] Goodyear had already started construction on the *Macon*, the second and larger of the Navy ships, which was christened on March 11, 1933 by the wife of Rear Admiral

William Moffett, who was chief of the Navy's Bureau of Aeronautics.[53] With the *Akron* and *Macon*, the United States seemed on the way to establishing one of Paul Litchfield's most cherished dreams: a transoceanic airship service.

Supported enthusiastically by Dr. Karl Arnstein, the idea of an ocean-crossing passenger and freight airship fleet seemed feasible in the early 1930s. In some respects, the rigid airship was more suitable for long-distance flights than the airplane.

In a paper presented in 1930 at the National Aeronautic Meeting of the Society of Automotive Engineers, J.C. Hunsaker, vice president of Goodyear-Zeppelin, listed the potential problems of airplanes on ocean flights: loss of fuel, engine failure, loss of visibility and control, and failure of any number of structural parts or functions relating to lifting, stabilizing and control. In contrast, he said, "The Zeppelin or rigid airship seems to be inherently adapted for long overseas voyages for precisely those reasons which make the aeroplane unsuitable: safety and payload."[54] Because of its ability to retain buoyancy so that crew could

repair even rips in the gas bag, the rigid airship was less likely to crash due to mechanical difficulties. Furthermore, Hunsaker stressed, the larger size of the airship permitted it to carry larger loads of cargo as well as more passengers in comfort and luxury.

By this time, the Germans had their own commercial airship, the *Graf Zeppelin*, which had made regular trips from Germany to South America. It had also safely crossed both the Atlantic and the Pacific.[55] Furthermore, the Germans were drawing up plans for a second ship, to be named the *Hindenburg*. In 1935, the *New York Daily Mirror* asked its readers, "What's the matter with us?" in lagging behind the Germans in the use of rigid airships. The article suggested it would be desirable "to have fifty or a hundred such ships ... able to cross the Atlantic and return, without stopping, able to

---

Above: P.W. Litchfield, left, with Dr. Hugo Eckener, commander of the German *Graf Zeppelin*. Both men shared a passion for airships.

Below: A model of the proposed Goodyear-Zeppelin.

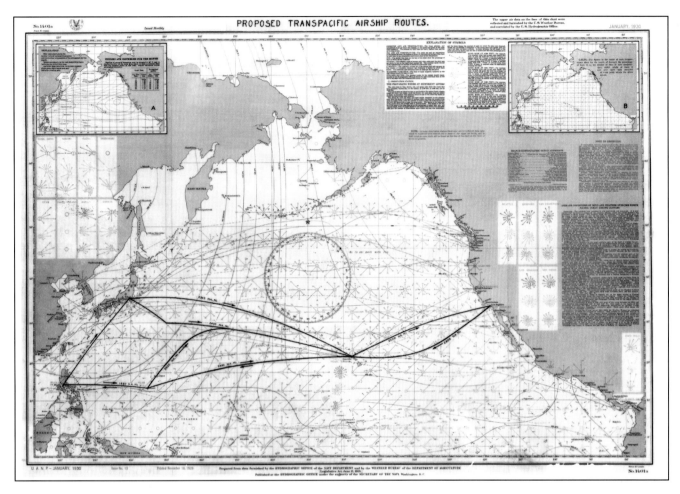

Above: Proposed routes for transatlantic airship passenger lines. After the *Hindenburg* disaster, the plan was dropped.

Center: Dr. Hugo Eckener, (far left), Fred Harpham, vice president of Goodyear-Zeppelin, and Dr. Karl Arnstein worked to make the joint venture a reality.

the service could count on 30,000 passengers per year.[57]

Goodyear-Zeppelin had developed plans for German and American passenger lines over the Atlantic, setting up separate companies which would share landing facilities and work together on schedules.[58] Commander Hunsaker worked to attract investors, and according to Litchfield, "had no difficulty interesting capital. The steamship people, the airlines, industries like the Aluminum Company, Carbon and Carbide, General Motors, banking houses like National City, G.M.P. Murphy, and Lehman Brothers, and California and Hawaii business houses took a similar

cross the Pacific to any part of Asia, drop 100 tons of explosives or poison gas and land, safe, in neutral territory."[56]

Litchfield and Arnstein were more interested in the airship's commercial abilities. In a 1936 article in *Aviation*, Arnstein outlined a vision of a "transoceanic express" that could revolutionize both passenger travel and freight shipments. He suggested that interest in the projected transpacific line. Goodyear-Zeppelin would provide engineering and fabrication, while experienced professionals in the shipping business would operate the ships."[59]

Early plans called for "two-and-a-half-day [trips] from Washington to Paris and, because of head-winds, six and a quarter [days] for the return. The Pacific route would start in California for Hawaii, Manila, Japan, and possibly China. This trip should require six and a half days — 36 hours from California to Hawaii, 72 more to Manila, then 48 to Japan. The return trip would probably take from four to six days, including a stop for mail and passengers in Honolulu."[60] The company produced booklets advertising "deluxe accommodations" for passengers on modern airships with capacities of 10 million cubic feet. These "Hotels of the Skies" could reach top speeds of 90 miles per hour.[61]

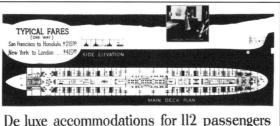

De luxe accommodations for 112 passengers

Deflating the Dream

Financial backing was easier to secure than legislative approval, and a series of Congressional mishaps delayed the important vote on a bill that would grant legal status to passenger airships, comparable to that of steamships.[62] As Litchfield recounted in his autobiography, passage of the bill seemed certain; it had already cleared the House, but in the Senate, a temporary chairman forgot about it and instead recognized a senator who began discussion on another matter, pushing the vote back a day.

As part of a publicity stunt, Goodyear invited Seminole Indians to fly on its blimps in 1930.

"There was one more day before adjournment, but that night a distinguished senator from a western state died of a heart attack on a train. The Senate adjourned in respect to his memory, and the measure had to go over until the next session. By which time other things had happened.

"I will always believe that if we could have gotten the program under way at this time, and if airships had had anything like the attention given to airplanes, fleets of both types would be patrolling world air routes today."[63]

The "other things" that impeded the development of a transoceanic airship line were the failure of airships themselves. On October 5, 1930, a British airship crashed in France, killing 48 people and causing the British government to cease development of rigid airships.[64] On April 4, 1933, the *Akron* plummeted into the Atlantic during a thunderstorm off the Jersey coast, killing 73 of the 76 men aboard, including Rear Admiral Moffett, whose wife had recently christened the *Macon*.[65] A Congressional committee set up to investigate airship disasters concluded that the *Akron* had been "ably built" and had failed due to pilot error in difficult weather conditions.[66]

A 1935 report of the Federal Aviation Commission recommended that the United States government proceed with airship construction and testing. The report said:

"We regard the arts of airship construction and operation as being still somewhat experimental. The only hope of making further progress is through the construction and operation of airships. The outcome of our consideration of the subject is a conviction that the chance of securing results of immense value is sufficient to justify proceeding with the work."[67]

One month later, in February 1935, the *Macon*, lost in a storm, plunged into the Pacific off the coast of San Francisco, after its crew battled for more than 30 minutes to keep control of the ship. All but two of the 81 crew members were saved by ships of the U.S. Pacific Fleet that had answered the S.O.S. call.[68]

Amid growing public skepticism and government reticence, Goodyear continued its campaign to set up the ocean lines. In April 1937, the *Akron Times Press* reported that Goodyear-Zeppelin had announced plans to construct two transatlantic ships like the German *Hindenburg* .

A few weeks later, on May 6, 1937, the era of the rigid airship was extinguished when the *Hindenburg* caught fire seconds before landing at Lakehurst, New Jersey, at the end of an ocean crossing. Unlike the American ships, the *Hindenburg* was filled with hydrogen, and once a spark from the engine ignited a piece of the envelope, the ship was devoured in flames as the crowd gasped, newspaper cameras clicked, and film cameras rolled. Thirty-five people were killed. Litchfield's vision of a fleet of flying yachts had come to an abrupt end.

Litchfield's disappointment was intense. The *Hindenburg* burned because of the German's use of hydrogen, which had a greater buoyancy than helium but was highly flammable. In the 1930s, the United States had the world's only large supply of helium, but would not sell it to Germany. Litchfield wrote, "It is my considered opinion that it was not the loss of the *Hindenburg* or the two American airships which brought the program to a halt in 1938, but the denial of helium gas to the German airships, which were then the connecting line with the opening of American lines."[69]

Litchfield believed it was a "tragic mistake" to abandon the rigid airship, both for commercial and defensive purposes. He agreed with Arnstein that the world should build on Count Zeppelin's dream that the dirigible be a "means of communication among the people of the world."[70] Following the Japanese attack on Pearl Harbor, Litchfield wrote that the dirigible could have played a significant role in World War II.

"The rigid airship is not a combat ship, except incidentally, any more than is the cargo airplane or the lightly armed merchantman. But it could have carried great loads of fuel and oil, vital replacement parts, and key staff people across the Pacific nonstop, landed anywhere where there was air cover. Two or three reconnaissance airships, able to patrol the ocean from Alaska to Panama, might have prevented the tragedy of Pearl Harbor."[71]

Although the 1930s were dominated by economic and labor strife, Goodyear remained "The Greatest Name In Rubber."

CHAPTER SEVEN

WEATHERING THE STORM

1930–1938

"I remember some guy heaved a brick through the window of our next-door neighbor when he was sitting in a chair, darned near killing him. I remember the tent cities, with the unions picketing this place."

— James Barnett, 1996[1]

ALTHOUGH POSITIONED to survive the Depression, the economic turmoil of the thirties took its toll on Goodyear, and eventually led to the Great Strike of 1936. The tire industry, linked so closely with automobile sales, was hit hard by the economic crisis. Between 1928 and 1935, the public's consumption of replacement tires fell 35 percent, from 50 million to 33 million.[2] To make matters worse, tire manufacturers had improved their products to the detriment of sales. In 1916, the average automobile used up eight tires per year, but by 1936, the number had fallen to 1.2.[3] Furthermore, since a 1926 plunge in crude rubber prices, a series of price wars had further reduced industry profits. In a July 1936 statement to the *Wingfoot Clan*, P.W. Litchfield said a good tire cost one-fourth as much as it had before World War I and lasted 10 times longer. "In 1908, a dollar spent for rubber tires bought 50 miles worth of tire travel. In 1936 a dollar spent for rubber tires buys 2,000 miles worth of travel."[4]

Between 1929 and 1933, manufacturing in the United States fell 37 percent. Automobile production fell by 64 percent, and tire manufacture fell by 34 percent.[5] The stock market crash caught B.F. Goodrich in the middle of a costly diversification plan, and the company had to struggle to survive its expansion. U.S. Rubber's financial straits were so dire that President Francis Davis agreed to supply General Motors with 50 percent of its original equipment tires at prices below cost.[6] For Goodyear, average daily tire production fell from 75,000 tires a day in 1929 to 25,000 a day in 1932.[7] Over the same four-year period, sales plummeted an average of $50 million a year, from $256 million in 1929 to $109 million in 1932.

Yet the Depression that redefined the middle class as poor and drove once-wealthy men to leap from buildings rather than face insolvency was simply one more challenge for Goodyear. Due to a firm financial structure that allowed it to pay dividends until 1932, the company avoided the nearly fatal difficulties it had experienced during the 1921 downturn.[8] It had already divested excess expansion and interests, and paid down its debt.

Still, the proverbial belt needed to be pulled even tighter. Total employment in the Akron rub-

---

As the public became fascinated with all things motorized, the motorcycle grew in popularity. During the thirties, Goodyear came out with the Straight-Side tire for motorcycles.

ber plants fell more than 50 percent from 1929 to 1933, and even workers who kept their jobs faced declining income because of shorter hours.[9]

Litchfield was one of the first industrialists to adopt the "share-the-work" plan, which became standard in the rubber industry.[10] To avoid mass layoffs, workers were put on six-hour days. The plan had been approved by the Industrial Assembly and put to a vote of Goodyear employees, who approved it overwhelmingly.[11] As a result, rubber workers who were not laid off made an average of 37 percent less between March 1932 and March 1933 than they had in 1928.[12] Yet under the atmosphere of emergency evoked by the Depression, the plan, which kept 3,000 workers on the payroll, was popular. In fact, the company's attempt to modify it would become a major factor in the 1936 strike.[13]

Cautious Expansion

Goodyear not only survived the Depression, but also expanded cautiously. Just eight months prior to Black Monday, the company had opened a plant in Gadsden, Alabama, and doubled its capacity for fabric production with the addition of two Georgia mills.[14] In 1931, Goodyear opened its first plant in South America, the company's fifth overseas factory. Litchfield had selected the site in a suburb of Buenos Aires before the 1929 crash, and management determined that the

Above: Goodyear went ahead with building a plant in Buenos Aires, Argentina, despite the general worldwide depression.

Below: The new Gadsden, Alabama plant in 1930. Due to Akron's high labor rates, the south was more cost-effective.

business potential was great enough to justify proceeding with the project.[15] In 1933, with the advent of a slow but promising economic recovery, the company acquired its fourth southern

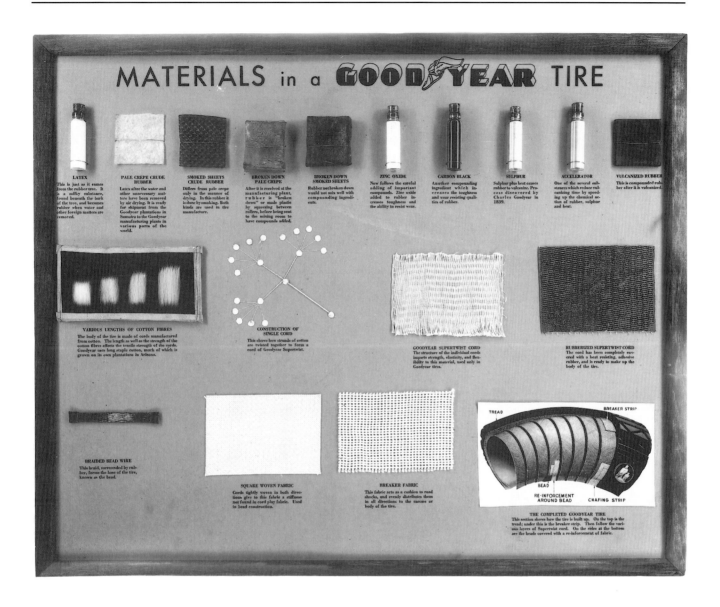

This demonstration board shows all of the materials required to build a high-quality tire.

textile mill in Decatur, Alabama, and set in motion plans to start a tire factory in Java, which began production on April 29, 1935.[16]

In 1935, Goodyear completed its first acquisition of an entire company when it bought Kelly-Springfield.[17] The company was an outgrowth of the Rubber Wheel Tire Company, partially owned by Frank Seiberling's former nemesis, Edwin Kelly. Kelly-Springfield started in Akron but had moved to Cumberland, Maryland. Damaged by the Depression, Kelly-Springfield was going bankrupt when it was purchased by Goodyear.[18] The subsidiary would return to profitability, and become an invaluable asset to Goodyear in years to come.

Product innovations in the early years of the decade included the straight-side tire for motorcycles and pneumatic tires for tractors.[19] In aeronautics, the Airwheel, a super-low-pressure airplane tire, was introduced in 1929, and hydraulic disc brakes for planes came out in 1933.[20] Beginning in the late 1920s, Goodyear researchers began looking for a new tire fabric, and in 1937, rayon tires were introduced after they were tested on Greyhound buses during long-distance, high-speed runs.[21]

No man in the world can buy a better tire than you can— simply because no better tire can now be made than the Goodyear Double Eagle. It was designed and built without regard to cost, in order to show how much could be accomplished, when the science, skill, and resources of the world's greatest rubber company were focused upon a single aim. You can buy it today for much less money than we originally believed possible, purely for the reason that vastly more people are demanding Double Eagle excellence than we dared expect. It is the outstanding product not alone of the industry but of the company whose standard quality is so superior that "More people ride on Goodyear Tires than on any other kind."

Above: The success of Goodyear's Double Eagle tire was proclaimed by this barely-clad Wingfoot. Soaring demand allowed Goodyear to offer the tire "for much less money than we originally believed possible."

Left: P. W. Litchfield inspects an early copy of Hugh Allen's *The House of Goodyear*, a corporate history published in 1936.

The Sears Contract Dispute

Goodyear's slow but steady expansion was made possible in part by its contract with Sears, Roebuck, a deal that would put the company under fire shortly after the worst of the Depression had passed. In 1926, Goodyear had signed a contract with Sears to provide tires for mail order sales. The Sears catalog was already an American icon, making its way into millions of American homes. In *The House of Goodyear*, Hugh Allen relates the story, most likely apocryphal, of a Montana rancher who added "a wife" to his Sears order form and found a female vol-

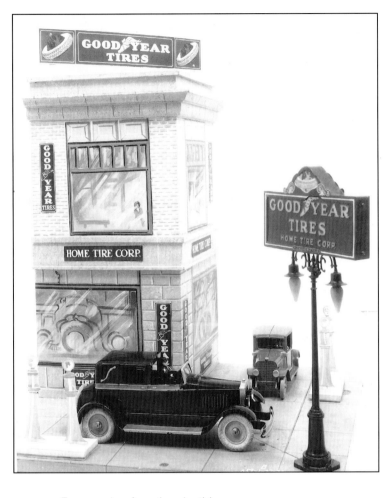

unteer accompanying his shipment.[22] The Sears contract created a large volume of business for Goodyear, and to sweeten the deal, Sears agreed to pay between $9.25 million and $10 million of overhead expenses per year, plus a profit bonus ranging from 6 to 6.5 percent.[23] From 1926 until the relationship was severed in 1936, the contract brought in $122 million of business for Goodyear, compared to total business in that period of $1.4 billion.[24] In return, Goodyear granted Sears price concessions not given to Goodyear tire dealers.

The Sears-Goodyear contract made national — and negative — headlines in the early 1930s. President Franklin D. Roosevelt's National Recovery Act granted the government broad powers to ensure fair competition and decent wages, and in 1933 the Federal Trade Commission filed a complaint charging that the quantity discounts Goodyear granted to Sears were in violation of the Clayton Anti-Trust Act.[25] Goodyear argued that Sears' 2.77 percent of the replacement tire market did not constitute a monopoly.[26] FTC hearings began January 15, 1934 and ended March 18, 1935. Independent retailers urged Congress to support the Robinson-Patman bill, which would abolish the system of quantity price discounting.[27]

Two examples of creative advertising.

Above: A toy Goodyear service station. The miniature station was available to children to attract the future buyers of tires.

Right: Circus elephants display their allegiance to Goodyear.

The "world's largest tire," built in 1930. During a time of slow sales and sagging mood, Goodyear sought to raise spirits with national gimmicks.

The FTC's ruling, released in March 1936, found that Goodyear gave Sears a price break as high as 35 percent. The government ordered a "cease and desist" act against the contract.[28] Goodyear appealed, but on June 19, 1936, the Robinson-Patman Act became law with a special addendum referring to volume discounts clearly aimed at nullifying the Goodyear contract.[29] Sears signed with Armstrong Rubber, a small manufacturer able to grant price discounts without discriminating against other customers.[30]

It was a blow for Goodyear. The contract had provided much-needed revenue during the financial crunch of the Depression, and its demise was ill-timed. In a July 22 message to Akron employees, Litchfield acknowledged that the lost Sears business would have to be replaced by either new business or by layoffs.[31] The announcement was seen by some employees as a thinly veiled threat, for 1936 was the year of Goodyear's greatest crisis in labor relations.

The Great Strike of 1936

Since the 1913 strike, Goodyear had been largely free of labor disturbances, partly as a result of the good wages paid to rubber workers and partly because of the company's efforts to establish harmonious employee relations. Rather than an uprising against a heartless authoritarian employer, the 1936 strike seems to have been part of the ongoing gestation of the United Rubber Workers Union. As in 1913, most of the strikers were concerned with such practicalities as retaining the six-hour day and preventing further wage cuts, but the underlying issue was the battle over the nature of collective bargaining.

The National Recovery Act of 1933 had guaranteed employees the right to organize and bargain with employers. Its agency evolved into the National Labor Relations Board under the 1935 Wagner Act. The guarantees provided by the NLRB encouraged unions. Goodyear, in spite of its record of fairness in harmonizing industrial relations, "became a battleground for an acid test of the New Deal's labor relations philosophies."[32]

After the economic nadir of 1932, Goodyear began a slow recovery in 1933. By 1937 yearly net sales would again pass the $200 million mark.[33] With the health of the industry taking a slow but positive turn, the American Federation of Labor began a drive to organize Akron rubber employees in 1933.[34] On June 30, a mass meeting at the Akron armory attracted about 5 percent of the city's rubber workers, who left with petitions and resolve. By fall, union locals had been established at the three major plants as well as nine smaller companies, including India Tire and Seiberling.[35] According to Harold S. Roberts, author of *The Rubber Workers: Labor Organization and Collective Bargaining in the Rubber Industry*, Goodyear was considered the main target.

"Particular attention was given to Goodyear, since it was the largest rubber plant in the city. The first union leaflets were distributed among Goodyear workers. The first Akron local to be chartered by the American Federation of Labor was the Goodyear local. Membership at the time the charter was granted was in the neighborhood of 200, and 600 by the time the charter was installed. By October 1, the local claimed more than 3,000 members."[36]

Initially, Goodyear executives tolerated the local union, but emphasized the tradition of the Industrial Assembly, which it saw as the workers' true connection to management. Union leaders' overtures to the company were met with polite but determined refusals. Because much of the business of the Industrial Assembly was conducted on company time, resulting in lost piece work wages for some of the members, the company was paying representatives and senators for their Assembly work, a practice union

Right: The 1931 heavy-duty All Weather tire, used for heavy trucks, like the fire engine below, tractors and earth-moving equipment.

leaders deemed unfair.[37] The union pushed harder for recognition.

The clash between Goodyear Local 2 and the "company union," as American Federation of Labor leaders called the Industrial Assembly, intensified in 1934 as union leaders at Goodyear, Firestone and Goodrich demanded the companies hold elections to determine employee representation. Firestone and Goodrich refused, and the AFL appealed to the National Labor Relations Board, which ordered in November that elections be held within three weeks.[38] At Goodyear, a confident Industrial Assembly agreed to run against the local, and in September, more than 10,000 workers voted in the Assembly primary.[39]

AFL leaders began to get nervous. Factory manager Cliff Slusser told Goodyear local president John House that the company "was ready for the vote tomorrow because we can lick the hell out of you."[40] The AF of L backed out, instead calling on the NLRB to "rule the Industrial Assembly off the ballot" because it was a company union.[41]

John House asserted that the locals were "not going to take no for an answer."[42] By March 1935, locals at the Big Three tire companies were determined to win recognition, a 30-hour work week, and seniority rights in deciding layoffs — even if they had to strike to achieve these goals.[43]

Plans to strike were made openly, and in April, United States Secretary of Labor Frances Perkins stepped in, urging manufacturers to withdraw resistance and legal challenges to the union. They refused. On April 12, she met separately with union officials and company representatives — Slusser spoke for Goodyear — and the parties struck the famous "teacup agreement," so named because Perkins served coffee and sandwiches from a tea set near her desk. The compromise stated that the strike would be called off, the elections postponed until the lawsuits were settled, and manufacturers would negotiate "individual grievances and terminate financial support for the company unions until the courts determined their legality."[44]

The contentious atmosphere led to scattered protests and sit-downs for months to come. In October 1935, Litchfield initiated a plan to return to the eight-hour work day, increasing the work week from 30 to 36 hours with a corresponding reduction in piece-rate wages to increase company profits still hampered by the price wars.

Goodyear employees, believing the additional hours would necessitate layoffs, were furious with the plan. John House charged that a 12 percent reduction in labor force would be the result and stated, "With several thousand men now on relief in Akron, this represents a serious problem."[45] Even the Industrial Assembly protested, calling for the six-hour day to become standard or for an employee vote on the matter.[46]

On November 15, Frances Perkins announced the formation of a fact-finding board, led by Fred Croxton of Ohio State University, to investigate the unrest at Goodyear. Croxton's report, not released until January 6, 1936, found that the company was at fault. Calling management's explanations "evasive and confusing," the board called the return to the 36-hour week "unjustified and in violation of [Goodyear's] truce

Strikers withstood severe weather to protest what they viewed as callous treatment by executives.

with organized labor."[47] The board also found that Goodyear discriminated against the American Federation of Labor unions in favor of the Industrial Assembly.

The report left a feeling of ill will between workers and management. On January 31, 100 workers in the tire curing department stopped the line to protest a 10 percent reduction in piece-work wages, initiating a wave of protests.[48] Litchfield bluntly stated that the wage reductions had been carefully studied and would not be overturned. He expressed disappointment that "the long era of mutual confidence between the company and employee has been marred."[49]

On February 14, the foreman of the tire room passed out pink slips to 50 fourth-shift workers. Angry at the proposed layoffs, the workers ceased production.[50] When the men left the next morning, John House met them at the gate and offered the assistance of the union. At noon, the second-shift tire builders sat down to support the grievances of the fourth-shift. At 6 p.m., the third-shift workers also stopped working.[51]

At 8:30 that night, Personnel Manager Fred Climer appeared with a stopwatch and told the men they had 30 minutes to get back to work. Three members of the Flying Squadron went to their machines, but the other 136 sat. An hour later, they received slips of paper marked, "Quit, no notice." Finally, the men stood up and defiantly built a single tire.[52]

Climer announced that the suspended workers could reapply at the unemployment office, but other employees were incensed at what they viewed as management's cavalier attitude. On February 18, after scattered sit-downs in other departments and union-led evening rallies, 500 Plant I tire builders shut down the plant, as more than 1,000 marchers streamed out of a meeting and down Martha Avenue, blocking entrances to the factory.[53] The protesters threw up picket lines, and the great strike of 1936 had begun.

For five weeks, more than 15,000 Goodyearites were thrown out of work. At one point, the picket patrol extended eleven miles.[54] Litchfield demanded police action, but Akron Mayor Lee D. Schroy told the police captain to maintain a "strict neutrality" between the interests of the company and of the strikers.[55] Throughout the protest, during which the factories were closed, Goodyear executives grew increasingly annoyed at the reluctance of Schroy and the police to enforce a court decision to limit the number of pickets.[56]

Litchfield was especially dismayed because the strike let loose employees' long-smoldering resentments toward his pet projects, the Flying Squadron and the Industrial Assembly. The Assembly was accused of being in the company's pocket, and the Squadron was attacked as a pampered group of "teacher's pets."[57]

Believing the strikers were a minority of militants, Litchfield initially refused to meet with strike representatives, a hard line similar to the one taken by Frank Seiberling in the 1913 dispute. For the first weeks of the strike, Litchfield refused to leave the plant, instead sleeping in his office on a cot brought in from the factory hospital and taking meals at the cafeteria with other managers and workers who remained inside.[58]

Nearly as militant as the strikers were the nonstrikers, who held mass meetings and pressured the mayor and sheriff to use force to help them pass the picket line. Despite Litchfield's hope that pressure from the nonstrikers and the Akron community would crumble strikers' resolve, progress toward a settlement was slow. In 1936, nearly 75 percent of the residents of the Rubber Capital of the World had either worked for a rubber company or knew someone who did, so although public sentiment was not necessarily pro-union, it was "pro-employee."[59] Many citizens sympathized with workers' complaints that longer hours and reduced pay

Strikers mob the Willard Street gate. Union leaders targeted Goodyear since it was the industry leader.

required them to "speed up" production and exhaust themselves physically. The Akron newspapers were more tolerant of strikers' complaints than they had been in 1913.

Deadlock

A February 22, 1936, *Cleveland Plain Dealer* article outlined the positions of the two sides. The union's complaints were summarized as a list of allegations against Goodyear. According to disgruntled workers, the company:

1. *Discriminated against union members and in favor of members of the Industrial Assembly.*
2. *Intimidated union members.*
3. *Lengthened work hours without considering the protests of workers.*
4. *Disregarded seniority rights in determining layoffs in favor of company union members.*
5. *Replaced older employees with younger Flying Squadron members at reduced wages.*
7. *Held a "high-handed" attitude toward union members.*
8. *Violated the labor agreement of April 1935.*
9. *Refused to negotiate with strikers, thus denying the principle of collective bargaining.*

The article also presented the position of the company, which maintained that:

1. *Eighty percent of Goodyear workers wished to return to work.*
2. *Collective bargaining had been honored during meetings conducted with various departments since the sit-down strikes began.*
3. *Wage rates had been adjusted because of industry competition.*
4. *Present grievances of strikers were not to be addressed until the men returned to work.*
5. *The Industrial Assembly was the collective bargaining agency of Goodyear.*
6. *Goodyear instituted the "share-the-work" program and was willing to continue it as much as possible.*
7. *Workers had been laid off because of business conditions.*
8. *The company's objective was to institute an average 36-hour workweek.*

9. *The strikers intimidated nonunion members and endangered the company with the shut down.*[60]

On February 26, 1936, the United States Department of Labor's "ace mediator," Edward McGrady, began a series of meetings with strike leaders and Goodyear managers in an attempt to achieve a settlement.[61] The next day, Akron labor leaders met and empowered a committee of 25 to call a general labor strike of 105 locals if any steps were taken to "break the peaceful picket line" that was keeping the Goodyear plants closed.[62]

At the urging of Fred Climer and E.J. Thomas, the company proposed its first settlement terms on March 1. Union leaders rejected the plan and hoped to enter into negotiations, but the company withdrew the offer.[63] Leaving the plant for the first time since the beginning of the strike, Litchfield met with reporters at the Mayflower Hotel on March 2. He insisted he would never sign an agreement with the United Rubber Workers of America.[64]

With tensions mounting and the two sides deadlocked, the formerly peaceful demonstration was marred by violence. E.C. Pace, a striking worker in the pit preparation department, was hospitalized after being beaten with a club by nonstrikers on March 4.[65]

On March 6, a frustrated Mayor Schroy ordered city sanitation workers to destroy the shanties the strikers had erected near the picket line to protect themselves from the bitter Ohio winter. The sanitation workers destroyed four shanties, then were met by more than 2,000 angry men. In the ensuing struggle, two police officers were wounded.

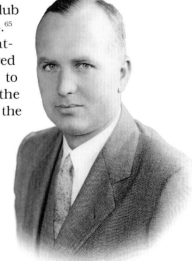

Edwin J. Thomas in 1930. Thomas joined Goodyear in 1930, and would be elected company president in 1940.

Schroy ordered extra police to go in and clean out the area, but when he was told the officers would have to "go back shooting," he called off the forces.[66]

Public tension further mounted with the formation of the Law and Order League, a citizens' committee devoted to forcing "out of town radical leaders" to get "the hell out of town."[67] *The Akron Beacon Journal* and *Akron Times Press* denounced the league as exacerbating an already volatile atmosphere.[68] In a statement issued to the press, Litchfield wrote that "Akron's reputation for lawlessness, its abject surrender to the defiant demands of a very small part of its population, is becoming so generally known that it will become increasingly difficult for us to convince our customers that they may depend upon us for an uninterrupted supply of rubber products."[69] The resulting loss of business, he chided, would prevent the company from hiring back all striking workers.

Long-time Goodyearite James Barnett vividly recalled that bitter and often violent time period. Barnett, who retired as chief of OEM sales worldwide in 1996, was a boy at the time of the strike, going to work for Goodyear in 1950. "I remember some guy heaved a brick through the window of our next-door neighbor when he was sitting in a

chair, darned near killing him. I remember the tent cities, with the unions picketing this place."[70]

It became clear to Goodyear executives that a settlement was necessary for the company and the city, and serious negotiations began on March 11. Climer and Thomas were actively involved, but Litchfield maintained his distance. On March 21, strikers voted enthusiastically to go back to work, throwing hats and cheering.[71] Under the terms of the settlement, which union officials considered a clear victory, striking workers were reinstated without loss of benefits or seniority rights. Management agreed to deal with "duly elected" worker representatives and post advance notice of wage changes and layoffs. In many departments the 36-hour week became standard, with future changes to be approved by employee referendum.[72]

The resolution was followed by months of labor disputes among former strikers and nonstrikers, with frequent sit-downs and protests interrupting plant operations. One local reporter criticized

The Great Strike of 1936 paralyzed the city of Akron, as strikers erected picket posts along the streets.

The strikers erected tents and shanties near the picket line to protect themselves from the bitter Ohio winter.

Goodyear employees for using the sit-down with "all the enthusiasm of a child with a new toy."[73]

The disputes sometimes turned violent. In early May, five men in Plant 3 were shot, receiving minor injuries.[74] On May 24, 28 tire builders at Plant 2 were arrested for kidnapping after they herded supervisors and former nonstrikers into a "bullpen" and prevented them from leaving or working during a 12-hour sit-down.[75] Goodyear's management worked hard to mend fractures between employees, and the *Wingfoot Clan* undertook a campaign to shame workers into better behavior. On May 6, an editorial on intolerance discussed "the denial of the inherent right of people to follow the dictates of their own consciences, or the right to worship to God as they believe they should, or the right to live and work without the interference of others." The article appealed to workers' patriotism by stating that intolerance had driven the Pilgrims across the ocean and spurred the colonists to fight the Revolutionary War. "Intolerance has no place in the United States of America," it concluded.[76]

With the strike finally resolved, the union had a new claim to legitimacy, making it the single powerful bargaining agent for Goodyear employees.[77] In agreeing to the settlement, Litchfield had insisted the Industrial Assembly would "occupy exactly the same position" it had in the past, but its powers had been diluted.[78] On August 31, 1937, the NLRB held an election asking Goodyear workers whether they wanted to be represented by Goodyear Local 2 of the United Rubber Workers of America. The vote was 8,464 yes to 3,192 no.[79] The Industrial Assembly was disbanded, and in October 1941, Goodyear inked its first formal contract with Local 2.[80]

At the time of the signing, Litchfield told Climer and Thomas he could not affix his name to such a contract. "Although he recognized that the Industrial Assembly — one of his proudest achievements — could never return, he felt a great sense of loss and a certain disappointment in his factory boys, as he called them, whose team he had led for so long. ... Thomas signed in Litchfield's place."[81]

1940 — Under the threat of war, Goodyear builds the nation's first synthetic rubber factory.

1941 — With war looming, Goodyear begins its greatest expansion in company history.

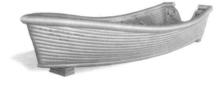

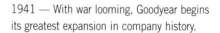

1940 — P. W. Litchfield steps down as president, and E.J. Thomas takes his place.

1942 — Japanese troops capture rubber plantations, as America's supplies dwindle. Synthetic rubber becomes increasingly important.

SAMIR G. GIBARA
CHAIRMAN OF THE BOARD
CHIEF EXECUTIVE OFFICER AND PRESIDENT

To Our Associates, Our Customers, and Our Friends Worldwide:

A clear vision of our future can be seen best through the filter of our own history. It is difficult to plan where we are going without knowing where we have been.

In an effort to better understand where we have been and where we are going — and for a host of other reasons ranging from the need to document a business milestone to the romantic emotion of pure nostalgia — we offer this literary time capsule of 100 years of Goodyear.

Thank you for your interest in The Goodyear Tire & Rubber Company. I hope this book will help you understand the unique attitude of family, our time-honored values, and the special corporate spirit that has carried this company to global greatness.

Fundamentally, the story brought to you by author Jeff Rodengen is a story of people:

— Goodyear people who made tough choices that proved to be pivotal decisions;

— Goodyear people whose spirit brightened the company's darkest hours;

— Goodyear people who celebrated success and learned from mistakes;

— And Goodyear people whose lives were forever linked, not because they worked for the same employer, but because they worked *together*.

Dr. Rodengen was given the key to our archives, our memories, and our critics. His is a report by an outside observer — an observer who is not only a talented writer, but also is a fair and impartial weaver of the threads of history.

This company first drew breath on the eve of a new century. Now, join with us in reliving the 100-year journey that brings us to the brink of a new millennium.

Most sincerely,

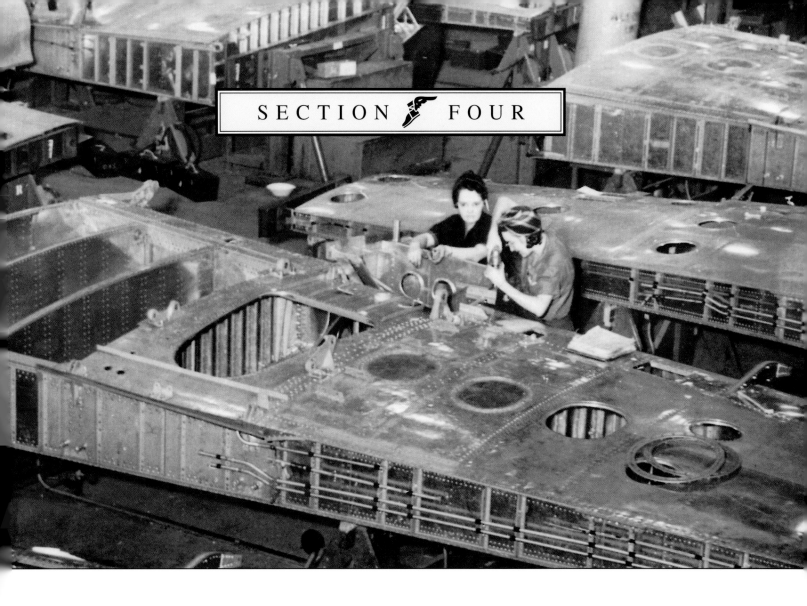

1943 — GAC begins production of the
B-29 Superfortress.

1948 — Goodyear celebrates its first
50 years.

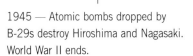

1945 — Atomic bombs dropped by
B-29s destroy Hiroshima and Nagasaki.
World War II ends.

1950 — Korean War breaks out; controls
on rubber once again go into effect.

Goodyear's 300 millionth tire, built in 1939, went on the massive *Snow Cruiser*, designed for Admiral Richard Byrd's expedition to Antarctica.

CHAPTER EIGHT

THE SEARCH FOR SYNTHETIC RUBBER

1937–1941

"Japan's staggering blow left us cut off from the sources of supply of more than 95 percent of our crude rubber — indispensable to modern industry and modern warfare. One brief weekend, and an economic crisis was upon us."

— G. Stocking and M.W. Watkins, *Cartels in Action*, 1946[1]

BY THE LATE 1930s, Goodyear's rubber factories dotted the globe with ever-increasing density. Tire plants had been established in Bowmanville and New Toronto, Canada; Bogor and Java, Indonesia; Buenos Aires, Argentina; Wolverhampton, England; and in Australia. Another international factory, 50 miles from Stockholm, Sweden, was completed in 1938. Goodyear's need for raw rubber continued to grow. By 1939, the company had produced its 300 millionth pneumatic tire. The tire was historic for another reason as well. It was one of a set of six 120X33.5-66s built to fit the giant car dubbed the *Snow Cruiser*, to be used on Admiral Richard Byrd's expedition to Antarctica. With diameters of 10 feet, the tires were the largest the company had ever made.[2]

Production of the special tires coincided with Goodyear's 40th anniversary celebration and the centennial of Charles Goodyear's discovery of vulcanization. To honor his accomplishments, a statue of Goodyear was unveiled in a park near Akron's Summit County Courthouse. Charles and Frank Seiberling acted as masters of ceremonies.[3]

Coming just seven months before Germany's invasion of Poland, the anniversary celebration foreshadowed the beginning of a new era. Even as Goodyearites were enjoying the event, the Industrial Products Department, under the guid-

ance of Herman Morse, was hard at work designing a new type of gas mask.[4] The first of many war products orders, the masks were tested by a pilot production team of 15 employees until late summer, when the Army demanded an increased production of 200,000 masks per month. More than 2,000 employees were assigned to the project. By the end of the war in 1945, Goodyear had made or supplied parts for more than 5 million gas masks, which actually proved unnecessary during World War II, since gas warfare had been abandoned as an impractical strategy.[5]

Events in Europe unfolded rapidly as the German Wehrmacht rolled over Poland in September 1939. At the same time, relations between the United States and Japan had reached a critical point. Tensions had been simmering ever since the Japanese invaded China in 1931, and the situation deteriorated as evidence mounted of brutality against Chinese residents. Nevertheless, Americans were more concerned about a war with industrialized Germany, dismissing Japan as too backwards to be much of a threat. Ironically, the United States depended on

The development of synthetic rubber material, like this inner tube, became increasingly important as war loomed.

Above: E.J. Thomas and two members of the Wingfoot basketball team in 1949. Thomas was a sports enthusiast.

Right: Dr. Ray Dinsmore, vice president of Research and Development, was vital to Goodyear's search for synthetic rubber.

islands in the Pacific for some of the most critical natural resources not found in the nation, including rubber and oil.

E.J. Thomas

In August 1940, P.W. Litchfield announced that he was stepping down as company president, a post he had held for 14 years.[6] While remaining chairman, he relinquished the president's desk to E.J. Thomas. With United States involvement in the war seemingly imminent, the 65-year-old Litchfield felt the challenge of running Goodyear was too much for one man to manage.[7]

The choice of Thomas was a popular one. Born in 1899, Thomas had grown up on Akron's Johnson Street "in the shadow of the smokestacks" of the Goodyear factory. His relationship with Litchfield dated back to the day when the 15-year-old Thomas rode his bicycle over to Goodyear Heights to check out the construction of the Scout Lodge.[8] He had left the University of Akron at age 17 to work in Goodyear's chemical lab.[9]

After serving in World War I, Thomas had returned to Goodyear as Litchfield's assistant and had progressed rapidly through company ranks, taking over Personnel in 1926, serving as general superintendent of the Los Angeles plant, and as managing director of the Goodyear Company of Great Britain in 1935. In 1937, he had become the company's first executive vice president. Genial and enthusiastic, Thomas had also played on the company's baseball and basketball teams. The *Wingfoot Clan* called him "one of the best liked men in all Goodyear."[10] He became Goodyear's eighth president on September 1, 1940.

Synthetic Rubber

One of the company's greatest technological advances, the development of synthetic rubber, was well under way by the time Thomas took office. The search for a synthetic had begun even before Charles Goodyear made natural rubber a workable material. In 1826, an English blacksmith, Michael Faraday, broke down crude rubber and discovered that its composition was five atoms of carbon and eight of hydrogen.[11] Faraday and others then worked on "distilling" rubber to what they believed were its essences of "spirit, oil and tar."[12]

By 1860, the British chemist Grenville Williams had devised a heat process to obtain a liquid with the same chemical composition of rubber, a substance he called isoprene.[13] In the 1880s, Sir William Tilden created isoprene from turpentine. The flimsy rubber-like pieces formed in the turpentine were useless, but Tilden's experiment marked the first time a rubber-like material had been made from something other than rubber.[14]

With the growth of the auto industry, the search for man-made rubber intensified, since natural rubber was inconvenient to obtain for the western world. The British blockade during World War I prompted Germany's development of a viable synthetic, and until the early 1940s, the country remained the world's leader in synthetic rubber production, operating a plant with an annual capacity of 1,800 tons by 1915.[15]

Goodyear joined the search for synthetic rubber during the 1920s, when natural rubber

Left: Chemigum was a primitive synthetic, developed in the lab by Dr. Ray Dinsmore.

A WINNER ON THE COURT

N THE DAYS BEFORE multimillion-dollar player contracts, sneaker commercials and Dennis Rodman, there were basketball enthusiasts such as Russ Ochsenshirt. Ochsenshirt, a Goodyear employee, played on the company basketball team, the Wingfoots. Led by Coach Clifton "Lefty" Byers, the Wingfoots won the Midwest Conference championship in 1936-37, and the National Basketball League title the following year.[1]

As predecessor to today's NBA, the NBL featured corporate-sponsored teams that were "professional" because the players had jobs with the companies. Having put in a full day's work, the players traveled by car to face teams such as the Duffy Florists and the Chicago Fast Freight.[2] Ochsenshirt recalled the dilemma of not being paid to play. Since he earned only $10 to $12 a week at the Goodyear factory and paid $15 per week to rent a room at the University Club, Ochsenshirt said, "After a year I owed so much money there I had to pay 'em back so much every week."[3]

The success of the Wingfoots — interrupted in 1940 when the Firestone Non-Skids won the title — built a bridge between employees and managers, most of whom attended games en masse. The tradition continued until 1970, when the team was disbanded. In its four-decade history, the Wingfoots won two national Amateur Athletic Union championships (1964 and 1967) and three consecutive World International Cups (1967-69).[4] Five Goodyear players made Olympic teams: Larry Brown, Dick Davies, and Pete McCaffrey in 1964; and Cal Fowler and Jim King in 1968.

Like the blimps, the Wingfoots were public relations marvels who carried the name Goodyear across the country and around the world. During the 1950s and 1960s, the team played exhibition games throughout the United States, and in Mexico, the Far East, the Middle East and Europe.[5]

prices fluctuated wildly. In 1929, Goodyear chemist Ray P. Dinsmore obtained patents for the basic processes to produce Chemigum, a primitive synthetic derived from a petroleum-cracking process.[16] Dinsmore's experiments were curtailed, however, when natural rubber prices fell. Synthetic rubber was expensive to produce and performed poorly in comparison to natural rubber.[17]

But as international relations grew increasingly unstable, obtaining a viable synthetic became a goal of paramount national importance. In 1935, relying on its friendly relations with Germany during the airship project, Goodyear sent Dinsmore to visit the German lab that was producing Buna-S in large quantities. Dinsmore inspected samples and returned to Akron to set up a small production line able to turn out 10 pounds per day of what many believe was the first synthetic rubber made in the United States.[18] In 1940, Goodyear's first complete Chemigum production plant — the country's first synthetic rubber factory — was built in Akron and had an annual production capacity of 2,000 tons.[19]

Litchfield was bothered by Germany's dominance in synthetic rubber. Rubber had become such a staple of military products that Litchfield warned the Trade Council in 1937 that Germany was "looking back upon the disastrous shortage which plagued her during the World War and looking forward to the time when she will have low-cost plants ready to produce."[20] By 1937, she already did. Imposing an additional 22-cent import duty on crude rubber products, Germany used the tax to fund construction of several domestic synthetic rubber plants in preparation for war.[21]

Goodyear's contribution was an early one, but several other companies were experimenting with synthetics as well. In addition to Goodyear's Chemigum there was Thiokol, produced by a Kansas City chemist, Joseph C. Patrick, who had been trying to make antifreeze; Duprene, later called Neoprene, produced by Du Pont; and B.F. Goodrich's Ameripol which, like Chemigum, had been successfully used to make tires.[22]

The various technical advances and the competitive jockeying for position in a new and promising industry, resulted in patent disputes and disagreements until 1942, when the United States government stepped in because of the exigent circumstances of war. In 1940, the U.S. Government Rubber Reserve had asked Goodyear, Goodrich, U.S Rubber and Firestone to construct synthetic rubber plants with annual capacities of 10,000 tons. By 1941, the companies were told to raise that capacity to 40,000 tons.[23]

Although they scrambled to create a large-scale industry overnight, at the time Pearl Harbor was attacked the United States had stockpiled about a year's worth of natural rubber, not nearly enough to supply a large nation at war. Plants that could manufacture synthetic rubber in large quantities did not exist.[24] The Pacific theater was, of course, the site of the world's source of crude rubber, and Goodyear's plantations in the Philippines and Sumatra were seized by the Japanese.[25] Obtaining a secure source of synthetic rubber was crucial, as discussed in the 1946 book, *Cartels in Action*.

"Pearl Harbor signaled a setback on the economic front scarcely less disturbing than on the military front. Japan's staggering blow left us cut off from the sources of supply of more than 95 percent of our crude rubber — indispensable to modern industry and modern warfare. One brief weekend, and an economic crisis was upon us."[26]

To encourage a unified synthetic rubber program, Congress appointed a committee headed by financial wizard Bernard M. Baruch, which outlined a plan for federal "dictatorial power within the fields of rubber production and rubber plant construction."[27] The tone of the committee's report, which was issued in the dark days of 1942, was urgent. "Let there be no doubt that only actual needs, not fancied wants, can, or should be satisfied. To dissipate our stocks of rubber is to destroy one of our chief weapons of war. We have the choice! ... In rubber, the United States must be listed as a 'have not' nation."[28]

Under the committee's plan, 49 private companies became involved in the synthetic project, creating one of the largest and most rapid of American industry's success stories.[29] The Big Four rubber companies operated government-

THE LIFEGUARD TIRE

URING THE SECOND half of the 1930s, Goodyear scored a public relations coup with its demonstrations of the LifeGuard tire, which featured a double tube that provided two air chambers separated by two layers of rubberized fabric.[1] The LifeGuard lessened the danger of blowouts. If the outer casing punctured, the inner tube provided enough cushioning to maintain steering stability until the driver could pull the car safely off the road.

To persuade a public skeptical of yet another advertised puncture-proof tire, Goodyear staged high-speed demonstrations during which drivers deliberately blew out tires. Paul Faulkner, one of Goodyear's expert drivers, typically destroyed eight to ten tires per demonstration, using dynamite or running over planks studded with iron spikes, often at speeds in excess of 70 miles per hour. Rather than careening off the side of the road or into an opposing lane, Faulkner blew the tire and took his hands off the steering wheel, calmly slowing the car amid the crowd's applause.[2]

LIFEGUARDS   PREVENT   ACCIDENTS!

CASING FAILS!   TUBE BLOWS!   SAFE ON LIFEGUARD!

NOT A TIRE... NOT A TUBE... BUT AN ENTIRELY NEW SAFETY INVENTION!
Modern successor to the inner tube, LifeGuard is a 2-ply *safety tire* inside a tube. If casing and tube fail, the inner tire holds enough air to support the car until it can be brought to a stop.
LifeGuard-equipped cars may be identified by the yellow and blue valve stems.

funded factories; Standard Oil and Du Pont ran the butyl and neoprene plants that provided the raw materials; and various oil companies supplied the necessary petroleum to produce butadiene.[30] The U.S. Defense Plant Corporation appropriated funds for the rubber companies to "select the sites, design the installations, and complete the construction" of synthetic rubber factories.[31] The plants were then leased to Goodyear, Goodrich, Firestone and U.S. Rubber at the rate of $1 per year, with the manufacturers agreeing to produce various copolymers and raw materials for the government's use.[32]

The companies agreed to produce a synthetic copolymer of butadiene and styrene, similar to the German's Buna-S. Goodyear, with an annual production of approximately 150,000 long tons (a long ton is 2,240 pounds, compared to a standard ton of 2,000 pounds), supervised and operated plants in Akron, Houston, and Torrance, California, and oversaw construction of a factory in Baytown, Texas that was subsequently run by General Tire.[33] In his autobiography, Litchfield recalled the "unprecedented teamwork" of the synthetic rubber project.

"Synthetic rubber was a bigger job than the industry had tackled, but not a different one. I have sometimes thought since of the contrast between this plan of voluntary teamwork on the part of many men, a distinctively American approach, as against the German system, where all direction came from the top. More men, more ideas — plus the fact that men usually work better when they are themselves creating something, rather than merely following orders. ... Most of these factories had to be built from the ground up. In the meanwhile our supply of natural rubber went down ... to 60,000 tons,

"Our car's safer'n yours... it's got LifeGuards!"

GOODYEAR LIFEGUARDS

The LifeGuard Safety Shield was Goodyear's most innovative development in tire technology during the 1930s. The principle behind the tire was used to develop a puncture-seal tube for aircraft tires.

two or three weeks' supply, when synthetic began to come in quantities."[34]

The success of the synthetic rubber project was illustrated by the fact that, from a "meager production of 5,400 long tons of synthetic rubber in 1941, the industry was capable of producing more than a million long tons annually by the end of 1944."[35] Other than those made by Goodyear's pilot plant, in 1941 virtually no American products were manufactured using synthetic rubber. By October 1945, 89 percent of rubber used in the United States was synthetic.[36] The 5 million gas masks, the 4,008 Corsair fighter planes, the tires for countless military and civilian vehicles, the 125,000 "Mae West" life jackets and 200,000 rubber boats and pontoons, the 4,880 barrage balloons and 168 blimps, and the 1 million bullet-sealing fuel tanks that were some of Goodyear's most important wartime products, were made possible by an even more essential one: the rubber itself.[37]

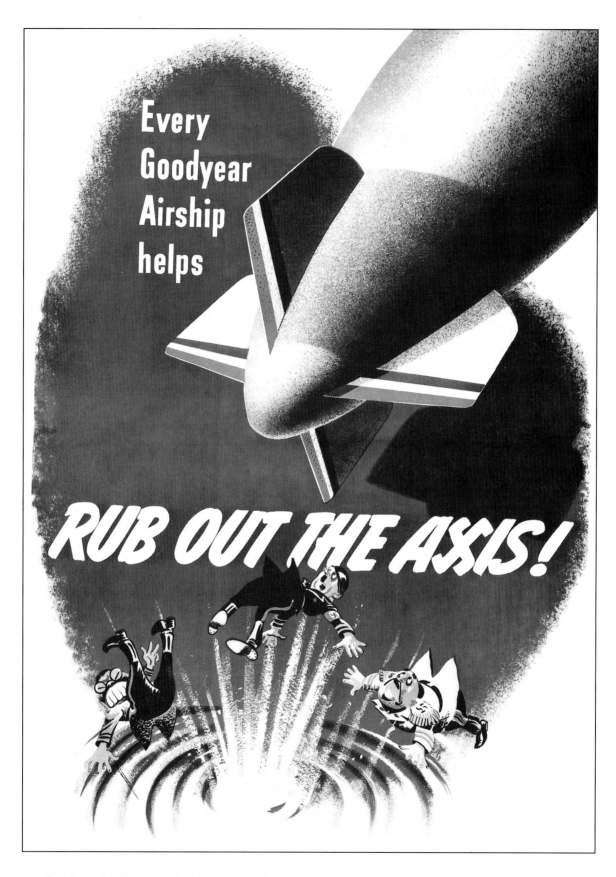

One of many inspirational and patriotic posters, this campaign used a play on words to exhort rubber workers to victory.

CHAPTER NINE

THE WAR YEARS

1939–1945

"We are at War. ... Every resource and facility owned by Goodyear, every bit of our talent and man power is the President's to command. This is offered without reservation or qualification. As individuals and as a corporation, we have worked hard during the past months to be ready for this situation. Now we shall double and redouble our efforts."

— *Wingfoot Clan*, December 10, 1941[1]

WHEN HITLER'S army attacked Poland on September 1, 1939, more than 18,000 of Goodyear's 46,000 employees worked outside the United States.[2] The foreign plants were quickly converted to wartime production. Although the factory in Wolverhampton, England, lay in a combat zone, it produced 22 percent of England's aircraft tires, and its engineers developed the Run-Flat Tire, which could run 50 to 100 miles after it had been punctured. The tire was so sturdy that it prompted German Field Marshal Erwin Rommel, called the "Desert Fox" for his tactical brilliance, to instruct his men to capture English trucks, since "German trucks get stuck in the sand too often."[3] To fill war orders, Wolverhampton employees worked 20 days with only one day of rest. However, their shifts were interrupted by frequent Luftwaffe raids that sent them fleeing to company-erected shelters.[4]

The six-month-old Swedish factory faced an extreme rubber shortage, producing just 630 tires in 1944, but kept busy reclaiming rubber and repairing worn tires.[5] In Argentina, the Goodyear plant "made bricks without straw," producing tires to move much-needed resources to the troops even though the country's supply of natural rubber was as little as 250 pounds per year. In normal times that amount would have run the Goodyear factory for just three weeks.[6] The Indonesian plant served the defense needs of the Netherlands East Indies; the Australian factory produced tires for military vehicles.[7] Beginning September 3, 1939, Goodyear-Canada blackened the windows of its factories and went into 24-hour production of defense materials including military tires, LifeGuard tubes, rubber rafts, life vests, fuel cells, and developed a five-ton armored tank called the Snowmobile, which could traverse deep snow, swamps and marshlands.[8]

The *Wingfoot Clan* brought the war home to Goodyearites through stories of its impact on their colleagues overseas. In mid-September 1939, workers were cheered by pictures of 17 American families returning to Akron from Wolverhampton. Three Goodyear blimps met the passenger ship outside New York Harbor and escorted its 1,700 passengers — nearly double the ship's carrying capacity — to shore.[9] Several months later, the *Clan* announced Goodyear's first war casualty, the death of 19-year-old Ronald Parker of the British Flying Corps, whose

Goodyear's 250,000,001st tire, built less than two months after the Great Strike of 1936 ended. Goodyear needed a reason to celebrate.

father Hugh was a Goodyear cotton buyer.[10] In October 1940, the magazine carried a request from C.N. Hurst, former general line salesman at London, who was imprisoned in a German POW camp. Hurst asked his Goodyear brothers and sisters to send chocolate, hard biscuits and cigarettes to make his captivity easier to bear.[11]

Until the attack on Pearl Harbor, the majority of Americans were isolationists, viewing the war as yet another bloody chapter in European history. According to one 1940 poll, only 2.5 percent of Americans favored United States involvement in the European conflict.[12] Likewise, although the United States officially deplored the Japanese invasion of China, few if any Americans wanted to see their sons killed in an overseas war.[13]

American industry, though, was already preparing for the inevitable. By January 1941, Germany conquered Poland, Norway, Denmark,

Luxembourg, Holland, Belgium and France, provoking the United States into a massive defense buildup.[14] That month, P.W. Litchfield advised employees about the role industry must play. "In this critical period, every man is called into the country's service, whether he is in uniform, in overalls, or wherever needed. Industry must forget its own interest, subordinate everything else to the national interest."[15]

As the war escalated, America's strict position of neutrality was losing popularity, although groups such as the America First party continued to argue against involvement. President Franklin Roosevelt asked for $1.9 billion for defense in 1940. Later that year, Congress approved $17 billion.

Essentially the "national interest" was industry. On a tour of the Akron plants just prior to Pearl Harbor, Lt. Colonel Robert Ginsburgh, representing the office of the assistant secretary of war, impressed upon Goodyear workers their crucial part in an Allied victory, saying, "The conflict must be won in our factories. This is a war of production."[16]

The First World War had advanced the concept of machine warfare, but at its conclusion the airplane was still in its infancy, the automobile an adolescent. Two decades later, World War II became what one historian called "the battle of the drawing boards ..."

"... fought between rival scientists — designers, researchers and engineers — in a never-ending struggle to provide their armies with superior weapons. Competition was especially keen in aircraft and tank design, in the velocity of shells, destructiveness of bombs, and the accuracy of fire control. It grew fiercer at such an accelerating rate that toward the end of the war no new battle was won with the same weapons that had won the last. God, Napoleon had said, is on the side of the big battalions, but in this war He seemed to favor the latest models."[17]

A worker constructs an aircraft tire in 1940. As aircraft grew heavier, the company experimented with rayon, then nylon fabric, which had better strength-to-weight ratios than cotton.

The importance of technology — in the form of new and better weapons, crucial innovations such as the development of synthetic rubber, and American industry's success in providing both — could be counted in the comparatively low toll of American casualties in relation to the size of the war. With more than 11.2 million Americans in uniform, the United States suffered roughly 261,000 battle deaths.[18]

Gearing Up for War

As the world's largest rubber company, Goodyear was in the thick of preparations. By the summer of 1941, the first peacetime draft in American history had built the Army's numbers to 1.4 million men, and Goodyear had embarked on the biggest period of expansion in its history.[19] Under contract to produce airplane parts, gas masks, barrage balloons, blimps, and tank, truck, and plane tires, Goodyear was faced with a serious shortage of space. The huge Airdock had been converted to a manufacturing cen-

Above: Goodyearites sew and check the seams on barrage balloons in the "balloon room."

Below: Barrage balloons were floated above ships and cities to entangle and distract enemy aircraft.

ter for control surfaces, ailerons, flaps and empennages for the Glenn L. Martin Company's B-26 bomber, but additional orders with Grumman and Consolidated required even more space.[20]

The unused textile mill in New Bedford, Massachusetts, roared to life in 1940 and became the primary site of balloon manufacturing, supplemented by Akron workers who set up makeshift "balloon rooms" in the gymnasium and on one floor of Goodyear Hall.[21] In the spring of 1941, in cooperation with the Defense Plant Corporation, a government agency that funded much of the country's building boom, Goodyear turned the area surrounding the Airdock into a manufacturing complex, adding two adjacent factories and smaller storage buildings.[22]

In November 1941, the *Clan* broke the flurry of activity into numbers:

> *"Excepting the 1916 boom when Plant 2 and other buildings were erected in Akron, the year 1941 is witnessing the greatest building expansion in Goodyear's history. ... [Goodyear] has completed or is in the process of completing 10 separate building projects, which provide 1,219,000 additional square feet of floor space.*
>
> *The Akron expansion requires:*
> - *12,662 tons of steel*
> - *45,530 barrels of cement*
> - *296,000 cubic yards of sand and gravel*
> - *More than two million bricks.*
>
> *Buildings being erected in Akron are:*
> - *D.P.C. Aircraft plant, 504,000 square feet*
> - *Brake and wheel assembly building at Aircraft, 244,450 square feet*
> - *Hydraulic press building at the airdock, 12,600 square feet*
> - *Shops and offices in the airdock, 86,600 square feet*
> - *Chemical plant addition, 1,200 square feet*
> - *Chemigum plant, 14,600 square feet (completed)*
> - *D.P.C. Chemigum plant, 55,000 square feet."*[23]

In 1941, sales were up 52 percent from the previous year, topping $330 million.[24] The company touted its contributions in a 20-minute film, *Goodyear Shoulders Arms*, which toured trade fairs and conferences throughout the country. On Monday, July 28, workers in every Goodyear factory and district office in the country were greeted with new metal plaques bearing the "Protect Our Good Name" company slogan.[25] "To every employee there was brought a deeper sense of responsibility and obligation," wrote the *Clan*. "For perhaps more than ever before all of us realized that upon our good work depends our good name."[26]

With United States entry into the war appearing more and more likely, the company purchased a factory in Mexico City in January 1942 and built a larger plant in nearby Lecheria.[27] To secure supply of the rich resources of Peru, Goodyear planned its fourth Latin American plant near Lima. It began production in 1942.[28]

The *Wingfoot Clan* kept workers informed about how their productivity was winning the war, and advertised patriotic rallies.

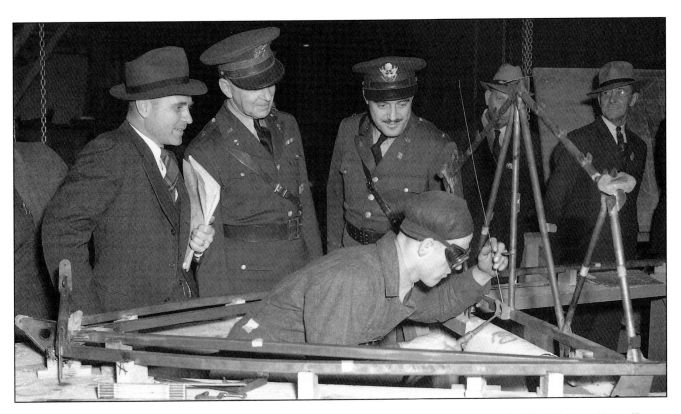

The Goodyear Engineering Corporation

Just days before the Japanese attacked Pearl Harbor, military officers toured GAC.

The most surprising of Goodyear's prewar construction projects was a $35 million bag-loading plant near Charlestown, Indiana.[29] While relaxing at home on December 31, 1940, E.J. Thomas received a cryptic telephone call from Colonel Miles of the Army Ordnance Department. Miles asked Thomas to send someone to meet him that night at the Cincinnati train station, but he would not reveal the purpose of the meeting. When pressed, Miles said the Army wanted Goodyear to plan and operate a major Midwestern bag-loading plant. Thomas, uncertain exactly what bag-loading meant, sent J.M. Linforth, vice president in charge of government sales, to meet the train.

Having served aboard a warship in World War I, Linforth knew a little about bag-loading. The army's project consisted of two plants to be built along the Ohio River: In one, Du Pont would make smokeless powder; in the other, Goodyear would make and load bags for 60 types of artillery, weighing anywhere from three pounds to 800.[30] Linforth was told the process was like "putting sugar in a bag ... except you have to be more careful."[31]

A new subsidiary, the Goodyear Engineering Corporation, was incorporated to operate the plant under the management of Harry Hillman, who had experience working with government contracts.[32] More than 40 engineers and supervisors were transferred to Indiana.[33] Construction was begun immediately, and the first bags were sewn and loaded on Labor Day in 1941, three weeks ahead of schedule.[34]

The job turned out to be more complicated than bagging sugar, and Goodyear workers received a crash course in the handling of explosives. Called the Hoosier Ordnance Plant, the two factories were built on a nine-square-mile site which was divided into an "explosive area" and an "inert area." The explosive section consumed more than 75 percent of the floor space. The fabric bags were made in the inert section, which was equipped with 1,500 power-driven sewing machines and a laundry for washing uniforms. The black-powder workers wore white

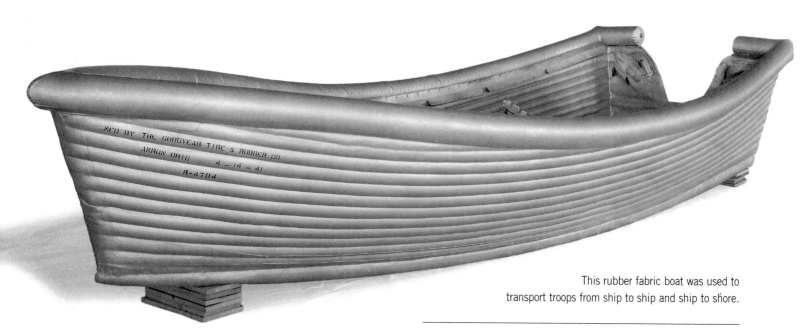

This rubber fabric boat was used to transport troops from ship to ship and ship to shore.

uniforms so that any trace of spilled powder would easily show.

The dangerous area was partitioned into sections, so that only a certain quantity of explosive material and so many workers would be contained in any one area. Working closely with the Ordnance Department, Goodyear employees laid out eight loading lines for the smokeless powder, four for black powder, and 177 "igloos," concrete buildings disguised with soil and grass that were used for storing the filled bags.

The company instituted strict safety standards. Goodyear engineers designed a storm indicator which showed the direction and intensity of lightning. If a storm threatened or a dangerous level of static accumulated in the atmosphere, a gong was sounded so that workers could seek shelter in one of the facility's 16 cafeterias. Also important was the "change house." Workers undressed on the inert side of the factory, leaving their street clothes in lockers and passing through the change house into the explosive area, where they donned pocketless uniforms.[35]

Bagging powder required a tremendous amount of precision.

"The manufacture of propellant charges actually is an almost endless process of checking powder moisture and the surrounding air, since powder must be kept dry and its weight must be controlled to specifications. Weighing tolerance on the loading line for many charges is one one-hundredth of an ounce. To achieve this accuracy in mass production, special weights for each powder lot must be calibrated in advance at the plant's master scale laboratory. Calibration of loading lone weights and powder cups is done by trained technicians on balances so precise that an accuracy of one part in a million is possible. These safeguards are necessary to assure charge that will propel an artillery projectile the precise distance predetermined when the gun is trained on a specific target."[36]

That Goodyear was chosen to oversee such a complicated operation in a field in which it had no experience reflected its reputation for quality and efficiency. The Charlestown plant was crucial to the war effort — but it had absolutely nothing to do with rubber.

"We are at War"

On December 7, 1941, more than 360 Japanese planes screamed down from the clouds, unleashing dive bombs and torpedoes on a surprised U.S. Navy. More than 2,400 Americans were killed. Three of the eight battleships — the backbone of the Navy — were sunk and the other five badly damaged. More than 150 planes were destroyed on the ground.

The December 10, 1941, issue of the *Wingfoot Clan* carried this message from Chairman of the Board Litchfield:

"We are at War.

The hour of war has struck.

Our people have been attacked by a foreign foe.

They must be given blow for blow — and more.

I do not say we must unite — I say we have united.

Internal differences are automatically resolved.

Capital, labor, and management are as one, shoulder to shoulder in the common and paramount determination — to wipe these sinister enemy forces from the face of the earth.

Every resource and facility owned by Goodyear, every bit of our talent and man power is the President's to command.

This is offered without reservation or qualification.

As individuals and as a corporation, we have worked hard during the past months to be ready for this situation. Now we shall double and redouble our efforts."[37]

Congress imposed immediate restrictions on rubber consumption. The synthetic program was still a scramble, and the United States had a stockpile of only 500,000 tons of natural rubber, less than a year's supply during peacetime.[38] The country had consumed more than 775,000 tons during the peaceful months of 1941.[39] When the Japanese captured Singapore in February 1942, gaining easy access to the Dutch East Indies and

Rubber assault craft enabled troops to hit beaches in shallow water, where larger landing craft would be disabled.

the world's primary supply of natural rubber, the rubber shortage became a crisis. Goodyear's own holdings in Java, Sumatra and the Philippines fell to the Japanese in quick succession.[40]

Automobile production came to a standstill, with auto manufacturers quickly converting their facilities to produce combat vehicles and mechanical parts. New tires were to be supplied only for military and "essential" vehicles.[41] Three weeks after Pearl Harbor, Goodyear introduced a passenger car tire made entirely of regenerated rubber.[42] Naming the tire Defense, the company made no claims for its quality and warned the public that it was a product of expediency and could not withstand speeds in excess of 35 miles per hour. Advertisements for the Defense also asked consumers to notice the symbolic "V" for victory in the tire's tread.[43]

In November 1941, 3.1 million passenger car tires were produced in the United States; the total fell to 1.9 million after restrictions took effect in December, then to 230,000 in January and only 61,000 in July 1942.[44] Goodyear's total tire production fell from 17 million in 1941 to 5 million the following year.[45] Tires were 60 percent of Goodyear's business and the company had 3.5 million of them stored in warehouses under government order.[46] Yet company sales for the war years, 1941 through 1945, reached a total volume of more than $3 billion.[47]

The Air War

Goodyear produced tires and tubes for military vehicles, but its foray into aeronautics proved its most important contribution to the Allied victory. In 1939, just three months after the invasion of Poland, the Goodyear Aircraft Company had been incorporated. GAC, which would eventually replace Goodyear-Zeppelin, was

The war tire, made entirely of reclaimed rubber. The Japanese cut off rubber resources when they overran Java, Sumatra and the Philippine Islands. The tire was limited to a maximum speed of 35 miles.

the direct descendent of the tiny aeronautical department started by Litchfield in 1910.[48] Overseen by Russell DeYoung and Dr. Karl Arnstein, vice presidents of Production and Engineering respectively, GAC began with only 30 employees, mostly transfers from the airship program. But with the 1941 contract to produce wings and engine nacelles for the B-26 Marauder — a project that called for 100 planes a month and required 7,000 employees — the subsidiary mushroomed in size.[49]

As the Japanese were invading French Indochina — later known as Vietnam — GAC found its production capacity falling short of projected orders, and under Litchfield's direction and with government funding Goodyear created Goodyear Aircraft-Arizona, a factory center near Phoenix.[50] At its peak in 1945, GAC-Arizona employed 7,668 workers in an 11-building, 900,000-square-foot complex.[51] Between 1942 and 1945, it produced more than 3 million pounds of airframes.[52]

By the time of Pearl Harbor, Goodyear Aircraft was already under contract with Grumman to manufacture empennages for the Avenger, the Navy's carrier-based torpedo bomber. After Pearl Harbor, GAC's payroll swelled to 30,000 and its contracts ballooned from $600,000 to more than $9 million.[53] War orders for 1942 would top $90 million, a figure that would triple before the war's end.[54]

By the end of the war, Goodyear — for which aeronautics had been a longtime but mostly

Above: The Navy's carrier-based Corsair. The Japanese dubbed it "Whistling Death," because of its maneuverability and the sound the engine made.

Below: GAC workers produced wheels, brakes, tires, fuselages and other parts for the Navy, Lockheed, Boeing, Mitchell and other aircraft companies.

Above: As men went off to war, production fell to women, collectively known as "Rosie the Riveter."

Right: Skilled hands were needed in the smallest of places. This little person takes a break from driving rivets into an aircraft's fuselage.

employed, housewives, mothers, and in many instances grandmothers and middle-age spinsters eager to 'do their bit' for the war effort."[58] According to company historian Clyde Schetter, skeptical male laborers and supervisors were won over by the "manual dexterity, technical comprehension, and dedication to purpose" of the "girls" — the majority of whom were enjoying their first opportunity to earn good wages.[59]

To find skilled workers, the company solicited names from its 2,500 tire dealers across the country and issued employment invitations. College students, male and female, were hired, as were retired men and high school boys and girls.[60] GAC put 20 blind people to work sorting nails and screws and doing other jobs they could accomplish by feel.[61] Midgets were hired for aircraft work because they could crawl into small spaces and drive rivets into plane wings and pontoons of flying boats.[62]

unprofitable sideline interest — had become among the 10 largest plane manufacturers in the United States.[55]

The company had to scramble to staff its production line. As young men were called to war, women stepped into the workforce in impressive numbers, making up more than 56.3 percent of all production workers by the end of 1944.[56] By comparison, in January 1942 — just after Pearl Harbor — only one woman was listed as a factory worker in the Akron plants.[57] Classes to train women in metal working were offered by Goodyear Industrial University, and the classrooms were quickly filled with "sales girls, waitresses, stenographers, beauticians, cooks, women from wealthy homes who had never been

All employees were packed into crowded manufacturing quarters, with machinery and workers being transferred into new buildings as soon as they were deemed safe by the construction foremen. Several plants received additions even before original construction was completed. To conserve space, cafeterias and hiring offices were moved outside and set up under circus tents. Hiring was temporarily halted one spring afternoon when a stiff wind picked up the employment office tent, blew it across a field, and left it draped over a barn.[63]

GAC's biggest contract was for the Navy's FG-1 Corsair fighter plane, the first plane for which the company was totally responsible. Production began in 1942 in Plant 3, the tire warehouse, and was transferred to Plant D as soon as the new building's roof was installed. The first Corsair was test flown in February 1943 before construction workers had completed the plant.[64] First of a new kind of heavy fighter, the Corsair featured a 2,300-horsepower engine and exceeded 470 miles per hour with full military equipment. Since it was designed for use on carriers, it needed a low landing speed — approximately 85 miles per hour — and its 41-foot wingspan could be folded to 17 feet to allow more of them to be stored aboard the carriers. The Corsair could carry six 50-caliber guns, which were later upgraded to cannons, and attachments for two 1,000-pound bombs plus a droppable 150-gallon fuel tank.

Goodyear was one of only three manufacturers of the Corsair. Chance Vought, the designer, and Brewster Aeronautical were the other two manufacturers.[65] Employed in the Pacific theater, the Corsair was first employed during the six-month battle of Guadalcanal in the South Pacific.[66]

Between February 1943 and September 1945, Goodyear produced 4,006 Corsairs and, was slated to begin manufacturing an improved design, the F2G, when V-J Day arrived.[67]

GAC also had a hand in the production of another legendary plane, the B-29 Superfortress. In July 1943, the contract for the B-26 Marauder was canceled in favor of the newly designed bomber, and Goodyear initiated a conversion of Plant C. While workers finished the last of the B-26 order on one side of the building, a wrecking ball was breaking the false floor on the other side to make room for the taller B-29.[68] Later in the war, when the Japanese home islands came under bomber attack, the B-29s were used in the fire-

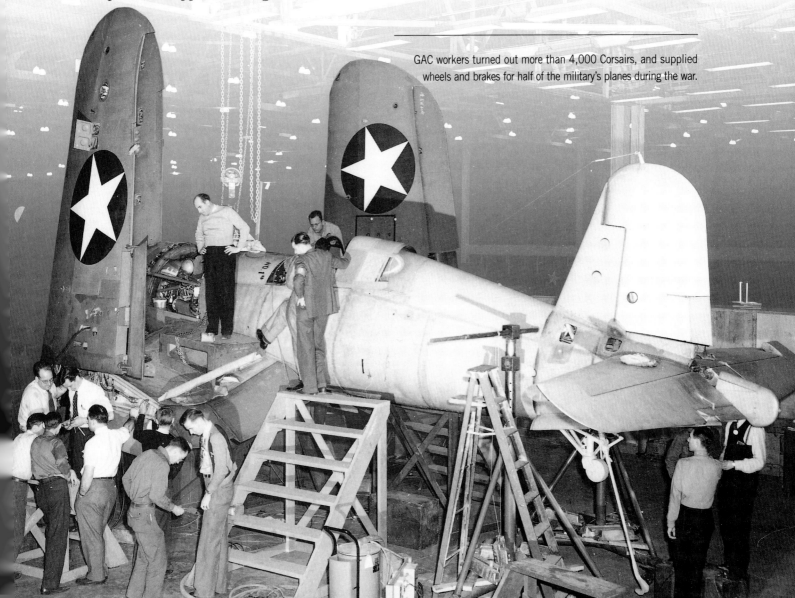

GAC workers turned out more than 4,000 Corsairs, and supplied wheels and brakes for half of the military's planes during the war.

bombing campaign, which in many respects caused worse damage than the atomic bomb. In a single raid, B-29s dropped enough ordnance to destroy 250,000 homes, killing nearly 84,000 people.[69] The *Enola Gay*, which dropped the world's first atomic bomb on Hiroshima, was also a B-29.

The Goodyear Blimp on Patrol

As the nation's only manufacturer of blimps, Goodyear delivered 168 lighter-than-air crafts to the U.S. Navy.[70] The blimps served a vital role in anti-submarine patrols. At the start of the war, the country was woefully ill-equipped to prevent sub attacks. In January 1942, Germany's Admiral Doenitz initiated a bold attack on American shipping, with U-boats sinking 568 Allied ships, some within sight of the coast.[71] Two weeks after Pearl Harbor, a Japanese submarine sank the SS *Medio*, a cargo vessel, off the California coast, and on February 23, 1942, another shelled an oil field near Santa Barbara.[72] On June 15, 1942, thousands of sunbathers at Virginia Beach were horrified to witness the torpedoing of two American freighters by a stealthy German sub.[73] With its own fleet having dwindled to just 10 airships, the Navy quickly drafted Goodyear's five blimps — the *Resolute*, the *Ranger*, the *Rainbow*, the *Reliance* and the *Enterprise*.[74] The *Resolute* started patrolling the southern California coast under

Above: The *Enola Gay*, the B-29 Superfortress that destroyed an entire city with one atomic bomb. (Photo courtesy of *Air Force Magazine*.)

Below: A Goodyear blimp on convoy patrol in 1942. Only one blimp was ever lost to enemy fire.

privateer status, armed only with the pilot's hunting rifle.[75]

Congress quickly authorized the purchase of 200 airships. By the end of 1942 more than 2,800 workers were building blimps at GAC, the tire plants, and the Wingfoot Lake hangar.[76] With their slow, silent approach, the airships were ideal for night patrols. By 1943, blimps cruised over more than 5,000 miles of sea from Newfoundland to Rio de Janeiro, also covering the Gulf of Mexico and the West Coast of the United States. The blimps were so effective that Congress cut back its order. In 1942 alone, 454 ships had been sunk by the enemy, but in 1944 the figure plummeted to just eight.[77] The blimps compiled an even more remarkable record as escorts for merchant vessels; of the 90,000 ships guarded by blimps, not one was lost.[78] Although 56 blimps were lost during the war, only one was lost to enemy fire. On July 18, 1943, the K-74 attacked a German U-boat off the coast of Florida but was riddled with machine gun bullets. Nine of the 10 crewman were rescued.

Blimps were also useful for rescues at sea. One incident reflected the ubiquity of Goodyear war products. Marine Captain Frank Baldwin, a former Goodyear employee, had recently returned from a Pacific tour during which he shot down 23 Japanese fighters. Baldwin was involved in a training mission off the California coast when he collided with another plane and was forced to parachute into the water.[79] Baldwin became coiled in the lines of his parachute and could not be reached by a rescue boat. Because of the choppiness and height of the waves, a seaplane was also unable to reach him. After nearly two hours of ducking high waves, Baldwin climbed out of the ocean via a harness lowered from a blimp that had been called in from the Santa Ana Air Station. Shivering and exhausted, Baldwin said to the men in the airship: "Here's one for Litchfield. A Goodyear man, flying a Goodyear Corsair, is kept afloat by a Goodyear life raft, then rescued by a Goodyear blimp.'"[80]

After the war's end, Baldwin returned to work for Goodyear.

D-Day

The company's most clandestine operation was also its most spectacular. Under J.F. Cooper, who died before the end of the war, Goodyear's balloon room had won fame for its national and international racing victories, as well as the colorful cartoon figures it created for the Macy's Thanksgiving Day Parade, an annual event since it began in 1924.[81] Toward the end of the war, the military gave Goodyear balloon designers an unusual assignment. They were to make reproductions of invasion craft: tanks, combat vehicles, PT boats and heavy artillery, constructed on a one-to-one scale.[82] Workers at Goodyear's Woonsocket, Rhode Island plant, where the "fleet" was produced, wondered what use the military would have for life-sized inflatable tanks.

By late spring of 1944, an Allied invasion of Europe was inevitable. The question for the enemy was: where on the coast of France would the invasion hit? For weeks prior to June 6 — D-Day — the Luftwaffe picked up signs of an invasion from one port, then another; amazingly, large numbers of combat equipment seemed to be gathering at entirely different sites around the English Channel and North Sea ports, sometimes appearing to spring up overnight.[83] The Germans grew increasingly confused. While the Phantom Fleet was repeatedly deflated and transported to new locations the true forces were coalescing across the Channel from Normandy. At the same time, radio signals and bombing campaigns were stepped up to point the finger at Calais, the most logical place for an attack because it was the narrowest part of the English Channel. Instead, the Germans were caught by surprise when the attack took place at Normandy.

Although GAC was more glamorous, the tire division performed well in a tough market, first facing a rubber shortage, then a sudden and crucial demand for product. By 1943, the entire supply of prewar tires had been used up, and existing factories could not produce tires fast enough to meet the military's needs.[84] The government authorized $70 million to build new tire factories to be run by the big rubber companies. As the largest, Goodyear was assigned four plants.[85] The Jackson and Kelly-Springfield factories, which had been making antitank guns, fuel cells and high explosive shells, were reconverted into tire plants; the Gadsden plant was doubled in size; and a new factory was opened in Topeka to produce large combat tires and rear tires for farm equipment.[86] The new plants went into production just as General George S. Patton's famous Third Army rolled into France.[87]

Yet in December 1944, General Brehon Somervel, chief of supply for the Army, informed rubber executives that the Army was facing a shortage of 472,000 tires for the first quarter of 1945.[88] The industry pledged a 120-day drive to maximize production, and by mid-February military tire output at the Akron plants reached the highest level of the war period,

A sailor demonstrates using the rescue ladder cast down from a Navy blimp.

with more than 9,000 employees having worked every day of the four-month pledge period.[89]

From 1940 to 1944, company sales mushroomed from slightly more than $217 million to more than $786.7 million, although war taxes reduced net earnings from 3.9 percent to 1.9 percent.[90] Wartime employment reached a high of 107,000 in 1944, but V-J Day also meant the immediate cancellation of government contracts amounting to $432.4 million, leading to widespread worker layoffs.[91]

For their war efforts, the coveted Army-Navy "E" Award, which was granted to only 5 percent of American industries, was given to 15 Goodyear plants: the Charlestown bagging plant, which received the award for five straight years beginning in 1940; Akron's Plant III, which had produced gas masks; GAC-Arizona; the Kelly-Springfield plant; the factories at St. Mary's, Ohio, and Gadsden, Alabama; all four of the cotton mills; and Goodyear Aircraft-Akron.[92] Individual Goodyearites recognized for outstanding contributions included Fred Climer, director of personnel at Akron, who served on the nation's War Production Board; and chemist R.C. Dinsmore, who joined the staff of the National Rubber Administration to coordinate the synthetic rubber program.[93] The highest award of the War Production Board, the Citation of Individual Production Merit, was presented to research chemist James A. Merrill for his innovative use of a nylon barrier to prevent gasoline in bullet-sealing fuel tanks from eating through layers of synthetic rubber. Merrill received his award from President Franklin D. Roosevelt at a December 1942 ceremony at the White House.[94]

By August 15, 1945, the last day of the war, battle lines had stretched across the globe, from the shores of Normandy and the skies of Tokyo, the islands of the Pacific and the snows of Russia, to the factory lines in Akron, Gadsden, Woonsocket, Los Angeles, Phoenix, Topeka, Bowmanville, Lima, and Wolverhampton. Buoyant with the Allied victory, Harry Blythe, vice president and general manager of Goodyear Aircraft, reminded employees of the service they had rendered.

"I am conscious of a feeling of humility as I think of the older women who had never worked in a factory before and who stuck by their guns when the going was tough; of the older men who had retired from an active life but who responded to the nation's needs; of hundreds of wives whose husbands were out fighting over the seven seas and the five continents involved. I tell you in all sincerity that this war could not have been won except for Americans like you. ...

"You came to us by the thousands from every walk of life, from every state in the union. Many of you did not know a punch press from a riveting gun when you came here. And we did not know anything about building airplanes. ... But you learned and we learned. We have been shipmates in an enterprise not often granted to men and women to experience in a lifetime. Your husbands, sons, and brothers can be as proud of you as you are of them."[95]

Top left: The coveted Army-Navy "E" Award.

Above: The bullet-seal fuel tank saved the lives of countless bomber pilots by preventing fuel from leaking after being hit by enemy fire. Workers turned out thousands of these tanks.

A Goodyear researcher experimenting with rubber compounds in 1949. Insatiable consumer appetite encouraged product development.

CHAPTER TEN

CONVERTING TO
A POSTWAR ECONOMY

1945–1951

"The death of C.W. Seiberling removes a truly great man from our midst. Whatever there is in this great business organization of comradeship, sportsmanship, loyalty, and the friendship between men and men, stems in large measure to Charley Seiberling."

— The *Wingfoot Clan*, 1946[1]

THE END OF THE WAR meant the end of Goodyear's frantic production schedule. Sales for 1945 fell more than $70 million from a peak of $786.7 million in 1944. This figure reflected the loss of more than $432.4 million in government contracts.[2] Goodyear Aircraft, which had enjoyed phenomenal growth during the war years, suffered an equally rapid decline after V-J Day. Employment for GAC-Akron, a division that had been fully committed to war products, plunged from 19,057 in July 1945 to 3,795 by the end of the year, bottoming out at 2,000 by the end of 1946.[3]

In an effort to establish a new raison d'etre, GAC shifted from its glamorous role as aircraft manufacturer to that of subcontractor for consumer goods. In February 1946, the division signed a contract with York Manufacturing, one of the nation's largest producers of refrigerators and freezers, to build thousands of storage bins for automatic ice makers.[4] For Montgomery Ward, GAC made steel sink cabinets. For the Army Quartermaster Corps, it provided $1 million worth of steel lockers.[5] In the late 1940s, GAC manufactured jukeboxes, storm doors and washing machine parts.[6] On a more somber note, GAC was awarded a $6.4 million government contract to provide 50,000 of the 250,000 caskets needed to bury the remains of the war dead.[7]

GAC did not leave the field of aeronautics altogether. It produced aircraft wheels and brakes, developed a plastic bubble canopy for cockpits — dubbed "optically perfect compound curved enclosures" — and worked for the military in the emerging field of rockets and guided missiles.[8] In 1948, GAC developed a cross-wind landing gear designed to allow aircraft to take off and land without regard to wind direction, making feasible the single-strip landing field and "forecasting the day when airports can be relocated closer to the heart of large cities."[9]

However, the search for non-military assignments would not endure. In 1949, the *Wingfoot Clan* introduced a series of articles with the ominous title: "Communism: The Enemy of Your Way of Life."[10] The Cold War had already begun, and the Korean War would erupt the following year.

Meeting the Demand for Goodyear Tires

As Goodyear-Aircraft sought new ventures, Goodyear Tire enjoyed a postwar boom. Conservation efforts had taken their toll on the national psyche. People wanted new cars, or at

A raincape made with the fashionable Plio-film, for women who wished to show off their dresses in all types of weather.

least new tires on which they could drive faster than 35 miles per hour. Civilian tire replacement sales, which had topped 34,000 in 1941, had dropped precipitously to 2,600 in 1942. The restrictions on commercial tire sales had left most existing automobiles with patched tires. As a result, the postwar period was a tire seller's market.[11]

As it had following World War I, Goodyear struggled to meet the demand. Although the company slashed the size of its Aircraft Division, many workers were either untrained for tire labor or elected not to transfer. Goodyear endured the irony of laying off thousands of workers even as it faced a labor shortage. The majority of female, retired and college-age workers returned to their prewar lives. Fortunately, return of war veterans helped avert a crisis. Prior to V-J Day, Goodyear had implemented a plan that guaranteed G.I.s their former jobs within 90 days of an honorable military discharge or, if the specific job was unavailable or the soldier had been wounded in battle, a position at a similar rate of pay.[12]

But the arrival of G.I.s was staggered and slow. To fill the gap, the company reverted to its practice of recruiting workers from neighboring states. Furthermore, the Goodyear local union demanded an immediate return to the prewar six-hour work day, and a series of disruptive sit-downs and other work stoppages ensued. Goodyear, along with much of the nation, was plagued by labor unrest and material shortages.[13]

Still, production rose rapidly. The war had left such a demand, both for replacement tires and original equipment for an invigorated auto industry, that not until 1948 could Vice President R.S. Wilson confidently state that the "vacuum created by the war shortages has been filled up. In the two years, 1946 and 1947, the rubber

Left: A couple enjoys the postwar years on a Goodyear-equipped motorcycle.

Below: A barbershop quartet celebrates the launch of the Crosby raincoat at Akron's O'Neil's Department Store in 1949.

industry sold enough tires to put a brand-new set on every car on the road.'"[14]

In each of those two years, Goodyear Tire's output increased by 25 million tires.[15] In 1946 the company set a peacetime sales record of $616.5 million in consolidated sales — the previous had been $330.5 million in 1941.[16] By 1948, that figure rose to $704.9 million.[17]

Losing Old Friends

In 1946, Goodyearites mourned the loss of three beloved members of the Old Guard. The "First Lady of Goodyear," Clara Bingham, died in

Above: In 1949, Goodyear built a Girl Scout lodge in Goodyear Heights, dedicating it to Charles Seiberling. Seiberling died in 1946.

Below: The 1949 Cleveland Air Races, sponsored by Goodyear. No longer in auto racing, Goodyear competed in the air.

May, ending a 48-year relationship with the company.[18] Bingham had been one of the Seiberling brothers' original hires in the fall of 1898. Throughout their friendship, Charles Seiberling had teased her that he had spied her walking up to the old strawboard factory and said to his brother, "She's a looker. Let's hire her."[19] Bingham first worked as a stenographer, then private secretary to the Seiberlings. She was put in charge of welfare work in 1916 and became the company's librarian in 1920, a position she held until her death. In 1948, the company dedicated a Goodyear Heights park in her name.[20]

Following Bingham in death was Goodyear's very first employee, Ed Hippensteal, who had originally been hired to replace the broken windows in the strawboard plant.[21]

In September 1946, Charles Seiberling died. Although he and his brother Frank had been absent from the company for more than a quarter-century, Charles had always considered himself a "Goodyear Man." He was remembered by workers as a man with scores of friends, who liked a good joke and a long poker game — a person who loaned money readily because he couldn't conceive of another man not paying

him back.[22] Seiberling was eulogized in the *Wingfoot Clan*:

> *"The death of C.W. Seiberling removes a truly great man from our midst. Whatever there is in this great business organization of comradeship, sportsmanship, loyalty, and the friendship between men and men, stems in large measure to Charley Seiberling."*[23]

Bringing Goodyear up to Date

In the three years following the war, Goodyear spent approximately $100 million in capital improvements, modernizing and expanding factories that had been converted back to peacetime production.[24] In 1945, Goodyear had opened small plants in Colombia, Venezuela and Cuba, and started construction of a tire and mechanical goods factory in Uitenhage, South Africa.[25] The company also purchased the Topeka tire plant from the government and made arrangements to obtain another at Lincoln, Nebraska.[26]

The New Bedford factory — a former textile mill converted into a manufacturing facility for barrage balloons, rubber boats, and fuel tanks — was converted again in order to produce bicycle tires.[27] Goodyear had discontinued production of bike tires in 1916 when the popularity of the bicycle declined as that of the automobile rose. However, during the war, conservation-minded Americans had rediscovered the fun and practicality of the two-wheeler.[28]

Getting Out the Message

The postwar years also witnessed Goodyear's entry into new fields of advertising. The blimp fleet resumed peacetime flights in 1946 when the company bought back three of its blimps — the *Ranger,* the *Enterprise* and the *Volunteer* — from the Navy, along with six additional K-ships it had made for the military which had been declared war surplus.[29] The blimps were used as "flying billboards," displaying an 18-foot-high Goodyear logo.[30]

In order to stimulate improved design and construction of light

airplanes, in 1947 the company began sponsoring a racing event during the annual National Air Races in Cleveland, awarding a trophy and $25,000 cash prize to the victor.[31]

Goodyear forayed into television broadcasting on October 5, 1946, when a football game between Army and Cornell was the first of nine games the company sponsored over the NBC airwaves that season.[32] As an underwriter of radio and television programs, Goodyear earned acclaim for a 30-minute public service series entitled "The Greatest Story Ever Told," which related Biblical stories. The program, which debuted in 1947, enjoyed a long and popular run on Sunday nights, ending in 1956.[33] Mark Woods, president of the American Broadcast Company, said it was the first time a sponsor of a major series elected to devote full air time to the program rather than interrupt it with advertisements.[34] The only recognition given to Goodyear was a single line at the beginning of the broadcast: "The Goodyear Tire & Rubber Company presents ..."[35]

Super Cushion

Goodyear's most successful product development of the time was the Super Cushion tire, which company spokesmen called the "most important engineering development in tires since the introduction of the low pressure or balloon tire in 1923."[36] The tire was an extension of both the cushioning principle of the balloon tire and the flotation principle of the Airwheel, for it featured a reduced air pressure and greater air volume.[37]

Standard air pressure for tires of the time was 28 to 32 pounds; the Super Cushion needed only 24. The cross-section was larger but the tire itself was shorter, the extra air volume made possible by shrinking the size of the doughnut. Since the tire was wide and soft, it provided a smooth ride, absorbing lateral shocks with an efficiency previous tires had lacked. Ample testing, which included driving the tire at speeds from 35 to 100 miles per hour over terrain as diverse as the southwestern desert, the Dakota badlands and Colorado's rocky Pike's Peak, had shown the tire

Above: The popular Super Cushion tire provided drivers and passengers with a bouncy, comfortable ride. Below: A typical Goodyear service station, this one in Tampa, Florida, in 1949.

Contractors apply Goodyear's Pliolite paint to Akron's Main Street in 1949.

to be cooler-running, thus more resistant to wear and blowouts.[38] Although the Super Cushion was slightly more expensive, its advantages soon won over auto manufacturers and consumers. In the six months following its debut, the company had to speed up production to build the 3.5 million Super Cushions consumers demanded.[39]

Converting the Chemical Products Division

In the postwar years, the Chemical Products Division, an outgrowth of P.W. Litchfield's early emphasis on research and development, began to assume a leadership role. In the first two decades of the company's history, the automobile tire had come into its own; in the following 30 years, aeronautics had emerged. Beginning in the late 1940s, the future — as the popular saying goes — would be in plastics.

The development of Chemigum and the manufacturing of GRS, the government-approved synthetic rubber, had opened Goodyear's eyes to a promising new field. The Goodyear Research Laboratory had been built in 1943 to house the research required during the war, and in 1946 the company implemented a $4 million expansion to the site. About $1 million went toward a Chemical Products Development Laboratory, and the rest was spent on a plant that converted vinyl chloride copolymers and other resins into films, sheets and other products. Litchfield promised Goodyear employees that the new complex would house many "postwar wonders" in research and development.[40]

Rubber derivatives produced by Chemical Products — Airfoam, Pliofilm, Chemigum rubbers and latex and Pliolite resins — had been useful in making war products, and by 1946 the division had found domestic purposes for each.[41] Goodyear stepped up production of rubber flooring, vinyl garden hoses, Pliofilm shower curtains, garment bags and raincoats, and Neolite shoe soles, made of a material that was neither rubber nor plastic and offered exceptional traction and endurance.[42]

The flooring department was given a new name, Builders' Supplies, because the products could be used on kitchen drainboards, counters, desks and wall coverings. Vinyl products were brightly colored and made flame- and stain-resistant.[43]

Pliofilm, which was moistureproof, transparent, durable and thermoplastic — meaning it could be molded by heating and cooling to take any desired shape — was widely adopted as a packing material for food products, including produce and coffee.[44] Pliobond, a rubber cement that could "cement anything to anything," and a new Pliofilm tensilized thread which could be woven into upholstery and clothing for a "stylish, moistureproof" material, were introduced.[45] Airfoam, a latex that was originally developed by Dunlop of England, enjoyed great success as a component of furniture padding. Goodyear built a plant in Malaya to expedite delivery of natural latex to Akron's Plant C.[46] In 1947, holders of reserved seats in the New York Yankee's baseball park enjoyed the cushioned comfort of Goodyear's Airfoam padding.

The Home Market

Goodyear also mass-produced the ultimate domestic product: the home itself. During the Depression many families had been unable to afford homes. During the war, people moved to industrial cities and got decent jobs. They were eager to buy homes, but restrictions on building materials led to a shortage. During the war, Goodyear cooperated in a "balloon housing project," making half-balloons that could be inflated with helium, sprayed with cement, and used as

temporary, movable dwellings.[47] By 1946, these prefabricated homes, made in factories and assembled on the buyer's lot, had caught on with the public.

But Litchfield had an idea for a product that would combine the balloon-house's mobility with the prefab home's rigid construction. "He wanted a completely built and equipped house, ready to move into and live in once light and water and gas had been connected up, one which could be delivered intact to any point within practical hauling radius. It had to be a house a man could pick up and take with him if he moved to another city."[48] Since the maximum clearance load on United States highways was eight feet, Litchfield asked his engineers to devise a fold-up house.

A new subsidiary, Wingfoot Homes, was created in Litchfield Park, Arizona.[49] Its mass-produced homes were simple, small and uniform, featuring three rooms and a bath. Each house came completely furnished except for dishes,

Below and Right: During the war, Goodyear forayed into the housing industry. These portable housing projects provided families with a comfortable, but somewhat cramped, home at an affordable price.

bedding and curtains, and sold for $2,650 on a monthly installment plan. Folded for transportation, they fit the legal limit of 26 feet by 8 feet. Once on site, the sides could be expanded to 15 feet, giving a total square footage of 255.[50]

The housing venture was only modestly successful, with homes selling mostly in Arizona, New Mexico, Utah and California; some were shipped to Montana and the Dakotas and sold to contractors who needed units that could be transported from jobsite to jobsite.[51] In 1947, the Atomic Energy Commission purchased 125 to be delivered to Los Alamos, New Mexico, the testing ground for the atomic bomb.[52]

The First 50 Years

Goodyear marked its first half-century with a three-day celebration beginning on October 6, 1948. The elaborate festival featured pageants, parties and the building of the company's 450 millionth tire.[53] At the time Goodyear employed 53,000 people, 20,000 of them overseas. It boasted more than 45,700 shareholders and sold products through 30,000 domestic dealers.[54] In the years between 1898 and 1948, more than 600 tire companies had set up shop nationwide. Only one in 25 of those companies were still in business in 1948. Goodyear had sold more than $9 billion of manufactured products during its first 50 years.[55]

In an article titled "50 Years of Goodyear," Litchfield reminded stockholders of the distance Goodyear had traveled:

"Fifty years ago, electric trolleys were replacing horse-drawn streetcars in progressive American cities. The newly invented automobile was greeted with severe ridicule and the airplane was still a thing of the future. ... The American system of free enterprise had grown strong roots. There was a willingness to work, a desire to produce. Far from content with his lot, the American constantly strove to better his position. With the dawn of America's Golden Era, there began the saga of Goodyear."[56]

Balancing Strategic and Economic Needs

One of the most important issues facing the rubber industry in the postwar years was how to balance the country's consumption of natural and synthetic rubbers. The price of synthetic rubber had fallen dramatically since its debut, so that by 1946 it had fallen below the price for natural rubber.[57] Furthermore, maintaining an adequate capacity to produce synthetic rubber was a matter of national security. The economies of Britain and the Dutch Indies were dependent on the natural rubber trade, so the recovery of the world economy was also an issue.

After the war, the government took steps to slow production of synthetic rubber. Sales that had constituted 73 percent of the world's total consumption in 1946 slipped to 42 percent in 1948.[58] In the 1947 Annual Report, Chairman Litchfield and President E.J. Thomas discussed this debate with shareholders.

"Due to wartime investments by the Government in synthetic rubber plants in this

Pilot Gene Ziegler inspects a tire designed for the North American T-28. Although peace slowed GAC's frantic pace, the subsidiary remained an important supplier of aircraft tires, wheels and brakes.

country, the combined potential production of natural and synthetic rubber for a number of years at least will adequately take care of the world's needs. By keeping an annual capacity of 600,000 tons, under Government control, the synthetic plants should act as a stabilizer between supply and demand, and provide for an accumulation of a Government stockpile to the extent deemed advisable for national security. We do not know of any expenditure which the Government made during the late war which will show more valuable returns, measured by national security and economic values, than the three-quarters of a billion dollars in synthetic rub-

ber plants. They should be kept intact and sufficiently elastic in operation to promptly meet the varying national needs, both for consumption and stockpiling for national security."[59]

The output of synthetic rubber, still overseen by the government, fell short of the 600,000 ton mark, and by 1950 domestic and foreign demands for rubber reached record proportions. World consumption hit 2.2 million long tons, an astonishing 85 percent increase over the prewar years.[60] In the United States, automobile registration was up 44 percent over the 1941 figure, and Detroit produced 8 million new passenger cars and trucks in 1950 alone.[61] Under the weighty demand caused by the country's entry into the Korean War, the price structure of rubber toppled and the cost of natural rubber jumped nearly fourfold, to 80 cents a pound.[62] Industry executives had seen the increase coming; in the months preceding the Korean War, Litchfield issued a series of publications, *Notes on America's Rubber Industry*, in which he called for a more stable supply of rubber.

"There are two things radically wrong in the rubber situation today: 1. Our supply of raw rubber is too low from the standpoint of national security. 2. The price of natural rubber is too high for economic stability.

Both situations trace primarily to our national rubber policy, once so clear, decisive and effective, but now seemingly weakened by a creeping uncertainty of purpose. The remedies are immediately available if we will only apply them. They are: 1. Stepping up our output of synthetic rubber to 50,000 long tons per month from the present output of 40,000 tons. 2. Building up an inventory or stockpile of synthetic rubber to a minimum of 200,000 long tons."[63]

The Korean War

On June 25, 1950, North Korean troops crossed the 38th Parallel, the somewhat arbitrary dividing line between North and South Korea, in an attempt to forcibly reunite the country under Communist rule. Having learned from Europe's failed appeasement policy — which led to World

War II — President Harry Truman sent troops to bolster South Korean forces. After months of sometimes desperate fighting, victory seemed near after General Douglas MacArthur's army routed the Communist forces, and crossed the 38th Parallel into North Korea. But with the entry of China into the conflict, the war bogged down into a bloody contest of wills.

On August 25, 1950, the government reinstated federal controls on rubber consumption, and the industry's supply of both natural and synthetic rubber was slashed 20 percent in the midst of clamorous demand.[64] Goodyear resumed operations in the government-owned Akron synthetic plant, which along with several others nationwide, had been shut down in 1947.[65] In 1950, the company's three factories produced 210,000 long tons, nearly one-fourth the nation's supply.[66] With the country's inventory restored by May 1952, the government removed controls.[67]

The war put a strain on employees. The squadron concept, which Goodyear had used for years, gave college graduates the training they would need to enter fields such as manufacturing, chemistry or engineering. A part-time squadron allowed students to work at Goodyear while taking a full load of classes. The "squaddies," as they were called, helped balance the workforce, while the squaddie gained valuable experience in different parts of the company. The Korean War put an even greater strain on students, recalled James Barnett, who recently retired as chief of Original Equipment Manufacturer sales worldwide. Barnett started in his squadron a few months after the start of the war.

"By that time, they were working seven days a week continuously. If somebody was sick or on vacation, they'd send a squaddie up temporarily. The union always found this to be an irritant. I started part-time, and ended up working three and a half years until I graduated. My future mother-in-law got me into Goodyear by saying,

'Why don't you get a part-time job?' And here I am, 46 years later."[68]

The year 1950 also brought the return of the last of Goodyear's holdings lost during World War II: the Wingfoot Estate, the plantation in Sumatra, again came under company control.[69] That same year, Goodyear Aircraft was once again busy making war products.

GAC no longer had to search for non-military business. In November 1948, it had procured a contract with Boeing to make nose cones and other parts for the B-50 bomber.[70]

By 1951, GAC was devoted 100 percent to the war effort.[71] The subsidiary built the first successful autopilots for helicopters, which had been designed by the Air Force; a prototype of the escape capsule, a shell that protected pilots during ejection from aircraft at high altitudes or speeds; various wings, empennages, assemblies, stabilizers, elevators and canopies for the T-28 Air Force Trainer, the F-84 Thunderjet fighter-bomber, and the F-89D Scorpion jet-interceptor; and fuel tanks and anti-icing systems for the Boeing B-47B bomber. The company also provided flooring, hatches and other parts for the Navy's Grumman S2F-1, an anti-sub search-and-attack aircraft; radomes for the Air Force's giant cargo plane, the Douglas C-124 Globemaster; and fuel tanks for the C-97 Stratofreighter, an in-flight jet refueler.[72] Tires for military vehicles and airplanes, aircraft brakes and wheels, blimps, and radar equipment were also important war products.[73] Employment at Goodyear-Aircraft, at only 3,500 when North Korea invaded its southern neighbor in 1950, climbed to 10,300 by the time the truce was signed on July 26, 1953.[74]

With GAC's revival, Goodyear set a new sales record of $845.1 million in 1950 and produced its 500 millionth pneumatic tire.[75] The company entered its 53rd year poised to pass another milestone: in 1951, Goodyear would become the world's first billion-dollar rubber company.

1952 — Goodyear introduces the high-quality nylon tire, strengthened using the 3-T process.

1960 — Goodyear begins challenging Michelin after completion of a new tire plant in France, begun a year earlier.

1959 — P.W. Litchfield dies following surgery.

1964 — Russell DeYoung named chairman and CEO of Goodyear; Victor Holt is named president.

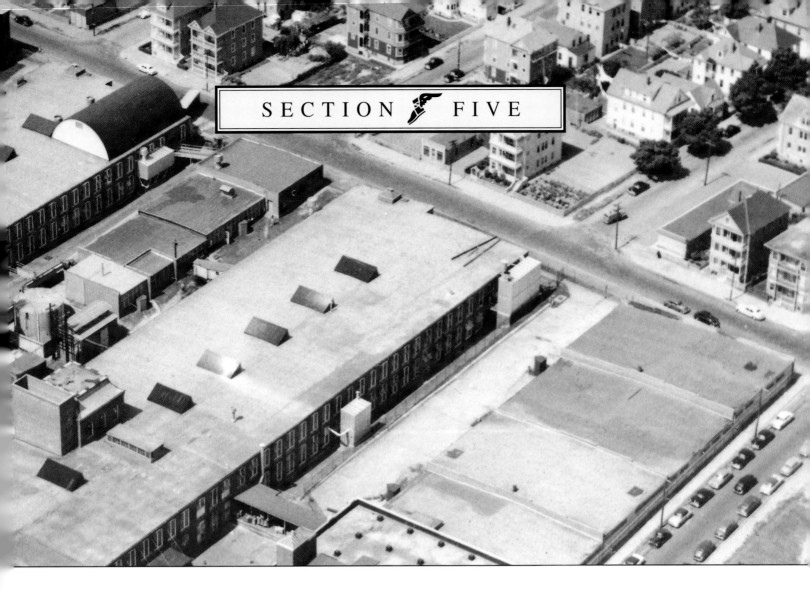

 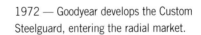
1969 — Goodyear Aerospace helps send astronauts to the moon and return them safely to earth.

1972 — Goodyear develops the Custom Steelguard, entering the radial market.

1977 — The $300 million Lawton, Oklahoma plant opens.

1971 — Goodyear tires make tracks on the moon.

1973 — Charles Pilliod becomes chairman and CEO.

To demonstrate the revolutionary tubeless tire, a nail is driven into the carcass to show its strength at a press conference in Detroit, held in 1954.

CHAPTER ELEVEN

WORLDWIDE EXPANSION

1951–1959

*"Great as are the prospects in the domestic markets for our goods, I
believe the field of our foreign operations will probably expand even faster."*

— President E.J. Thomas, 1955[1]

N ITS FIRST 50 years of
business, Goodyear had
sold approximately $9 bil-
lion worth of products. In just
nine years, between 1949 to 1958,
total sales topped $11.5 billion.[2]

On February 18, 1952, the national press
announced that Goodyear had become the
world's first billion-dollar rubber company by
achieving total sales of $1,101,141,000 for 1951.[3]
Three days after the news was shared with stockholders and the public, Chairman P.W. Litchfield
spoke before a packed audience at the Goodyear
Theater, thanking employees for having made
"Goodyear's greatest year" possible.[4]

It was the first of a series of "greatest" years.
During the prosperous 1950s, Americans purchased automobiles in record numbers, settled
comfortably into the nation's new suburbs, continued the postwar population boom, and
watched countries in Europe and Asia recover
economically from the devastating consequences
of the war. It was during this unprecedented period of calm and prosperity that Goodyear set one
sales record after another, passing the $1.5-bil-
lion-dollar threshold during 1959.[5] Company historian Clyde Schetter, writing in 1965, said of
the 1950s boom years: "In reviewing some of the
highlights of the period ... it is difficult to refrain
from the use of hyperbole, cliches, or extravagant superlatives."[6]

A Nation on Wheels
— And Rubber

The 1951 sales figures represented a 30 percent increase over
the previous year, made possible in part
by the rapid jump in automobile production.[7]
The fifties are often remembered as a time of
drive-in movies and roller skating car hops, for
the automobile became a centerpiece of pop culture, an icon of American mobility and prosperity. In 1951, passenger car registration stood at
39.5 million, an increase of more than 10 million in less than 10 years.[8] Truck registration
had nearly doubled during the same period, topping 8.5 million in 1951.[9] Domestic auto production increased 40 percent from 1952 to
1953, and the growing popularity of two-car
families kept executives of the automotive and
rubber industries smiling.[10] By 1954, the average passenger car came equipped with 115
pounds of rubber — 65 in tires and 50 pounds
in hoses, gaskets, floor mats, seals, rubber foam
cushioning and belts.[11]

Globally, the news was even better. While
domestic sales increased 25 percent in 1951, for-

A Goodyear sign in Arabic, outside an Egyptian dealership, advertising
the world's most popular tire.

eign business grew an amazing 46 percent.[12] The Marshall Plan, developed by General George C. Marshall and authorized by President Harry Truman, had enlivened European markets, and the "economic miracles" of Germany, Italy and Japan were under way.[13] Developing or recovering nations embraced modern infrastructure, transportation and manufacturing, all of which required rubber. Between 1950 and 1959, world rubber consumption rose from 2,303,000 long tons to 3,693,000.[14] Goodyear President E.J. Thomas told a gathering of reporters in 1955 that even better times lie ahead.

"Great as are the prospects in the domestic markets for our goods, I believe the field of our foreign operations will probably expand even faster. When you stop to think that in this country there are about 20 pounds of rubber used per person per year, and the figure for the rest of the world is only a little over one pound, you can realize why I feel as I do on this point."[15]

With the opening of a tire factory in Luxembourg in 1951, Goodyear strengthened its position in Europe, a market that was still dominated by such indigenous companies as Dunlop in Great Britain, Michelin in France, Continental and Metzler in Germany, Pirelli and Ceat in Italy, Semperit in Austria, and Englebert in Belgium.[16] In 1949, Goodyear had arranged with Dunlop to make tires in New Zealand, and in 1951 had contracted with Continental Gummiwerke in Hanover, West Germany, for the production of Goodyear tires.[17]

Also in 1951, the company entered the burgeoning Japanese market through a contract that allowed Bridgestone to make Goodyear tires. During World War II, operating under the name of The Nippon Tire Company, Bridgestone had operated the captured Goodyear factory in Bogor, Indonesia, for the Japanese army, producing nearly half a million tires — printed with both Japanese characters and the name "Goodyear" — before abandoning the factory in 1945.[18] Under the new agreement, Bridgestone made tires under close technical supervision by Goodyear, with John J. Hartz serving as the production manager in Japan.[19]

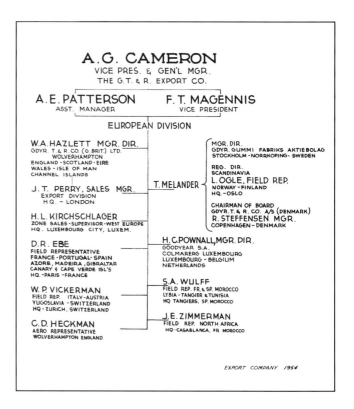

Flow charts from the Goodyear Export Company show the scope of Goodyear's non-U.S. holdings in 1954. As it grew, the subsidiary would be reorganized into Goodyear International.

Taking Part in the Atomic Age

The world had entered the atomic age on July 16, 1945, triggered by the massive detonation at Trinity Site near Alamogordo, New Mexico. Seven years later, Goodyear entered the atomic business. On August 12, 1952, the Atomic Energy Commission announced that Pike County, Ohio, a rural area near Portsmouth, would be the site of a proposed $1.2 billion plant to produce the fissionable isotope uranium 235.[20] With the country embroiled in the Korean War and the public increasingly fearful of the "Red Menace," the government wanted to speed production of atomic weapons. The Ohio site was designed to be the country's largest producer of uranium and would accelerate weapons production by four to five years.[21] The Pike County plant would join gaseous diffusion plants in Paducah,

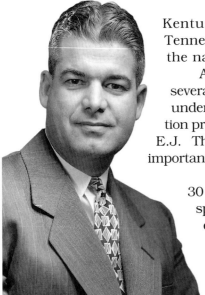

Kentucky, and Oak Ridge, Tennessee, as the backbone of the nation's nuclear defense.

After soliciting bids from several top industries, the AEC undertook a complicated selection process. Goodyear President E.J. Thomas took part in all important negotiations.[22]

On September 18, 1952, 30 minutes before the AEC spoke to the national media, employees were ushered into Goodyear Theater and shown a film on the power of atomic weaponry. When the house lights were raised, Thomas strode to the lectern and said:

"You have just seen the unleashing of one of the most powerful forces in the history of the world — atomic energy. Strong emphasis at the present time is upon its use as a weapon in which we presently hold leadership and which it is hoped can be used as a force to make future wars improbable, but of equal importance is its application as a force to be put to peaceful use in the interests of mankind."[23]

The *Wingfoot Clan* reported the crowd was "electrified" as Thomas and Chairman P.W. Litchfield told Akron employees the company had been selected to run the Pike County plant. Litchfield said Goodyear would meet the future challenge by relying on the legacy of its past.

"Goodyear is going into the field of atomic energy — the most significant force developed in our lifetime — with the same spirit of pioneering and determination that has propelled the compa-

---

Above: Russell DeYoung in 1949, two years after he became vice president in charge of production. DeYoung would become chairman in 1958.

Right: A.J. Gracia, the first factory manager for the Portsmouth, Ohio atomic energy plant.

ny to leadership through the past half-century. We took our meager profits from the manufacture of bicycle and carriage tires and hitched our star to the horseless carriage in the early days of our company. That is the reason we rose to become the world's largest tire manufacturer and the world's largest rubber company. Again, when the airplane came along, we developed tires for the flying machine and in other ways tied closely with aeronautics. ... Now, in taking a leading part in the atomic energy program, we have reached another landmark in the progress of Goodyear. We are keeping pace with the latest developments in this new atomic era."[24]

Because of the immensity of the project, a new subsidiary, Goodyear Atomic Corporation, was established, with plant manager A.J. Gracia reporting to Russell DeYoung, vice president in charge of production for the parent company.[25] Under Goodyear's supervision, prime contractor Peter Kiewit Sons of Omaha, Nebraska, completed the plant six months ahead of schedule and more than $4.6 million under the estimated cost.[26] In September 1954, the first phase went into production. To make room for the plant, three tiny Ohio towns with a combined population of 300 were leveled.

The importance of the project caused some Pike County residents to worry about being targeted by Russian missiles; others welcomed a new employer seeking to hire 4,000 workers.[27] When completed, the 4,000-acre site was enclosed by 11 miles of fence, with an additional 3.7 miles of fencing surrounding the actual area of production.[28] The buildings' total floor space came to 220 acres, with each of the three main buildings stretching for more than a half-mile. Equipment included 90,000 recording instruments, 600 miles of pipe, 1,000 miles of copper tubing and 4,600 miles of wire and cable. The produc-

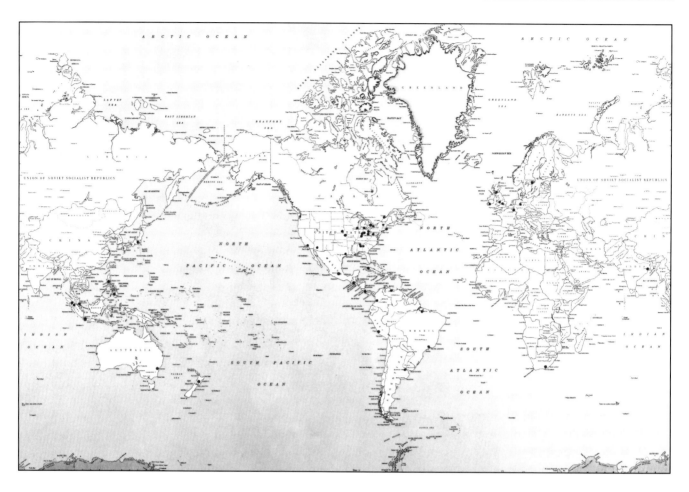

The world map in 1957 was dotted with Goodyear holdings, with the corporate flag flying on every continent except Antarctica.

tion process required more than 30 million gallons of water per day, and the yearly electric bill was approximately $72 million. "The total power consumed by the plant represented two-thirds of all required by the state of Ohio and three percent of the total generated in the United States."[29]

The plant produced explosive uranium through the gaseous diffusion process by separating uranium 235 from non-fissionable uranium 238. Because U-235 atoms are slightly lighter (235 times heavier than hydrogen, as opposed to 238 times for U-238) and thus travel more quickly, uranium hexafluoride in gas form was pumped through a complex series of "filters," microscopic screens with millions of holes per square inch. The U-235 atoms sped through the filters, but the heavier U-238 atoms were slowed.[30]

The process was complex and time-consuming. A.J. Gracia noted at the time that "10 tons of raw material going into the system for processing on any given day will yield something less than

one quart of the desired product, U-235, at the other end of the system three months later."[31]

Other Technological Endeavors

Not to be outdone by the young Goodyear Atomic Corporation, Goodyear Aircraft introduced another marvel of technology in 1952, an improved "electronic differential analyzer," or "mechanical brain."[32] The new computer, called L3 GEDA, represented a crucial step in space exploration — using GEDA, flight engineers could program and analyze electronic data dealing with potential problems of space flight, simulating flights and translating various factors into mathematical solutions that could be tried on the screen.[33] GEDA was in use five years before the country's space program was galvanized by the blastoff of *Sputnik.*

By the middle of the decade, Goodyear stood as a force in the field of missile science, and in 1955 the company undertook a $3 million construction campaign to provide engineering labs at GAC-Akron and GAC-Arizona for the study and development of guided missiles and other implements of "push-button" warfare.[34]

By that time, GAC had become a major producer of booster metal parts for such military missiles as the Nike-Ajax, Nike-Hercules, Hawk, Matador, Mace, Farside, and Genie. In 1956, the Air Force signed a multimillion-dollar contract with GAC for Atran, an all-weather navigation system for manned aircraft and unmanned missiles. It was the result of 10 years of R & D efforts and was widely recognized as the most highly perfected all-weather navigation system yet produced.

In the late 1950s, GAC also supplied a wide range of missile support equipment for the Army and Navy and the Air Force's Strategic Air Command, including nose cones for the Army's Jupiter, the first successful U.S. Intermediate Range Ballistic Missile. On January 31, 1958, Jupiter put the first U.S. satellite in orbit.[35]

The company's 1958 Annual Report assured shareholders that Goodyear was doing its part for the nation in "the space age race for superiority and survival."[36]

With business conditions prosperous and forecasts promising, Goodyear undertook another massive expansion project in the 1950s, spending nearly $500 million on capital improvements.[37] In 1951 alone, capital expenditures exceeded $44 million, an increase of more than 30 percent over the previous year. Five years later, capital spending peaked at $100 million.[38] The Topeka plant was given a capacity boost of 25 percent, the Akron Chemigum plant was expand-

Above: The Scotland tire plant was the second in Great Britain; the first was in Wolverhampton, England.

Below: The Pathfinder Chemical Plant was established in Niagara Falls, New York, in 1946.

ed by 50 percent, and production at the Niagara Falls vinyl resin facility increased 100 percent.[39] The factory at Gadsden, Alabama, became the country's largest tire manufacturing plant with the addition of a building and equipment improvements that totaled $11.5 million.[40]

In 1956, under terms of the Rubber Producing Facilities Disposal Act, Goodyear bought from the government the two synthetic rubber plants at Akron and Houston, at a cost of $14 million.[41] That same year, Goodyear opened a major distribution center in Brook Park, Ohio, a suburb of Cleveland, and began manufacturing industrial products at a recently purchased factory in North Chicago, Illinois.[42]

By 1957, Goodyear was operating 30 factories in 23 foreign countries: Australia, Argentina, Brazil,

Canada, Colombia, Costa Rica, Cuba, England, Germany, India, Indonesia, Ireland, Japan, Luxembourg, Malaya, Mexico, New Zealand, Peru, the Philippines, Scotland, South Africa, Sweden and Venezuela.[43] Two years later, Goodyear started construction on facilities in Amiens, France; and Medicine Hat, Alberta, Canada.[44] Goodyear products were sold in every country outside the Communist bloc, and the company adopted variations of the slogan, "Around the World, More People Ride on Goodyear Tires than On Any Other Kind."[45]

The company's success overseas had much to do with the way management encouraged employees and the local community to think of the Goodyear plant as "theirs," noted Scott Buzby, who retired in 1989 as an executive vice president.

"I found that often when I was in a country, the locals thought Goodyear was a Colombian company, or Brazilian or Australian. They considered it theirs, and of course that's what we wanted. It gave our people a great deal of self-confidence and pride without arrogance."[46]

The Suburbanite was a winter tire that offered up to twice the traction of conventional tire treads, and performed admirably in both loose and packed snow, as well as on ice.

MORE TRACTION where there's snow... **MORE MILEAGE** where there isn't !

GOODYEAR SUBURBANITES—the true all-winter tires—bite through snow that is hubcap deep, yet give you Turnpike-Proved mileage like all Goodyear tires.

Even in the roughest winter, you're usually only *yards* away from *miles* of cleared roads. That's why it pays you doubly to have Goodyear Suburbanites.

More traction. When you're up to your hubcaps in snow, 260 deep-cut cleats get you out and moving. When you need to stop, over 3,700 individual biting edges go to work to grip the road.

More Mileage. When the roads are clear, you get the kind of mileage you get with all Goodyear tires . . . Turnpike-Proved! How does Goodyear do it? With the best combination of tread rubber and tread design for winter driving. Plus exclusive 3-T triple-tempered cords.

Beat winter to the punch. See your Goodyear dealer *now.*

GOODYEAR

MORE PEOPLE RIDE ON GOODYEAR TIRES THAN ON ANY OTHER KIND!

3-T SUBURBANITE PRICES START AT **$15.95** black, tube-type 6.70 x 15 rayon plus tax and tire off your car

TURNPIKE-**PROVED** for extra safety

Suburbanite T. M., The Goodyear Tire & Rubber Company, Akron 16, Ohio.

In 1957, with foreign sales accounting for nearly one-third of the company's total, Goodyear consolidated The Goodyear Tire & Rubber Export Company, responsible for foreign sales, and Goodyear Foreign Operations, Inc., the supervisor of foreign manufacturing, into a new subsidiary, Goodyear International Corporation.[47] Frank Magennis became the first president of GIC, moving up from the vice presidency of Goodyear Export and Goodyear Foreign Operations, and became responsible for international operations involving more than 40,500 employees.[48]

From Nylon to Tubeless

At home, Goodyear held its edge in tire sales with continued introductions of improved products. Reflecting a demographic trend of the period, the aptly-named Suburbanite Tire was introduced in 1952. Developed with the commuter or city traveler in mind, the Suburbanite was a winter tire that offered up to twice the traction of conventional tire treads and provided "superior traction in both loose and hard-packed snow, as well as on icy roads."[49] Also in 1952, the company announced the new All Nylon Double Eagle, its highest-grade premium tire, followed the next year by the All Nylon Super Cushion, the first all-nylon priced only slightly above original equipment tires.[50]

The new nylons represented major improvements in the use of nylon fabric and were produced through a process called 3-T, the culmination of five years of research and an investment of more than $50 million.[51] Dr. R.P. Dinsmore, vice president of Research, said of the new tires:

"Nylon is the perfect tire cord if the stretch can be controlled. Goodyear has developed a method of chemically treating the nylon cord and then putting it through a triple action tempering process involving tension, tempera-

Above: The 3-T machine preconditioned tire cord as it traveled one-third of a mile through the million dollar unit.

Below: Introduced in 1952, the All Nylon Double Eagle was the company's premium passenger tire.

ture, and time — the three T's. Thus we are able to take advantage of nylon's many advantages in strength, lightness, and heat and fatigue resistance. The result is the strongest, lightest-weight, and coolest-running tire cord ever developed."[52]

Melvin Kilgore, the assistant engineering manager who supervised the building of the 3-T machines, called them "a factory within a factory," as each was four stories high and 150 feet long at the base.[53] One-third of a mile of fabric was fed into the entrance station of the machine before emerging at the exit point. The machines were installed at Akron, Cartersville and Rockmart, Georgia, at an initial cost of $1 million per plant.[54]

With the success of the 3-T process, Goodyear introduced an entire line of nylon tires, including the All Nylon

Above and inset: A 1953 curb test of a white-sidewall, tubeless tire demonstrated the strength that the 3-T process provided. Hitting the curb might have resulted in a blowout, but was reduced to a leak.

Super Eagle, for motorcycles. In 1957 — the same year the New Bedford factory produced its 30 millionth bike tire — the first all-nylon bicycle tire, called the Suburbanite 175, was introduced.[55]

The 3-T process also paved the way for the biggest revolution in tires since the balloon tire had replaced the old high-pressure tire in 1923. At a Detroit press conference in August 1954, E.J. Thomas unveiled a full line of tubeless tires, calling it "the milestone the industry has looked forward to for 25 years."[56]

While the tubeless tire was as old as the industry — Robert William Thomson of Middlesex, England, had patented the first in 1845 and Litchfield had received a 1903 United States patent for an early Goodyear model — the 1954 design embodied a radically different concept.[57] Whereas other tubeless tires held air via a heavy sealant or rubber lining, Goodyear's tubeless relied on a completely unified, airtight construction of the carcass. The tire was made with the triple-tempered preconditioned cord of the 3-T process, which offered puncture protection, mileage up to 12 percent higher than standard tire cord, and blowout protection.

Because air was held within the body of the tire, a puncture resulted only in a slow leak. Because of the efficient 3-T machines, Goodyear could offer a tire with these advantages at a price comparable to that of standard tires.[58]

Believing the tubeless tire would change the industry, Goodyear flooded dealers with a full line, for everything from passenger car tires to trucks, tractors, buses, wheelbarrows and motorcycles.[59] During the next few months, Thomas and other top executives formed a sort of traveling show, demonstrating sample tires at elaborately staged sales meetings in cities from New York to Los Angeles.[60] A few short months after the announcement to the press, Goodyear factories were devoting 50 percent of their facilities to manufacturing the tubeless tires. The Air Force and Navy ordered tubeless tires for fighter jets such as the Republic F-105 and the F9F-9 Tiger.[61]

Creating Better Tires

During the 1950s, Goodyear also introduced the Lifeguard Blowout Shield, a double air chamber in the premium Double Eagle tire that allowed motorists to drive 100 miles on a puncture; the Unisteel, a belted truck tire; the Blue Streak Special for police vehicles; the All-Weather

Raceway and All-Weather Speedway for stock car racing; and the multi-sized rugged Terra Tire, designed for missile-transport vehicles, tractors, golf carts and mining equipment.[62]

In 1955, Goodyear's researchers developed a synthetic rubber, polyisoprene, that closely simulated the properties of tree-grown rubber.[63] Called Natsyn, the new product was put to a widely publicized highway test that revived the old road demonstrations begun in 1917 with the Wingfoot Express.[64] A tractor-trailer equipped with natural rubber tires on one side and Natsyn tires on the other was driven from San Angelo, Texas, to California, then to the Atlantic Coast and back to Texas. Goodyear analysts determined at journey's end that the Natsyn tires fared well when compared to the performance of natural rubber tires.

Since 1944, Goodyear had centralized its tire-testing facilities near San Angelo, using local desert highways for test drives, but in 1957 the company built a 7,200-acre site in the area.[65] The new multimillion-dollar complex fea-

tured a banked, circular roadway that earned the name "The Turnpike that Never Ends" and allowed speeds in excess of 140 miles per hour, a 20-mile paved course in a distorted figure-8 shape, a 2½-mile straightaway for tractor tires, five miles of gravel road, and a headquarters building and garage.[66]

A Diversity of Products

By 1958, sales of tires and tubes accounted for only 60 percent of Goodyear's total business.[67] In one five-year period, from 1949 to 1953, Chemical Division sales quadrupled, establishing Goodyear as a prime supplier of raw materials such as paint, rubber, plastic and paper to major industries.[68] The average American came in contact with Goodyear chemical products every day,

During the postwar years, Goodyear focused on less-glamorous products, such as conveyor belts.

as shown by a short list of their applications: Pliolite S-5, a basic resin resistant to acids and alkalis, was used in traffic paints, stucco finishes, plaster sealers and concrete enamels; Chemigum was added to water-based paints as well as coatings to make oil-resistant rubbers for fuel cells, hose, storage tanks, shoe soles and conveyor belts; Pliovic resins were used to improve vinyl products such as plastic films and sheeting, garden hose, flooring, automobile crash pads, upholstery, floor mats and seat belts; and Plio-Tuf added durability and high-impact resistance to such plastic items as football helmets and golf ball covers.[69]

The Industrial Products Division enjoyed a new kind of success that gained recognition by the national media. Since the late 1940s, Goodyear had been supplying conveyor belting to mining operations, including the world's longest steel cord belt — 22,000 feet — for the Weirton Steel Company near Morgantown, West Virginia, and the highest lift conveyor — a two-mile belt with a vertical lift of 862 feet — at a Waltonville, Illinois mine.[70] In May 1954, Goodyear unveiled a new type of conveyor, one built to carry people rather than coal. Designed in conjunction with the Stephens Adamson Manufacturing Company, the world's first passenger belt began carrying Hudson & Manhattan Railroad customers through a 227-foot tunnel built beneath the Hudson River.[71] The Jersey City "moving sidewalk," dubbed the Speedwalk, was capable of transporting more than 300 persons per minute.[72]

In 1954, Goodyear's brisk manufacturing pace was interrupted by the company's first nationwide strike. Contract negotiations between management and the United Rubber Workers stalled, and on July 7 workers at 10 different plants around the country, including Akron, initiated a 52-day sit-out that paralyzed company operations and caused the first drop in domestic sales of the decade.[73] The first serious labor disturbance since 1936, the strike was settled on August 27 and company operations resumed on September 1. Despite the breach between management and workers, more than 50,000 employees and their families attended the annual Goodyear picnic held at Euclid Beach on the Lake Erie shore. President Thomas spoke of the resilience of the Goodyear spirit: "It is too bad that certain conditions had to prevail in our organization at this time. However, we have had these picnics year after year and something more important than what is in progress now would have to occur to cause cancellation of this traditional affair for our employees — this annual family picnic."[74]

Above: Even during the strike, E.J. Thomas invited Goodyear workers to the annual company picnic, held at Euclid Beach.

Left: The Speedwalk, a sort of human conveyor belt, was capable of moving more than 300 people a minute.

Al Cunnington was one of the first men Frank Seiberling hired after founding Goodyear. Cunnington had celebrated his 51st year at the company in 1949.

Death of Founder F.A. Seiberling

The decade — and the industry — witnessed a somber changing of the guard. In 1953, Goodyear lost its "Grand Old Man," Al Cunnington, who died October 1, just one week after being honored for 55 years of service.[75] At 89, Cunnington was the oldest Goodyear employee and had served as head receptionist in the main lobby of the general offices for the previous 15 years.

Longtime Goodyearites mourned again the following year when founder Frank A. Seiberling died of respiratory failure on August 11 at Akron General Hospital.[76] Although his tenure at Goodyear had ended more than three decades earlier, the *Clan* devoted its front page and several columns to the spirit of "Little Napoleon," so enthusiastic that he had remained chairman of the board of the Seiberling Rubber Company until he was 90 years old. The *Wingfoot Clan* credited Seiberling with possessing "one of the rubber

industry's greatest inventive minds." Goodyear flags were flown at half-mast.[77] Another testament to his continued influence on the company was the presence of two of his grandsons, J.F. Seiberling, Jr., of the company's law department, and W.C. Seiberling, who worked in advertising.[78]

In 1957 the company initiated a policy of mandatory retirement at age 65 for hourly workers and 68 for salaried ones; the first wave of employees who transferred from the payroll to the pension list numbered 1,200 men and women, 75 percent of them from the old Akron plants.[79]

Beginning the previous year, seasoned management gave way to younger executives who were rising through the ranks when P.W. Litchfield retired from the position of chief executive officer, a post he had held for 30 years.[80] Litchfield remained chairman of the board, but Thomas stepped into the role of CEO. Thomas — who had been the company's only executive vice president — created three new positions of executive vice president: R.S. Wilson was put in charge of sales; P.E.H. Leroy of finance and accounting; and Russell DeYoung of production, personnel and research and development. Victor Holt, Jr., L.E. Spencer and F.J. Carter were made vice presidents of the parent company.[81]

Fighting the Cold War

The 1950s, remembered for sock hops and economic expansion, had a dark side in which school children practiced air raid drills, crouching in hallways to shelter their heads from nuclear fallout. The McCarthy hearings and the communist presence in East Asia led to an almost paranoid national mindset. The country's fears were manifested in two crucial technological fields: the race into space, intended to prove the superiority of democracy over communism; and the buildup of advanced methods of warfare. Goodyear played a starring role in both.

The Russians won the first round in space technology by launching *Sputnik* in October 1957, but Goodyear aerodynamic scientists managed to steal some of the public relations thunder. Darrel Romick, head of the astronautics group of GAC's weapon systems department, was scheduled to speak at the eighth annual conference of the

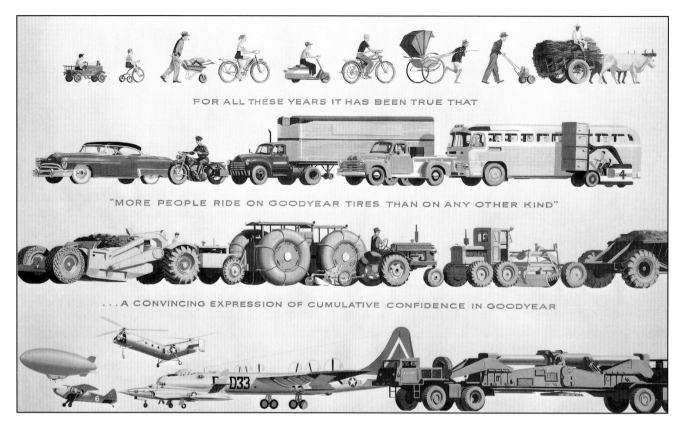

FOR ALL THESE YEARS IT HAS BEEN TRUE THAT

"MORE PEOPLE RIDE ON GOODYEAR TIRES THAN ON ANY OTHER KIND"

...A CONVINCING EXPRESSION OF CUMULATIVE CONFIDENCE IN GOODYEAR

A poster of tire applications showing the wide range of tire types and sizes produced by Goodyear.

International Astronautical Federation in Barcelona, Spain, on Wednesday, October 9.[82] Romick, aided by aerodynamicists Richard Knight and Samuel Black, planned to present a 68-page proposal for a three-stage ferry rocket system for establishing a manned earth satellite. Called Meteor Junior, an acronym for "Manned Earth-satellite Terminal evolving from Earth to Orbit ferry Rocket," the proposed system would boost a satellite into a constant 16,660-mile-per-hour orbit for the purposes of research, communication and observation.[83]

Goodyear's public relations department released an advance story that the media were to use on October 6. But on October 4, the Russian *Sputnik* began the first successful orbit of a man-made satellite. Goodyear publicists allowed American reporters to announce Meteor Junior a few days early, and articles carried artists' renderings of moon landings and space travel that

the system was designed to make possible.[84] "The result was the greatest amount of newspaper space ever devoted to a single news release issued by Goodyear's News Service."[85] The country was eager for news of United States success in space technology, even if only on paper.

More proof of Goodyear's technical prowess came the next year, when GAC beat out 63 competitors to win one of the most important contracts in its history: a $65 million assignment from the Navy's Bureau of Ordnance to develop an anti-submarine missile system.[86] Called Subroc, the system was to be part torpedo, part rocket. With a range of approximately 200 miles, Subroc could be launched from conventional torpedo tubes, sending a rocket first through the water. At a predetermined point, the casing would fall away, causing the rocket to propel upwards into the air, where it would gather speed. When the spent rocket fell away, the warhead would dive undersea to destroy the enemy submarine.[87]

T.A. Knowles, president of GAC, assigned Richard L. Burtner as project manager, and GAC researchers worked with the Naval Ordnance Laboratory in White Oak, Silver Springs,

Maryland.[88] The Subroc contract was given top priority by the Navy, as experts had estimated that Russia possessed more than 500 submarines compared to 100 active and 50 inactive subs for the United States.[89] Except for the Polaris ocean-to-ground missile system being developed by a subsidiary of General Tire, the Subroc contract was the Navy's most expensive and essential project.[90] Missile expert Erik Bergaust wrote of Subroc: "The significant point ... is that it can be fitted into the existing structure without any modification to existing equipment. It can be carried by present-day subs; it can utilize nuclear warheads."[91]

Diamond Jubilee

To celebrate its 60th anniversary in 1958, Goodyear created the "Diamond Jubilee Double Eagle," a top-line tire featuring a 3-T nylon carcass said to be 50 percent stronger than standard four-ply nylon. Thomas said that for every 1,000 miles of driving on an ordinary tire, "our designers flatly state that most drivers can add up to 500 miles with a set of the new Double Eagles."[92]

On October 6, Goodyear marked the end of an era when the 83-year old P.W. Litchfield, who had joined the company prior to its second birthday, resigned as chairman of the board. E.J. Thomas stepped into the chairmanship, vacating the presidency to be assumed by Russell DeYoung, the ninth man to serve in that position. Executive Vice President P.E.H. Leroy was elected vice chairman and continued to serve as the chief financial officer. An honorary chairmanship was created for Litchfield.[93]

Announcing the management shuffle to employees in the Goodyear Theater, Thomas ended his speech with the following:

"The only really important part of any business is its people, and the strongest asset we have always had is the loyalty and spirit of our Goodyear men and women. ... Let us bring this meeting to a close by rising and giving a great ovation to a man who, for 58 years, has contributed

mightily to the cause of Goodyear with a record unsurpassed in this, or any other, industry
— Mr. Paul W. Litchfield."[94]

Five months later, on March 18, 1959, Litchfield died unexpectedly following an operation at a hospital in Phoenix. His last function for Goodyear was attending the February 18 meeting, at which officers had voted to commission a bronze sculpture of him that would be placed in the Akron offices. More than 2,000 mourners in Akron attended a memorial service held on March 25.[95]

The *Wingfoot Clan* and the *Beacon Journal* carried large tributes to "Litch," listing his numerous accomplishments and contributions to the growth of Goodyear and American industry. Citing his initiation of the Industrial Assembly and the *Wingfoot Clan*, the Goodyear association with Boy Scouts, as well as his many innovations in research and development, the *Beacon Journal* called Litchfield a "human capitalist kingpin."[96]

In his 1954 autobiography, *Industrial Voyage*, Litchfield spoke of what he saw as mankind's mission, an almost poetic belief that explained his purpose in creating a paternalistic relationship between corporation and worker:

"There is more to life than making a living for those we cherish and being a decent neighbor to those similarly engaged. Civilization advances as each generation leaves the world a little better than the one it found. There are impulses in every man, deep rooted and pressing ones, to move ahead to the limit of his capacity, great or small, from the things he came into a Point Beyond."[97]

In his 58-year association with The Goodyear Tire & Rubber Company, Paul Litchfield, dedicated to pushing himself to the point beyond, supervised the purchase and processing of more than one-eighth of all the rubber that had been produced in the world.[98]

P.W. Litchfield's autobiography, published in 1954 by Doubleday, describes his tenure with Goodyear.

During the day-glo sixties, Goodyear's experiments with synthetic resins led to polyester tire cord, clothing and other products.

CHAPTER TWELVE

GLOBAL DOMINANCE

1960–1970

*"In the sixties we seemed to have no competition. ... We built more plants
in that 10-year span than probably in the history of the company."*

— Fred Steel, 1997[1]

I N 1960, JOHN F. KENNEDY campaigned on the theme that the nation was standing "on the edge of a New Frontier."[2] The "frontier" would take different and sometimes tragic forms — such as the Bay of Pigs fiasco and racial strife — but among its most soaring manifestations was a rejuvenated and highly successful U.S. space program.

For Goodyear, the sixties would be a period of unparalleled growth. Chairman Edwin J. Thomas, dubbed by *The New York Times* as the "Chief Optimist on Wheels," ignored doomsayers of the time and predicted in 1960 that the rubber industry would surpass previous records. He correctly predicted that Goodyear's sales, which had hit a record of almost $1.58 billion in 1959, would proceed to the $2 billion milepost "within the next four or five years."[3]

Yet even Thomas did not foresee Goodyear's dramatic growth spurt during the 1960s. His prediction of $2 billion in net sales came true in 1964, but that accomplishment seemed modest just five years later when sales soared to a remarkable $3.2 billion.[4] From 1960 to 1969, net income more than doubled, from $71 million to $155 million.[5] During the 1950s, Goodyear had advanced at a healthy trot, but now it was in an all-out sprint. Between 1951 and 1961, pneumatic tire production had increased from 29.5 million to 41.8 mil-

lion. By 1966, it topped $77.8 million.[6] Fred Steel, recruited by Goodyear in 1960, was still working in his management-trainee squadron at Jackson, Michigan, at the time. Steel, who gradually moved up to plant manager of the Topeka, Kansas facility, recalled the excitement of the period.

"In the sixties we seemed to have no competition, really. And we seemed to have so much money, we didn't know what to do with it. We built Union City, Fayetteville, Danville, Philipsburg, Freeport. ... I mean, we built more plants in that 10-year span than probably in the history of the company. Tremendous opportunity for people willing to go forward, and hell, I did it all. I worked as a night supervisor for three years, never saw the light of day. I never ever dreamed that someday I'd be sitting in a corner office."[7]

As *The New York Times* put it, in a rather backhanded compliment to Akron, "The odor of rubber that hangs over this city, no matter how

An inhabitant of Yellowstone National Park inspects a Goodyear tire.

Above: Chairman E.J. Thomas (left) and President Russell DeYoung with Goodyear's 1 billionth tire, constructed on November 20, 1963.

Right: Victor Holt, holding the Vytacord tire, served as president of Goodyear from 1964 to 1972.

unpleasant it may seem to the nostrils, is the sweet smell of success."[8]

Russell DeYoung

Joining Thomas at the helm of Goodyear during this period was Russell DeYoung, who had been made president in 1958 when Thomas assumed the chairmanship vacated by Paul Litchfield. As Thomas had personified the benign optimism of the 1950s, DeYoung's energetic style fit the youthful spirit of the sixties.

Born in 1909 in Rutherford, New Jersey, DeYoung had attended 13 grade schools across the country before his family settled in Akron. To pay tuition at the University of Akron, where he earned a degree in industrial engineering, DeYoung worked in the Goodyear factory, where he was recognized as a budding young talent, receiving the Litchfield Award of Merit as the outstanding member of his production squadron class.[9]

After graduation, DeYoung oversaw the construction of the tire plant in Java; won a Sloane Fellowship to the Massachusetts Institute of Technology, where he earned a master's degree in business administration; and, as assistant to the president of GAC, directed the company's massive wartime manufacturing of planes, blimps, and other materials.[10] From 1947 to 1956, he served as production vice president of the parent company and as a director. In 1956, he became an executive vice president, becoming president in 1958.

DeYoung's philosophy was to get done yesterday what needed to be done today. His competitive spirit found outlet in a regimen of physical activity that included several games of handball per

The new Polyglas tire gives you up to double the mileage.

1. Squirm rubs out tires.
You can't see it but an automobile tire squirms like a worm. The tread constantly wriggles and writhes on the road... rubs itself away like an eraser.

2. Polyglas fights squirm.
Polyglas stands for a combination of a polyester cord body plus a fiberglass cord belt. Together, they hold the wide tread firm on the road. It squirms less ...so it wears less.

3. With Polyglas. Without Polyglas.
Both these tires went 20,037 miles under identical conditions. The Polyglas tire still has plenty of tread left, while the other tire's bald. See? The Polyglas tire gives you up to double the mileage of the tires that come on many new cars.

POLYESTER CORD BODY   FIBERGLAS BELT

GOOD **YEAR**

4. Only Goodyear makes it.
Nobody else has Polyglas construction. Get it now in Goodyear's new Custom Wide Tread. Where? Where you see the Goodyear sign.

week and a daily half-mile around his swimming pool. He once said, "If there's anything I can't stand it's an executive who lets himself get sloppy, overweight and out of shape. I expect each man in our company to keep himself fit and do a hard day's work. That's what we pay him for."[11]

On April 6, 1964, after 48 years with Goodyear — 24 as president or chairman and CEO — Thomas relinquished the chairmanship, but continued as a director and chair of the executive and finance committee at the request of other board members. Victor Holt, Jr. was promoted from executive vice president to president, and DeYoung assumed the top post as chairman and CEO.[12] In his first interview as chief of Goodyear, he was asked if he thought the company could maintain its world leadership. "I wasn't hired to put Goodyear in second place," he answered.[13]

Building a Better Tire

In the early sixties, Goodyear improved on its most popular product by introducing a new tire that was stronger and more economical.

From the debut of the pneumatic tire at the turn of the century until 1938, cotton had been the king of tire cords, woven into the rubber to reinforce it, much the way steel reinforces concrete.[14] Synthetic fabrics proved

more resilient, and tire companies turned first to rayon, then nylon, in its search for a strong and cost-effective cord. In trials at Goodyear and other companies, polyester had passed the four-point test with flying colors; a tire cord had to provide: "a smooth, quiet ride to complement the quieter cars rolling out of U.S. factories; a high-speed, cool-running tire for use on long stretches of expressways and turnpikes; resistance to cuts and bruises; and improved economy."[15]

Polyester was more expensive than rayon or nylon, but allowed the use of less rubber in the tire body.[16] Using the triple-tempered process, Goodyear engineers developed a polyester cord, Vytacord, that was used in the 1962 premium

Above: Goodyear introduced the Custom Wide Polyglas, a transition between the bias-ply and the radial.

Below: The polyester molecule, which made the Vytacord tire possible. Vytacord was introduced in 1962.

tire, the Double Eagle with LifeGuard Safety Shield.[17] Performance of the Double Eagle was so promising that the company began manufacturing Vytacord at its Point Pleasant, West Virginia, factory. By the end of 1962, Vytacord was used in eight of Goodyear's 14 auto tire lines, and in 1967, Goodyear opened the Polyester Technical Center in Akron, a wing of the Research Laboratory.[18] Other companies followed suit. In 1962, the United States used just one million pounds of polyester tire cord, but by 1969, the figure had soared to 170 million pounds.[19]

Worldwide Expansion

Record sales and demand for products spurred the largest period of capital expansion in the company's history. In 1960, Goodyear's holdings included 30 domestic and 27 foreign plants. By 1969, the company flag flew in 53 American cities and 40 overseas locations, as well as at manufacturing affiliates in 13 countries.[20] Many Goodyearites found their best opportunities overseas, gaining experience for the eventual emergence of a global economy. One such person was Bill Massey, who entered the International Division in 1966, spending all but five of his years outside the United States.

"I have had the good fortune to have worked and lived in eight countries outside the United States, some of them more than once. This is the opportunity I sought when I graduated from Harvard. It has made life one continuous, pleasant learning experience for me and my family. And it has made work fun."[21]

In 1959, Goodyear boldly invaded Michelin territory by breaking ground for a $10 million tire plant in Amiens, France.[22] On the surface, it appeared that Goodyear was tempting fate by challenging the number one tire producer in France on its home turf. But Samir Gibara, who became manager of Goodyear's Paris office in 1966, noted that many businesses — particularly car manufacturers — did not feel comfortable relying on a single source of equipment. Gibara, who was elected chairman of Goodyear in 1996, said that Michelin, in spite of its strong position in France, did not own a distribution network in that country. "We felt that Goodyear had an opportunity to expand faster than Michelin."[23]

Goodyear challenged Michelin, the clear leader in the French tire market, on its home turf in France, opening a new tire plant in Amiens in 1961.

"When I saw that Michelin was so strong in France, I felt that people wanted an alternative to Michelin. But no other brand had been able to establish a reputation as the alternative to Michelin. The essence of my efforts in France was to establish Goodyear as the only credible alternative to Michelin."[24]

Sylvain Valensi, today vice president of the European Region, said battling Michelin was one of his biggest challenges. "I spent hours and days training our sales force to present themselves as different from Michelin. ... Not to sell the old-fashioned ways, but to present a very professional explanation of why manufacturers would want to work with us, a systematic approach."[25]

In 1962, Goodyear acquired the German tiremaker Gummiwerke Fulda, located just 20 miles from the Iron Curtain, and began manufacturing tires under the Fulda brand name.[26] Using an Italian sales company, Goodyear Italiana SpA, Goodyear challenged Italy's leading tire company, Pirelli, with the 1965 construction of a tire and tube plant in Cisterna di Latina, 30 miles south of Rome.[27] On hand at the opening ceremony were DeYoung, Goodyear International President Richard Thomas, the future prime minister of Italy Giulio Andreotti (then minister of defense), and Eugene Cardinal Tisserant, dean of the Roman Catholic church's college of cardinals.[28]

In 1967, the company opened its biggest foreign factory to date in Philippsburg, West Germany, a $15 million investment capable of producing 2,400 tires per day.[29] Facilities in the United Kingdom, Luxembourg, France, Italy and West Germany, served markets that were very different from the United States, where most of the company's research and development was based, as Maurice O'Reilly noted in *The Goodyear Story*.

"The smaller cars, narrow roads, and high speed limits of Europe brought new and different technological requirements to U.S. tire engineers, who had to spend much time on the Continent studying several dissimilar markets there and their peculiar requirements."[30]

The Goodyear Technical Center-Europe, established in 1957 at Colmar-Berg, Luxembourg with a technical staff of three, grew in both size and scope during the sixties.[31] By the end of the decade, the center employed 300 people of various nationalities, and by the late sixties, it would develop products for all of Goodyear International's markets.[32] In 1969, it received a new name, the Goodyear International Tire Center, to reflect this broader mission.[33]

Since 1910, Goodyear had been a strong presence in the Canadian market. During the 1960s, it added tire factories at Medicine Hat, Alberta, and one at Valleyfield, Quebec, along with an industrial products plant at Collingwood, Ontario, and a foam products facility at Owen Sound, Ontario.[34] In 1964, Goodyear acquired all shares of the Seiberling Rubber Company of Canada, assuming control of its Toronto factory and more than 1,500 dealers and distributors.[35]

New factories were also constructed at Morant Bay, Jamaica; Izmit, Turkey; Salonika, Greece; and Melbourne, Australia. But the company lost holdings in Cuba and, temporarily, in Indonesia.[36] After fighting for three years against a right-wing dictator, Fidel Castro quickly dashed American hopes that he would institute democracy.[37] Instead, Castro embraced the Soviet sphere of influence and seized American-held assets, including the San Jose plant, which Goodyear had started operating shortly after World War II.

In Indonesia, the government appropriated the factory in Bogor, Java — the same one that had fallen under Bridgestone's control during World War II — as well the Dolok Merangir and Wingfoot Estate plantations on Sumatra.[38] Dolok Merangir, the company's first plantation, was returned in 1967 by the Suharto government, along with two adjacent properties, in exchange for the Wingfoot Estate.[39]

While new plants sprouted up worldwide, existing ones were extensively modernized. In 1966 alone, capital expenditures exceeded $189 million, funding factory improvements in the United States, Mexico, England, Scotland, Sweden, Luxembourg, France, India, the Philippines, Turkey, Australia, Peru and Venezuela. Even the year-old plant in Valleyfield, Quebec, was enlarged.[40]

The expansion was in preparation for predicted massive growth in overseas markets. As *The New York Times* reported in 1968, "By the mid-1970s the European tire market is expected to be much larger than the American tire market. Even by the end of this year, auto registrations outside the United States will exceed registrations within the United States for the first time in history."[41] Goodyear President Victor Holt looked ahead to a "5 to 8 percent growth in tire sales every year for 'as long as I can see.'"[42] Goodyear was already the top American tire manufacturer in Western Europe, holding 13 percent of the market. Firestone was second with 11 percent.[43]

Growth through Acquisitions

Throughout the sixties, Goodyear acquired companies related to its tire business. In 1961, Goodyear purchased the Geneva Metal Wheel Company of Geneva, Ohio, which made wheels for lawn mowers, boat trailers and farm implements.

Three years later, it acquired the seven plants of the Motor Wheel Corporation of Lansing, Michigan.[44] Motor Wheel had a history of rapid growth and success. Founded in 1920 as the union of four companies — Prudden Wheel, Auto Wheel, Grier Pressed Steel and Weis & Lesh Manufacturing Company of Memphis — it was, by 1924, the world's leading producer of wooden and steel wheels. By the late 1920s, it had diversified into brake drums, heating and air conditioning units, and wheels for heavy machinery.[45] Under Goodyear, Motor Wheel operated as a wholly-owned subsidiary. John H. Gerstenmaier, later to become Goodyear's president and vice chairman, was named the fifth president of Motor Wheel in 1964.[46]

In 1965, Goodyear purchased a Lee National Corporation plant in Conshohocken, Pennsylvania, which had closed down after a 1963 strike. The plant became a subsidiary called the Lee Tire & Rubber Company.[47] Lee had been founded in 1883 by J. Elwood Lee to make surgical implements.

Above: A new factory was established in 1963 in the town of Logan, Ohio, to produce foam automobile parts.

Below: Throughout the sixties and early seventies, the Windsor shoe factory was hurt by low-priced foreign imports.

Merging with Johnson & Johnson in 1905, Elwood Lee began to manufacture tires. In 1962, Lee Tire & Rubber Corporation was taken over by New York interests and renamed the Lee National Corporation.[48]

Goodyear added two tire factories to its Kelly-Springfield subsidiary, one in Tyler, Texas, and the second in Freeport, Illinois, and two to the foam products division, in Logan, Ohio, and Bakersfield, California.[49] The Logan plant produced items for car interiors, including padded dashboards, which were made with Neothane, a leather-like synthetic rubber developed by the Chemical Products Division.[50] A new tire factory in Danville, Virginia, was completed in 1966, as was a reinforced plastics plant in Jackson, Ohio.[51] That year, ground was broken for a shoe products facility at Madisonville, Kentucky, and an industrial products plant at Marysville, Ohio.[52]

In 1967, the company announced the largest construction project in its history to date — a $73 million, 593-acre site in Union City, Tennessee, with a capacity of 37,000 tires per day.[53] At its inception, the Union City plant reflected Goodyear's commitment to build its lead in domestic sales. In the 1970s, it would become a crucial weapon in the radial tire war.

In Air and Space

In 1962, the world appeared to be on the brink of war, as the United States and the Soviet Union stood toe-to-toe over the issue of Soviet missiles in Cuba. After six agonizing days, the Soviet Union backed down and removed the missiles, but by then tensions in Southeast Asia were rising. During the same period, President Kennedy proposed to achieve what was considered one of the greatest challenges in human history: to land a man on the moon and safely return him to earth.

In 1963, a new subsidiary was created under the name of Goodyear Aerospace, replacing Goodyear Aircraft.[54] The name change reflected the division's continuing role in military and space projects, embracing plastics, missiles,

guidance systems, radar systems, advanced electronics, flight simulators and trainers, aerospace ground support equipment, communications structures and interplanetary systems.[55]

Goodyear Aerospace became involved in a number of highly successful military contracts in addition to the highly successful Subroc weapon system.[56] Goodyear Aerospace helped develop an all-weather, high-resolution radar system for aircraft, which was adopted by the Air Force in 1962 for the RF4C fighter jet.[57]

In 1966, Goodyear helped build a system that rapidly processed reconnaissance photographs. Sixteen of these units were deployed in Vietnam.[58] Goodyear was also one of several companies that helped develop a fiber flak jacket worn by American fliers in Vietnam. The glass-and-ceramic vest was more efficient than steel and could stop bullets at speeds of 1,250 feet per second.[59]

Moon tire prototypes, which Goodyearites spent 10 years developing.

"The Eagle Has Landed"

During the second half of the decade, the nation's imagination was captured by the Apollo space missions, which culminated in the summer of 1969 with Apollo 11's lunar landing and Neil Armstrong's "giant step for mankind." Most Americans were too awestruck to notice, but Goodyear Aerospace supplied essential products for the Apollo spacecraft. When the missiles moved into place on the launch pads, the huge transporters supporting them slowed and stopped on Goodyear brakes; in flight the engines ran on GAC's "purge-and-conditioning" system that carried air and heated nitrogen in and excess concentrations of hydrogen and oxygen out. The window frames of the command modules were GAC-manufactured, as was the Bondolite panel on which landing instruments were mounted.[60]

When Apollo 11 returned to earth, splashing nose-down into the ocean, it was righted by Goodyear-made flotation bags that kept the capsule upright while the astronauts crawled into life rafts.[61] Millions of Americans sat before their television screens, riveted to this display of technological mastery and human daring.

Two years later, millions would again watch, as astronauts Alan Shepard and Ed Mitchell explored the moon's surface while pulling a two-wheeled cart carrying cameras and film, digging equipment, and 35 numbered bags which they filled with lunar rock. The cart — which NASA

called the Modular Equipment Transporter — was fitted with 16-inch tires that were the result of a 10-year development project on which hundreds of Goodyearites had worked.[62] One of those men, Walter Curtiss, helped engineer the specially designed tires. Curtiss, today director of the Goodyear Technical Center, said the project had actually been shelved, until someone from the Apollo program came forward with a problem.

"This guy said, 'You know, every time we land on the moon, we spew out carbon all over for a radius of 200 to 300 feet. We have to get beyond that to get pure samples for carbon dating and it's too much of a load for the astronauts to walk out that distance and carry back between 20 and 50 pounds of rock.' So we thought we could make a little rickshaw and just put some rubber tires on it. But we found out that we couldn't have any carbon in our tires, and we use carbon black quite extensively. So we used silicon. The other problem was flotation. There was some dust up there and they didn't want a tire to sink in. The maximum inflation we could have was two pounds per square inch. What we literally had to do was inflate these tires here on earth in a vacuum chamber. Take them out of the vacuum chamber, where they would collapse. Put them on the vehicle and send it to the moon."[63]

After 73 years traveling the roads of earth, Goodyear had made it to the moon.

Background: Tire tracks on the moon, the result of the Modular Equipment Transporter. The lack of natural erosion, with the exception of meteorite impacts, means these and other tracks will last for millions of years.

Far left: Victor Holt and Russell DeYoung pose with the specially designed moon tire and a model of the Modular Equipment Transporter the astronauts used.

Opposite left: The actual Modular Equipment Transporter used to carry equipment and rocks.

Above: Alan Shepard on the surface of the moon with fellow astronaut Ed Mitchell in 1971.

The $300 million Lawton, Oklahoma plant was the most modern factory in the country, and Goodyear's biggest investment in its history.

CHAPTER THIRTEEN

ROLLING INTO NEW MARKETS

1970–1980

"They told me it would never fly here, that they were just too expensive. I listened to that for two or three weeks, but I finally said, 'Look, I don't believe a thing you say. We're going for 100,000 a day just as fast as we can design the equipment and install it.' "

— Chuck Pilliod, 1996[1]

ON JULY 22, 1970, the New York Stock Exchange made history when the largest single block of stock ever traded on its floor crossed the tape shortly after noon. The stock was 1,184,300 shares of Goodyear traded at 24.5, two points down from the previous day's close. The trade came a few hours after Goodyear announced a sharp decline in quarterly earnings during a United Rubber Workers strike.[2]

The distinction of having such a record sounded an ominous note for a new decade that would test Goodyear's financial resilience and technological resolve as the rubber industry underwent a major reshuffling. The entire industry suffered severe losses, as one analyst would observe: "Between the end of 1969 and the end of 1979, the S&P 400 Index, which measures changes in the average stock prices of large U.S. companies competing in a wide variety of industries, rose 19 percent. During that period Uniroyal's stock dropped 70 percent; Firestone's dropped 65 percent; Goodyear's dropped 58 percent; and Goodrich's stock fell 40 percent."[3] Although Goodyear's annual sales would more than triple between 1970 to 1981, by the time Ronald Reagan was sworn in as president in 1981, Akron's boast of being the Rubber Capital of the World was on its way to becoming a quaint but inaccurate nickname.

The 1960s had been intensely profitable years, with auto registration doubling outside the United States.[4] Goodyear, Firestone and Goodrich supplied more than 75 percent of the North American tire market, with the rest belonging to small domestic manufacturers and some imports.[5] The seventies, by contrast, brought new challenges both in engineering and public relations, as foreign companies set their sights on the United States market, and political unrest at home fostered negative opinions of both government and big business.

A Return to Labor Unrest

For Goodyear, the decade began with its first sales backslide in eight years, triggered by an eight-week strike that held sales $24 million under 1969's record $3 billion mark.[6] Strikes were becoming common for the industry: between 1967 and 1977, 12 national rubber strikes interrupted production and aggravated relations between labor and management.[7]

The Hog was chosen as the mascot for Reclaim Division, which turned discarded tires from an environmental eyesore into workable rubber.

In 1970, Goodyear executives saw the strikes as annoying blips on a generally clear screen. There were plenty of reasons for optimism. GAC was flying high with a contract to produce components for Boeing's new 747 superjet, and new equipment at the Akron wheels and brakes plant made it the most modern aviation testing facility in the industry.[8] In 1970, the same year the moon tire was wheeled before the press, Aerospace introduced Staran, the "world's fastest computer," which was used for air traffic control.[9] For Goodyear International, a massive capital improvements project was under way:

Above: Goodyear International opened its Luxembourg Technical Center campus in 1970.

Below: The test track at the Technical Center put tires through a tough rubber-wearing regimen.

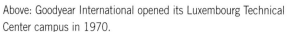

the new Technical Center had opened in Luxembourg complete with a factory, a research and development center, a test track and tire proving ground, two plants to make molds and steel wire, an airplane test development center, and a $13 million fabric mill.[10] Plans were announced to build tire factories in Morocco, Brazil and Zaire, expand both the Luxembourg tire plant adjacent to the Tech Center and the Indonesian tire plant, and enter into an agreement with the Indonesian government to operate two additional tire and tube facilities.[11]

The expansion of Goodyear International made it a unique training ground for the company's future leaders, who had to learn how to adapt to different cultures and currencies as the world moved toward a truly global market. The challenges were formidable, particularly in Brazil, which was in the throes of skyrocketing inflation, recalled George Strickler, treasurer of Goodyear Brazil in the late seventies and vice president of Finance for North America in 1997.

"We borrowed money on a nightly basis at rates that sometimes exceeded 240 percent. So we worked out a plan with suppliers, where we would borrow money for two days and then lend them money for three days just to flatten all this out. Inflation was sky-high, and we were losing a lot of money because we were under price controls. Eventually, we were able to cut back on our terms to dealers and get some discipline with them. All of a sudden, we were making money. From a business and learning experience, it was probably the best assignment I ever had because it forced our organization to do things differently from what we were trained to do."[12]

On January 1, 1971, the company's chief optimist, Edwin J. Thomas, ended 55 years of service at Goodyear by resigning as director and chairman of the finance and executive committees.[13] Since his retirement as chairman of the board seven years earlier, Thomas had embraced community activities. His commitment was honored when the University of Akron announced it would name its new $11.7 million performing arts center after him.[14]

Later that month, the U.S. Army awarded Goodyear with its highest civilian award, the Outstanding

Above: Opened in 1935, the Indonesian factory became the largest tire plant in Southeast Asia.

Below: The Morocco factory began tire production in 1974.

Civilian Service Medal, for the development of a crash-resistant and self-sealing helicopter fuel tank.[15] Presenting the award to Chairman Russell DeYoung at a ceremony in the Pentagon, U.S. Army Chief of Staff General William Westmoreland said: "In 20 major accidents suffered by aircraft equipped with the system, there have been no injuries or fatalities as a result of fire. Our crash investigators have determined that 50 percent of the aircraft in major crashes could have or would have been burned if it had not been for the crash-resistant tanks."[16]

Back on Track

Sales for 1971 put Goodyear back on the track for growth, swelling 12 percent to reach $3.6 billion.[17] The company had weathered the labor storm of 1970 in better shape than local competitors. Its sales increase of $400 million topped the increases of the other Big Four companies combined. Second-place Firestone had to content itself with a sales increase of $150 million, while Uniroyal increased $120 million and Goodrich increased $95 million.[18]

Much of Goodyear's success stemmed from its popular bias-belt tire, introduced in 1967 as a bridge between the traditional bias-ply and the more durable but expensive radial tire that was overtaking the European market. By the time Goodyear introduced its 13th line of bias belts, the Power Belt Polyglas, in 1971, the company had produced more than 56 million of the tires in little more than three years. In 1972, bias belts accounted for 50 percent of all automobile tires sold in the United States, bias-ply tires made up 42 percent and radial tires accounted for just 8 percent.[19]

Above: The Edwin J. Thomas Center for the Performing Arts, at the University of Akron, was named such to honor the former chairman's community involvement.

Below: The *Columbia*, reminding people to "pitch in" to keep America beautiful.

But the winds were shifting. The United States rubber industry had long enjoyed the success of the big kid on the block, but by the seventies that dominance was eroding. Spurred by inexpensive labor, foreign competition had already usurped 83 percent of the market for rubber shoe products. Between 1966 and 1971, imports had tripled to 9 percent of U.S. tire sales.[20] The domestic tire industry was losing ground: 1971 exports of 4.3 million car and truck tires fell woefully short of the imported figure of 19.4 million units.[21] Goodyear's director of Corporate Business Planning and Research, Edwin Sonnecken, paraphrased in a historical journal, explained what the alarming trend meant to the industry.

"[Sonnecken noted] that on the average every million tires imported meant 457 fewer tire industry jobs in the United States. Sonnecken also pointed out that in 1970, foreign cars accounted for 15 percent of the U.S. market, compared with 10 percent in 1959, and that in California one in every three cars sold in 1970 was an import.

"Further, greater gains abroad in output per worker and

*differences in labor costs were also major fac-
tors to be considered. Foreign labor costs per
hour, including wages and benefits, ranged
from $1.05 in Spain to $5 in Canada. In the
United States, these costs exceeded an average
of $6 an hour including wages and benefits.
Tariff differences and export subsidies by foreign governments ... accentuated the problem.*"[22]

The Ecology Movement

As American businesses faced tougher foreign competition, they also had to grapple with
new pressures at home. Anti-government sentiment roused by the war in Vietnam led to a mis-
trust of big business, and the ecology movement
directed public awareness toward the environmental costs of industry. Between 1966 and
1972, Goodyear spent more than $19 million
meeting tough new governmental pollution
standards.[23] By 1978, the amount would rise to
$60 million.[24]

In the Akron area alone, the company's pro-
environment projects included a million-dollar
cleaning facility to clear oil and debris from the
Little Cuyahoga River; $6.2 million electrostatic
precipators in the stacks of Plants 1 and 2 to
meet federal clean air emission standards; and

The water purification treatment plant eliminated pollution from
Goodyear's plants in Akron.

an energy-development program for which eight
wells were drilled around Akron to provide natural gas to supply the factories and nearby
homes.[25] Energy conservation initiatives implemented at all domestic plants resulted in the use
of 12.3 trillion fewer BTUs by the latter part of
the decade.[26] James Whiteley, vice president of
product quality and safety since 1993, said
Goodyear had an advantage over other mature
manufacturing companies when the environment became an issue.

*"For a long time we had quality control groups
who were supposed to catch everything bad. We
never got ourselves into any massive problems.
Our biggest problems were traditional manufacturing errors: rejects, slowed production, ineffi-
ciency, excessive costs rather than consumer
safety issues."*[27]

Goodyear had been involved in conservation
efforts since 1947, when it had instituted an
annual award program to encourage conservation

of land, water, forests and wildlife.[28] By 1970, the "shrinking world" phenomenon created by television and air travel prompted cries of "zero population growth" and "limited resources," and as a source of land pollution, tires became a scapegoat. The durability of Charles Goodyear's vulcanized rubber worked against itself; scrap tires heaped in landfills were eyesores that did not biodegrade. By 1978, the country was wearing out roughly 175 million tires each year. Disposing of them in an "environmentally acceptable manner," Goodyear Vice Chairman John Gerstenmaier told a University of Akron symposium in 1979, "is a real challenge."[29]

To meet the challenge, Goodyear sought to turn discarded tires into an economic resource rather than an environmental problem. In Akron, its reclaiming facilities were the largest in the industry, processing 66 million pounds of rubber annually from approximately 3 million tires and using the recycled material in such products as inner tubes, tires, shoe soles and industrial belting.[30]

Goodyear also tried burning tires in cement kilns, which was beneficial because the steel content from belts, wires and beads remained in the ash.[31] When burned, scrap tires generated 40 percent more energy than coal. One Goodyear spokesman said using tires for fuel is "like returning borrowed energy," since one percent of oil pumped from the earth is used to make synthetic rubber.[32] Tires as fuel became the sole energy source for the steam furnace at the Jackson, Michigan, plant, and this energy source was also used at the Akron electrical facility.[33]

Goodyear even began converting used tires into artificial reefs for aquatic life and into floating breakwaters to protect coastal land. Bundled and sunk to the ocean floor, tires could provide habitats for species propagation in formerly barren sections of lakes and oceans; when chained together and used as breakwaters, they could dissipate more than 80 percent of the eroding power of waves.[34]

In the 1970s, the ecology movement had a major impact on American industry. One EPA study estimated that American businesses would spend $26 billion to meet federal pollution requirements between 1975 and 1984, with an additional $140 billion needed to adhere to state and local laws.[35] Speaking before a group of students and community members in 1978, Gerstenmaier acknowledged that regulations were needed, but called for a balancing between costs and benefits.

Above: A model of a tire reef under construction, one of Goodyear's more creative solutions to the problems of scrap tire disposal.

Below: A diver examines the delicate life of coral, which turned discarded tires into a home.

Goodyear's 75th anniversary party, held in 1973, was a company-wide celebration.

"It is estimated that in 1977 this country paid about $103 billion for government regulation. That's $470 for each person living in the United States, 25 percent of the entire federal budget, nearly 75 percent as much as the annual private investment in plant and equipment. ... In these times of double-digit inflation, high energy costs, stagnant productivity and a weak dollar, this country can't afford single-minded pursuit of environmental objectives without regard for the cost and consequences of that pursuit."[36]

75th Anniversary

In 1973, Goodyear celebrated its 75th birthday with a new blimp, the *Europa*, stationed in Italy.[37] As part of the festivities, a restored 1916 Packard painted to look like the Wingfoot Express followed the course of its predecessor's 750-mile journey from Akron to Boston. The modern version completed the trip on a single set of tires, while the original had suffered blowouts about every 75 miles.[38]

The U.S. headquarters in Akron underwent impressive renovations. Goodyearites were proud to show off their new office to the 21,500 people who attended a February open house.[39] The most visible change was in the exterior of the building, for the entire 400 yards fronting Market Street received a facelift. "The only thing Litchfield would recognize from the outside is the address," recalled

one old-timer, alluding to Paul Litchfield's aversion to investing in office facilities.[40] Inside, improvements included a new terraced lobby, modernized offices and a Speedramp system connecting all five floors. The "model room" was also updated into a polished display center for replicas of Goodyear plants around the world. Each was built to 1/360 the size of the original and decorated with shrubbery, tiny pedestrians and cars.[41]

Although 1973 sales reached record levels and net earnings were the second-highest in the company's history, the year was marred by the OPEC oil embargo and a Watergate-related scandal that darkened Russell DeYoung's remaining months at Goodyear.[42] As part of the ongoing Watergate investigation, DeYoung became one of 21 American executives who admitted making illegal contributions to the Nixon campaign. Two of these executives went to jail, but DeYoung paid a $1,000 fine and resigned from Goodyear shortly before his mandatory retirement at age 65.[43]

Robert Mercer, who became chairman of Goodyear during the mid-eighties, said the incident was tragic for DeYoung, who was always known as a straight arrow.

"He had no bad habits at all. Didn't smoke, didn't drink, didn't go around with other women. ... The worst part was that his own legal counsel advised him to donate because the unions do it. He was Mr. Clean."[44]

Charles Pilliod

Stepping into the dual role of CEO and chairman was Charles J. Pilliod, who had been president since 1972. John Gerstenmaier assumed the presidency.[45] Pilliod combined personal ties to the community — he had grown up in nearby Cuyahoga Falls, attended Kent State University, and had earned 67 cents an hour as a Goodyear trainee — with the international perspective of a man who had flown bombers in World War II and served Goodyear International in both the Latin American jungle and the streets of Great Britain.[46] After he retired from Goodyear in 1983, Pilliod went on to become U.S. Ambassador to Mexico in 1986. Pilliod didn't have patience for anything that would slow down the progress of the company. His eventual replacement, Robert Mercer, who was then general manager of Industrial Products, recalled his first run-in with Pilliod as president.

"The day after Chuck became president, I waltzed into his office to present the budget for expanding a rubber hose plant in Lincoln, Nebraska, thinking it would be a breeze. His first question was, 'What manufacturing process are you going to use?' 'The tried and proven process we have in Lincoln, Nebraska,' I replied.

"Then Pilliod said, 'Get a passport, go to Europe, and visit all the radiator hose makers. When you come back and tell me your process

---

Above: The airship *Europa*, hovering over its base in Rome in 1972.

Right: A 1973 portrait of Charles Pilliod, who became CEO and chairman in 1974.

represents the latest state of the art in the industry then maybe we will discuss the plant.

"That was Monday. I passed him in the hall that Wednesday, and he said, 'I thought I told you to go to Europe.' Now you don't just show up in Berlin and say, 'Lead me to the nearest air hose manufacturer.' You make arrangements first. But believe me I was on an airplane that night."[47]

The selection of Pilliod reflected Goodyear's increasingly global nature, recalled John Perduyn, vice president of public affairs for Goodyear, who had joined the company in 1965 as editor of the internal publications *Go* and *Triangle*. Perduyn said Pilliod's ascension meant that international experience was recognized as critical for Goodyear's leaders.

"Russ DeYoung had real vision to pick Chuck Pilliod to succeed him. Pilliod was a real dark horse and nobody had thought it would happen. But he spent as much time overseas as Samir Gibara [Goodyear's current chairman and CEO]. We really started to look outside of the United States even then."[48]

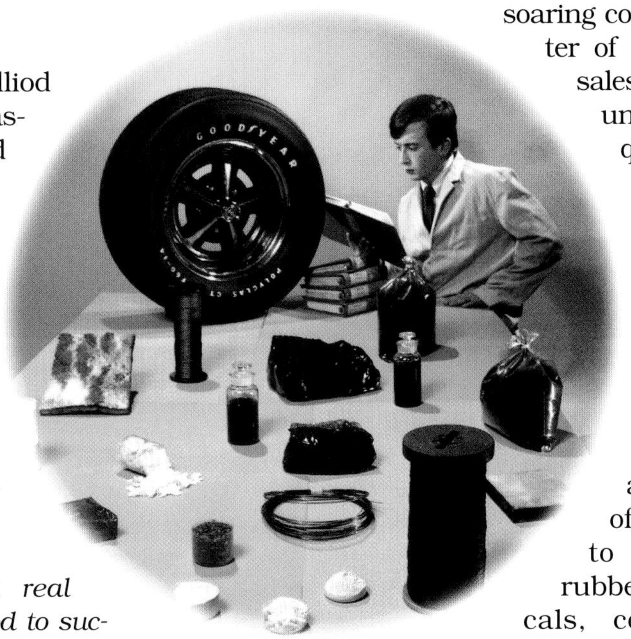

The Winds of Change

Pilliod assumed the helm at a time of great transition. Between 1969 and 1974, Goodyear's sales had grown 25 percent — from $3 billion to well over $4 billion — but this trend was changing.[49] Two major factors contributed to the shaking and eventual restructuring of the domestic tire industry: the oil crisis and the radial tire. Unluckily for Goodyear and its local competitors, they hit at about the same time.

In October 1973, five Arab nations attacked Israel during the Yom Kippur holiday. Emergency supplies — ranging from ammunition to medical equipment — flowed to the Jewish state. As the war gradually turned against the attacking nations, OPEC imposed an oil embargo on any nation that lent support to Israel, notably the United States.

The embargo slowed the nation's economy and afflicted tire manufacturers with a dual burden: decreased demand for product — particularly for the conventional bias-ply tire — and soaring costs. During the first quarter of 1974, original equipment sales fell from 15.9 million units to 10.7; in the same quarter, the replacement market fell off by 3 million units.[50] Consumers cut down on travel and slowed to the new 55-mile-per-hour speed limit designed to reduce gas consumption and increase the life of tires.[51]

Furthermore, since approximately 80 percent of the basic materials used to manufacture synthetic rubber tires were petrochemicals, costs escalated. Nearly seven gallons of oil were needed for production of each tire.[52] To offset higher costs, Goodyear instituted a 2 percent increase in tire prices.[53]

The embargo experience demonstrated that natural rubber tires would always be in demand. Natural rubber was a renewable resource that did not rely heavily on petrochemicals, noted Fred Kovac, who had been vice president of technology-business planning since 1992 and was interviewed shortly before he passed away in 1996. A Goodyearite since 1956, Kovac had been honored with the first-ever Tire Society Award, and was the first non-German to receive the Eric Konrad medal, both for significant contributions to the advancement of rubber science and technology.

The ingredients shown above are for a Custom Polyglas GT. Goodyear raced to catch up with Michelin in the radial market.

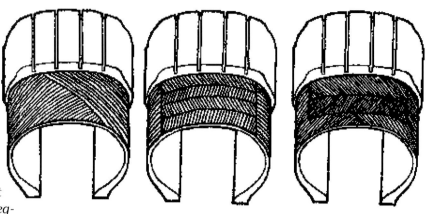

Bias-ply; radial (center): bias-belt

"When I was in college in the fifties, our professor in the polymer chemistry field told us to forget the natural rubber stuff. He said we could make any kind of synthetic you want, tailor it to your exact need. 'Natural rubber is out of the picture,' he said. But then the oil crisis hit. We realized that all synthetic rubber is made from oil. Natural rubber, on the other hand, is a renewable resource that comes from trees, the highest rating of vegetation because it has a canopy. Suddenly natural rubber was of great interest to us again."[54]

In addition to its availability, natural rubber contained some desirable properties that synthetic rubber has yet to match, said Gary Miller, vice president of Purchasing. Miller, a chemical engineer, was in charge of polyisoprene rubber. He noted that one of the distinguishing features of natural rubber is its ability to dissipate heat rapidly. "We still have not been able to develop a natural rubber substitute as a drop-in replacement," he said in 1997.[55] Tapping trees for use in making natural rubber had another benefit: the trees themselves manufactured oxygen for the environment. "Certainly, it is a green product that comes from a renewable resource, although it takes between five and seven years to mature a tree."[56]

The French Revolution: The Radial Tire

Meanwhile, a revolution was taking place within the tire industry. When Pierre Boudon, the uncle of Francois Michelin, obtained a patent for a radial tire in 1946, the idea was not new. In 1913, two Englishmen had filed a patent that described the advantages of the radial design. The advantages of the radial — better handling, a firmer, sportier ride, a seven percent increase in fuel economy and double the tread wear — were made possible by the lack of cross plies in the tire's carcass.[57] But until the seventies, no company had possessed the technology to build a radial without the risk of the components separating and the tire collapsing in pieces all over the road.[58] In the traditional bias-ply, the carcass was built of crisscrossed layers of fibers

and rubber that chafed under rolling stress and eventually wore through. Goodyear's innovative bias-belt added a layer of fiber or metal cord beneath the tread, but the carcass plies still rubbed. In contrast, the radial featured fiber cords that ran in parallel rings around the tire beneath a metal belt.[59]

The radial revolution caught domestic tiremakers off guard. In 1970 and 1971, just one percent of the U.S. replacement market went to radial tires; by the end of 1973, the figure had climbed to 14 percent.[60] Despite the increased cost — radials sold for 65 to 70 percent more than the conventional bias-ply — by 1975 one out of every four tires sold in the United States was a radial.[61] The fast switch represented a "belated recognition in the U.S. that the Michelin steel-belted radial introduced in Europe a quarter-century before" was simply a better product, and one capable of changing the industry.[62]

Michelin was determined to prove the point. Between 1970 and 1975, it spent more than $1 billion in global capital investments; at the end of 1973, half its 45 factories were less than six years old.[63] By 1975, when it opened its first American plant in South Carolina, Michelin made nothing but radial tires — more than 80 million of them — and had captured one-third of the European market, overtaking the giant Dunlop-Pirelli to stand as the number one tire manufacturer in Europe and the third-largest in the world.[64] In the United States, Michelin had been selling steel-belted radials through Sears, Roebuck, since the mid-sixties. Ford began fitting its Continentals with Michelins, and by 1974 used them on most of its new models. General Motors wasn't far behind.[65] Akron had to take decisive action to stop the bloodletting.

Fortunately for Goodyear, Chuck Pilliod's work in Great Britain had given him a ringside seat to Michelin's success. Upon returning to Akron in 1966, Pilliod had become "almost a Jeremiah in his insistence that Goodyear was falling behind the foreign competition and that its technology was old hat." So, although Goodyear lagged behind Michelin's technology, it had gotten a running start on its U.S. competition.[66] Gene Culler, executive vice president of North American Tires, recollected that Pilliod "came at just the right time," and was able to overcome much resistance to the new product.[67]

"He was telling them, 'Hey, there's this new tire,' and the people in Akron were saying, 'Oh, but this tire's hard riding. You run it up against the curb and it blows out.' That was because our original tires were hard riding and would blow out when you went up against the curb! We were benchmarking the concept against ourselves, which wasn't good. With Pilliod, we made the transition into radials. I think that if he had not become chairman, we would not have made the progress in the radialization of the market that we did."[68]

In a 1996 interview, Pilliod said several marketing and sales people had investigated whether the more expensive radial tire would have much of an impact in the United States.

"They told me it would never fly here, that the tires were just too expensive. I listened to that for two or three weeks, but I finally said, 'Look, I don't believe a thing you say. We're going for 100,000 a day just as fast as we can design the equipment and install it.'"[69]

In 1972, Goodyear entered the battle. The company introduced four lines of radials, including Custom Steelguard, the only steel-belted radial accepted by all Detroit automakers for 1973.[70] In 1974, Goodyear introduced the Custom

Polysteel Radial and a top-of-the-line Eagle Radial, with belts made of Flexten cord, a material also used by Goodyear Aerospace in a parachute landing craft for a proposed Mars expedition.[71] That year, Goodyear became the first tire manufacturer to exceed $5 billion in sales.[72]

But the transition in technology and equipment was enormously expensive. Under Pilliod's leadership, the company spent more than $2 billion converting at least half of its tire facilities, simply to catch up to Michelin's production capacity.[73] "We had to create the

A Double Eagle bias-belt being tested for tread strength. The plunger strikes the tread at 40 miles an hour.

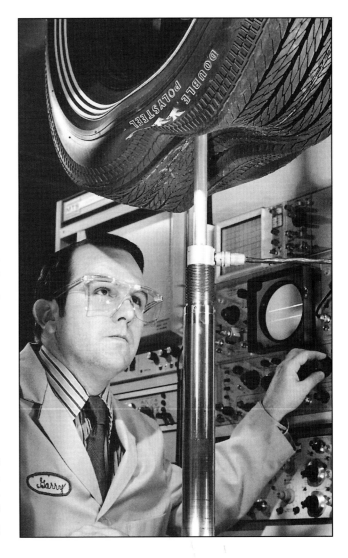

technology up front and as a result we spent some money," Pilliod recalled. "I wouldn't let anybody buy anything for the offices for a while, not even curtains, but instead socked capital into these factories."[74]

By 1976, when radial sales accounted for 45 percent of the market, Goodyear opened the two largest all-radial plants in the country, in Union City, Tennessee, and Fayetteville, North Carolina.[75] The Fayetteville plant was particularly difficult because it had originally been set up as a bias tire plant, and conversion from bias to radial was enormously difficult, recalled H. Clay Orme, division superintendent at the time. "The corporation was really stretched. We had new compounds that we had never worked with before. They were much more difficult to run and they burned the rubber more easily. We struggled to build the right equipment with the right parts, stuff that we would no more try to build today than to send a man to the moon by ourselves."[76]

Goodyear also planned a $69 million renovation and expansion of its Gadsden, Alabama, plant.[77] Ironically, the radial tire that represented a huge technological advancement in the industry also weakened it, explained one industry analyst.

"The initial effect that the shift from bias-ply to radial tires had on U.S. tire manufacturers was to weaken their balance sheets, because most of them found it necessary to borrow the funds needed to finance the conversion. Very soon after, it began to have an adverse effect on income statements as they found it necessary to accept the costs of closing dozens of bias-ply tire plants that had become obsolete. ... In addition, the widespread acceptance of the more durable radials has reduced sales opportunities in the higher margin tire replacement markets and has, therefore, increased the extent to which tire companies must rely on lower margin supply contracts

with manufacturers of new cars and trucks to sell the tires their plants produce."[78]

A New Management Model

In 1975, Goodyear's profits were helped when the company won the largest single contract in industry history, the entire service contract and a share of the tire supply for the Alaskan pipeline.[79] However, the following year, a United Rubber Workers strike closed factories for 130 days. An exasperated Chuck Pilliod was heard to mutter, "God must be a Frenchman."[80] Goodyear reported its first quarterly loss in 39 years, a $5.3 million slump on the heels of the strike.[81] Other domestic companies suffered even more.

In 1976, Michelin was number three worldwide and Japan's Bridgestone, with 16 plants and sales of $2 billion, was sixth.[82] Michelin had built two plants in Canada, two in South Carolina, and a truck tire factory in Littleton, Colorado. Since its United States facilities were nonunion, it was unaffected by the nationwide strike.[83] The factories were supported by 2,600 sales outlets, up from only 165 two decades earlier, and it was supplying original equipment tires to all major United States automakers.

Bridgestone was also making headway in the United States market. Between 1960 and 1976, it had opened nine factories in Japan to handle exports and established a center in Torrance, California.[84] By 1980, Bridgestone would have more than 1,000 retail outlets in the United States.[85] During the seventies, its profits would increase

Above: The company honored the nation's bicentennial with red, white and blue sidewalls.

Left: A Goodyear product display at Summit Mall, west of Akron.

Employees would gather at the Lawton plant's Learning Center to discuss product knowledge, operational problems and solutions.

fivefold, from under $20 million to over $100 million annually.[86]

In 1977, Goodyear took a bold approach when it broke ground in Lawton, Oklahoma, for what would become the most modern tire factory in the country.[87] The Lawton plant was necessary for two reasons: first, to upgrade Goodyear's radial capacity and second, to improve employee relations. One of only a few companies without a single nonunion plant, Goodyear had been hit hard by the strikes in 1973 and 1976, when rubber workers won a catch-up cost-of-living adjustment that approximated a 36 percent boost in wages and benefits.[88] Unhappy with the URW's practice of establishing an industry pattern by bargaining with a target company, Goodyear local delegates had sought increased local autonomy for bar-

gaining, but were outvoted.[89] Strikes had become so predictable that automakers demanded the rubber companies stockpile tires in advance of the start of negotiations, leaving tire companies caught in a cycle of paying costly overtime to make sufficient product to withstand a long work stoppage.[90] Furthermore, "the strikes and tire shortages ... enabled foreign producers to increase their penetration of the United States replacement market for tires from 4 percent in 1974 to 7 percent" in 1977.[91]

The $300 million Lawton plant represented the largest initial factory investment in Goodyear history.[92] The 1.4-million-square-foot plant, located on 500 acres, incorporated state-of-the-art manufacturing equipment and utilized computers for constant monitoring of raw materials, production processes and output.[93]

The plant was also an experiment in labor relations, according to a *Fortune* magazine article. It was the first factory to move "from what

The relaxed relationship between workers and management at Lawton made the plant a model for other factories to follow.

Goodyear calls 'control model' management to 'commitment model' — meaning that individual workers, rather than supervisors, are now responsible for quality. Working with management consultants from Harvard and MIT, Goodyear tried to change the relationship between supervisor and worker from what it calls 'parent-child' to 'adult-adult.'"[94] Toward this end, the company fostered discussion groups, goal-setting meetings, and problem-solving teams made up of managers and workers, and eliminated inspectors to make each worker responsible for his product.[95]

William Sharp, who was heavily involved in planning the operation, said everything about the plant was unique except its purpose. Consequently, the entire plant was on a learning curve.

"It was the first time we started up a facility where the vast majority of the machines, along with the controls and systems and processes, were brand new. Chuck Pilliod came to visit — he visited quite frequently — and he saw how many of the machines weren't even running. So he said to take him to a machine that works. We had one new machine, a ply cutter, that was brand new and working fabulously. We stopped and shook hands with the college-degree kid who was running the machine. He put it on manual, at which time the machine began to back up. Within a minute there was a holy mess. Pilliod looked at me and said, 'Just take me back to the office.' Because of all this new technology, we couldn't even show him one machine that would work."[96]

Sharp, who was elected president of Goodyear's global support operations in 1996, said the plant was operating brilliantly a short time later, partly because of the technology and partly because of the nonunion, enterprising management style. "Today, it is one of the leading facilities of any tire company in the world. It has been studied and analyzed by the industry on a global basis."[97]

In *The Goodyear Story,* Maurice O'Reilly explained the management philosophy adopted at Lawton.

"Managers were chosen for their proven 'people orientation,' even at the expense of experience or education. The aim was a highly productive workforce built on mutual understanding and consideration of both employee and company needs.

"The program was a success from the start, putting Goodyear among the leaders in enlightened industrial relations. By 1981, when the Lawton plant reached full capacity, turnover of manufacturing employees was less than 1 percent; it dropped to 1/3 of 1 percent by early 1983. The accident incident rate, which was 10.4 percent in 1981, was 2 percent at the start of

1983. In the 1981-83 period, controllable absenteeism declined from 1.5 to 1 percent. With the extension of the program to unionized plants, Goodyear entered a new era of employee-management relations which not only fostered harmonious industrial relations but also was instrumental in attainment of productivity and product quality goals."[98]

If Lawton represented the future, Akron symbolized the past. Between 1978 and 1981 domestic rubber companies closed 19 tire plants, including three by Goodyear.[99] Facilities such as the one in Los Angeles, built nearly six decades earlier, had been rendered obsolete. As a whole, the domestic tire industry was shaky; in 1973 tiremakers shipped 238 million tires but by 1980 the number was down to 180 million.[100] By 1979, Goodyear had laid off 10 percent of its 30,000 domestic workers, coinciding with the 100,000 production workers that the Big Three automakers had placed on indefinite furlough.[101] By June 1980, Ohio's jobless rate would stand at 9.4 percent, second only to Michigan's 14.4 percent.[102]

Goodyear had begun making automobile tires in Akron in 1901. In January 1978, the company announced it would begin a month-long phaseout of production at Plant 2, its oldest remaining manufacturing facility and the last one in Akron.[103] Seven hundred and thirty production and salaried personnel lost their jobs, with 1,100 workers retained to make industrial products and run the rubber reclamation operation. The only tires Goodyear continued to produce in Akron were experimental racing tires. In announcing the decision to close the plant, Pilliod blamed high manufacturing costs and the declining popularity of the bias tire, which accounted for 60 percent of the plant's output.

The smell of rubber was faint in Akron, but Goodyear continued its commitment to the city by converting Plant 2 into a Technical Center, a $125 million investment. The 700,000-square-foot factory became a center for innovation, with offices, laboratories, and test design and engineering facilities capable of producing as many as 1,200 experimental tires per day. A one-mile performance track was constructed less than a mile from the building.[104]

Although Goodyear's sales continued the upward march, topping $8 billion in 1980, the 1970s had been a costly decade for the tire industry.[105] Reeling from the government-mandated recall of 10 million of its Firestone 500 tires, Firestone in 1980 closed five plants, permanently released 20 percent of its workforce, forfeiting its position as the world's number two tire company to Michelin.[106] B.F. Goodrich quit supplying original equipment tires to Detroit, concentrating instead on high-quality performance tires and the replacement market, and investing heavily in chemicals and polyvinyl chloride.[107] Uniroyal was staggering under the weight of low profits and more than $500 million in unfunded pension liabilities; in 1978 it asked employees for wage concessions in order to survive.[108]

Emerging from the seventies much healthier than its Akron competitors, Goodyear nonetheless faced a new decade burdened with the cost of its success, a debt-to-equity ratio of nearly 50 percent.[109] As one industry executive told a *New York Times* reporter in 1981, "I don't know anyone who envies their balance sheet."[110]

The modern Lawton, Oklahoma facility, built in 1977, was an experiment in employee relations.

Photo by Kyle Newton

1902 — Goodyear Straight Sides were entered in a 2,500-mile race in England, which destroyed the tire. The event led to the Quick Detachable Straight Side tire.

1913 — Goodyear enters the Indy 500, with driver Charles Metz taking third place.

1921 — Facing financial difficulties, Goodyear abruptly pulls out of racing.

SPECIAL RACING EDITION

GOODYEAR TIRE NEWS

GOODYEAR TIRES WIN AT INDIANAPOLIS RACES

1911 — The first Indianapolis 500 race is held before 80,000 fans.

1919 — Every major race in the country is won on Goodyear tires, including the Indy 500.

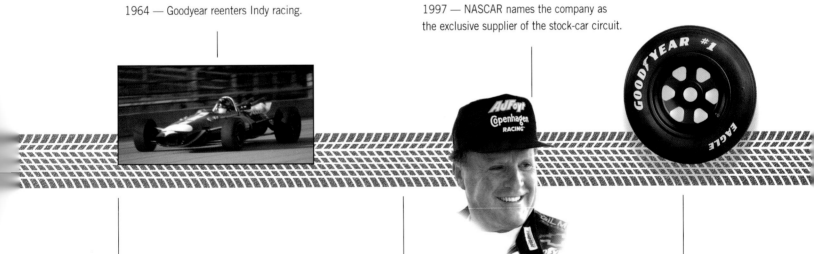

1964 — Goodyear reenters Indy racing.

1997 — NASCAR names the company as the exclusive supplier of the stock-car circuit.

1964 — Using Goodyear tires, Craig Breedlove becomes the first man to top 600 miles an hour (by .601 miles an hour).

1967 — A.J. Foyt becomes the first Goodyear driver to win the Indy 500 since Howdy Wilcox in 1919.

1997 — Goodyear achieves 350th Grand Prix win.

Al Unser, Jr., or "Little Al," prepares to take his Goodyears out of pit row at the Homestead Motorsports Complex in 1997. (Photo by Karine Rodengen.)

CHAPTER FOURTEEN

OFF TO THE RACES

1894–1997

"We would go to Indianapolis on a Goodyear tire test, and basically sit there waiting for one of their test guys to blow an engine or have some type of problem with the car. And we would cross our fingers, hoping that Goodyear would come to you and say, 'Hey, are you guys doing anything? Want to run some tires?' The slogan always has been, 'If you want to go fast, go test for Goodyear. You'll go fast!'"

— Al Unser, Jr.[1]

FROM THE EARLY footraces of the Greek Olympics to the Kentucky Derby to the roaring machines of the Indianapolis 500, men have pitted the skills of their bodies, their animals and later their inventions against one another. The invention of the automobile, with its ability to surpass even the horse's velocity, meant a new variation of the old obsession. From almost the beginning of the company, automobile racing has been a part of Goodyear — and Goodyear a part of racing.

The first organized automobile race took place on July 22, 1894, when more than 100 horseless carriages set off on a 77-mile journey from Paris to Rouen. Although most did not finish and the winner came in at something less than the speed of lightning — a dizzying 11 miles an hour — the race touched off a European craze.[2] The first American race may have occurred that same year, when the only two cars in the state of Ohio met in a field outside Dayton. The two cars set a precedent that continues to this day, as *Tire Wars* author William Neely explained:

"As the two men talked and compared machines, the talk undoubtedly turned to speed. Which motorized buckboard was faster?

"... Insurance records indicate that the meeting in the Ohio pasture was the first damage claim. ... [W]ith but two cars in the entire state of Ohio, they ran into one another. ... Unknowingly, the two men in that Ohio field were setting the stage for a century of automobile competition. They were, in fact, creating the Foyts and the Unsers and the Pettys, who would come along a couple of generations later."[3]

By the time Foyt, Unser and Petty came along, Goodyear had asserted itself as the dominant supplier of racing tires. In so doing, the company tested and demonstrated the quality of its products, while carving its brand name in the loyalties of racing fans.

The first race to feature Goodyear tires occurred in 1901, the same year the first ad for the company's new Straight Side tires appeared in the *Saturday Evening Post*.[4] Attending the International Exposition of the Automobile in New York, Henry Ford ran into Charles Seiberling. Ford, whose young company was

---

The 1966 Blue Streak racing tire, upon which Goodyear built its reputation for being "#1 in Racing."

already gaining a reputation for dependable quality (such as it was at the turn of the century), said he wanted to build a car that stressed speed over reliability, but couldn't find financial backers. Upon returning to Akron, Seiberling penned a letter to Ford striking a deal which could benefit both: "I am willing to throw away the profit of one set of tires in order to get you started and give you a chance to test them."[5]

Racing was a flashy way to attract attention and investors. In July 1901, Ford won the $1,000 prize of the Detroit Driving Club's one-mile race at Grosse Pointe.[6] It was a propitious omen for both Goodyear and Ford.

The early races were primarily testing grounds for both automotive and tire technology. In 1902, Goodyear Straight Sides were entered in a 2,500-mile race in England, attended by Paul Litchfield and a companion who had paid their own fares on a cattle boat to attend the event.[7] Litchfield was appalled with the poor performance of the tires, which disintegrated internally from the pressure of road contact.[8] While watching the race, however, Litchfield was struck with the idea that the tires were not too weak but too strong; a tire facing the ruts and stones in turn-of-the-century roads, particularly at advanced speeds, needed to absorb road shocks rather than resist them. He experimented with changes in air pressure, then with cord fabric, beginning the evolution to the oversized Quick Detachable Straight Side tire, the Tire that Made Goodyear. It marked the first time an automobile race would have a direct impact on the design and development of Goodyear passenger tires.[9]

When a new tire, made with rivet fabric to prevent tread separation, was ready to be tested in 1905, Goodyear persuaded Buick and Reo to use them in a five-day race between

LEO MEHL

Born: April 7, 1936
Retired from Goodyear as General Manager of Racing Worldwide in 1996
Vice President of Indy Motor Speedway
Helped develop tires that won 1967 Indy 500

ONE OF THE most respected men in motorsports isn't a race driver. He doesn't risk his life weekend after weekend, taking impossible curves at speeds that would turn the hair of most mortals white. He's H. Leo Mehl, a chemical engineer whose expertise and leadership in Goodyear's tire technology often kept those drivers from winding up on the wall.

Mehl's career at Goodyear began in 1959 after his graduation from West Virginia University and a three-year stint in the Air Force. He had been involved in Goodyear Racing for almost his entire career. Starting out as a trainee, Mehl moved into racing tire development in 1963. Since then, he served as racing manager in Europe, directing both race tire development and sales for Formula I Grand Prix, among other international series. Mehl was named Director of Racing in 1974, and took over the worldwide program in 1979. Retired from Goodyear since 1996, Mehl has since become vice president and a director of the Indianapolis Motor Speedway.

Foremost among Mehl's considerable accomplishments at Goodyear are the strong bonds he helped forge between Goodyear, the race car drivers and ultimately the fans. Mehl said Goodyear decided early on that it would support the drivers and motorsport first, and let the benefits of the publicity come afterwards. That meant a policy of supplying tires of the same quality to everybody. When Goodyear became dominant in racing, the policy proved to be a wise one, he said.

"The teams and drivers, Al Unser, Mario Andretti, Parnelli [Jones] and so forth — all the key Firestone drivers — were very, very con-

London and Scotland. The cars made strong showings; the Reo entrants endured the entire course without a single puncture.[10]

The Indianapolis 500

By 1913, the company was supplying tires to some of the drivers for the two-year-old Indianapolis 500. In 1909, boasting more than 100 car manufacturers, Indianapolis rivaled Detroit for the title of Motor City, and local businessmen led by Carl Fisher built a racetrack to advance its claim. The length of the race was set at 500 miles because it was as far as the cars could go during daylight hours.[11] Although Goodyear was not involved in the first race, held in 1911 before 80,000 fans, two years later Charles Metz became the first Goodyear driver to finish, taking third place. After a disappointing showing in 1914, a year dominated by

European cars and European tires, Goodyear roared into the sport with a vengeance following World War I.[12] The importance of auto racing as a development tool was widely recognized.

"The Germans had five cars in the French Grand Prix of 1914 at Paris, France, which was run just a few days before the outbreak of the war. It is now known that these cars were entered for the purpose of securing a final test for their engines, which so soon were to play such an important part in their military airplane program. The first three cars in the 500-mile-grind, humbling the best speed creations of other countries, were the German Mercedes entries. It is well known in racing circles that the Liberty motor used in thousands of our American airplanes was a development based largely on the motor in Ralph DePalma's racing car. ... The important relation

cerned because we had been their enemy for so many years. Since 1963, it had been an intense and fierce competition. Now, they're in the position where they've got to come to us for tires. From a long-term standpoint, it didn't make sense to punish these guys. The reason we were racing was to prove that technically we were the best company in the world, and if racing was becoming more commercial, then racing was becoming more useful from a sales standpoint. So we made the policy that we were going to give everybody the same tire. Now, our teams didn't like that. They said, 'You ought to make them pay.' But those guys I mentioned, and many more, became very good friends of Goodyear."[8]

At the time, however, drivers like Mario Andretti thought they had blown their chance with Goodyear. Andretti, interviewed in 1996, said Goodyear wanted to recruit him as a driver, but he elected to stay with Firestone.

"Then I heard that Firestone, which was undergoing some management changes, was going to pull out of racing, and I thought, 'Oh my God, now I'm really in trouble!' It proved to be true, and the only thing I could do was approach Leo Mehl and ask him, 'You know Firestone is out. What are you going to do with me?' He said, 'I'll make you one of our top testers, and I'll bring you in.' They could have played hardball with me and I would have totally understood, but they embraced me as if I had other options. That was a gesture that I think restored a lot of faith in the human element for me."[9]

which automobile racing bears toward the development of motors was keenly realized by the United States Government during the war, when it gave official sanction to wartime racing because of its great aid in developing high speed American motors and also for its value as a relaxation for the public.[13]

The Goodyear Racing Tire Department was created to take advantage of the engineering and advertising benefits of motorsports. In 1984, then-Director of Racing Leo Mehl explained the sport's importance in words that would have rung true 70 years earlier: "We get worthwhile spinoff in any area where tires are subject to high heat conditions, such as airplane tires, and any area where you need to learn about wet-weather traction, again for trucks and aircraft. In addition to that, we have made improvements in the technology we

used for manufacturing the tires, in terms of the machinery, the building equipment. And that sort of advance in technology applies to any sort of tire."[14]

Yet no company led by the fiery Frank Seiberling could be interested merely in product development. Goodyear wanted to win. Although tires were sold — not given — to the drivers, the company made an additional investment in time, sending a tire crew to the track several days before the scheduled race to inspect conditions and determine what the drivers would need. The Goodyear crews obtained the wire wheels and mounted the tires, checked the tubes and casings, and helped man the driver's pit during the race. With their reputation "on the line in the full glare of publicity,"[15] the Goodyear men embraced the spirit of competition:

"In the 150-lap race at Uniontown, Pennsylvania, October 20, 1917, with only a few more laps to go to win the race, Eddie Hearne's

Then and now: Though the speed has somewhat changed, the thrill has always remained the same, whether it was in this 1917 speedster or this 1997 Juan Manuel Fangio II CART car. (CART photo by Karine Rodengen.)

SPECIAL RACING EDITION

GOODYEAR TIRE NEWS

VOL. 8. No. 6. AKRON, OHIO, U. S. A. JUNE, 1919

GOODYEAR TIRES WIN
AT INDIANAPOLIS RACES

Howdy Wilcox's Indy 500 victory was Goodyear's last until A.J. Foyt took the race in 1967.

car threw a tire tread, a common occurrence on the race track. On the next lap Hearne stopped at his pit for a new tire, but the Goodyear man who was managing Hearne's pit that day, instead of getting him a new tire, picked up a hammer and shaking it at him, told him to get back in the race and win it. Hearne obeyed and won easily, completing the race without a stop. He did not know when he stopped at the pit that a Goodyear tire will make from 25 to 75 miles on the race track even after the tread is gone. If Hearne had taken time to make a tire change, he would have lost his lead."[16]

The peak of Goodyear's first racing era came in 1919, when every major race in the country was won on Goodyear tires.[17] The season began in February when Ralph DePalma broke every land-speed record from one to 20 miles on the sand at Daytona Beach; during his fastest race, he achieved a speed of 150 miles per hour.[18] That year, Howdy Wilcox won the celebrated Indy 500 in one of the 27 cars — in a field of 33 — running on Goodyear tires.[19]

Two years later, during the financial crisis which ousted the Seiberling brothers and brought the company temporarily under the control of bankers, Goodyear retired from racing saying it had "nothing left to prove."[20] It had already become the world's largest tire company on the basis of sales, and was well on its way to becoming the world's largest rubber company as well. Using racing as a testing ground, Goodyear had developed cord fabric, the detachable rim, and the balloon principle of low air pressure, and had helped advance the popularity of motorsports in America. It would be the lasting power of this popularity that eventually drew the company into its second motorsports era, and its second period of dominating the sport.

Sex Appeal

As a 1987 Goodyear press packet admitted, "tires don't have much inherent sex appeal."[21] During the prosperous years of the 1950s, a public opinion survey found that Goodyear was popular with middle-aged consumers attracted to quality and stability, but ran a dismal second to Firestone with young, affluent urbanites, demographically the fastest-growing segment of the population.[22] Firestone had inherited the racing crown. This may have been particularly irksome to Goodyear executives for Firestone was located just a few miles away, on the southern end of Akron. In the early years, Frank Seiberling and Harvey Firestone worked opposite sides of the streets trying to attract investors. Each year, Firestone set up elaborate displays celebrating another win on the Indianapolis Speedway. It was too much for Goodyear to take.

In little more than a decade, Goodyear would reenter racing, prove itself a force to be reckoned with, and usurp Firestone as king of the track. Through its affiliations with such glamorous drivers as A.J. Foyt, Lee and Richard Petty, Mickey Thompson, Craig Breedlove and Jackie Stewart, Goodyear added zing to its corporate image and numbers to its net sales. A survey conducted in the mid-eighties revealed that 28 percent of adults believed racing tire experience helped a company make better street tires; 42 percent of those who described themselves as racing fans shared that feeling.[23]

During the 1950s, motorsports caught fire in America. "More than 200,000 fans jammed the Indianapolis Speedway each Memorial Day for the classic and world-famous 500-mile race of races," wrote Maurice O'Reilly. "Attendance at Grand Prix events around the world averaged about 100,000 people per race. Marathon races for sports cars — such as the 24 Hours of Le Mans and the 12 Hours of Sebring — attracted even larger crowds. Drag racing became highly popular in the United States, and television began to cover all big racing events on a regular basis."[24]

Goodyear's reentry officially began in 1958 with a full line of stock car tires, a quiet inroad for the company as well as a necessary one.[25] Stock

car racing had begun on horse tracks in the southeast, according to author Neely:

"What these pioneer drivers lacked in skill, they made up in bravado and plain old nerve. They banged on each other and usually the one who won was the one who banged the hardest. ... The cars were stock in virtually every aspect — headlights, horns, fenders and tires. Many drove their cars to the track, put tape over the headlights to prevent breakage from flying rocks, and they simply lined up and raced for the checkered flag. And then they drove them home and probably to work the next day, providing, of course, there was enough left of them."[26]

Stock Car Racing

As the largest tire manufacturer, Goodyear was already an unofficial supplier of stock car tires, since most drivers simply raced on street tires. Goodyear was the favored choice of many, including drivers who never bothered to show up at a track but whose loudly expressed opinions mattered. Neely wrote of one theory of the origins of stock car racing:

"[It] stemmed from the illegal running of homemade liquor — moonshine — from mountain stills

Stock car racing in the 1950s was often equal parts dirt and speed.

to city customers. Drivers developed tremendous skills in high-speed runs on twisting two-lane blacktop mountain roads, followed by lawmen in hot pursuit. With the skills came the bragging about who could drive the best — and it was back to the country horse racing tracks to prove the point.

"The shine runners — 'wheelmen,' they were called — obviously had the best chance of winning races because they not only had high-speed experience, they had hot cars, usually modified to the hilt. One driver who limited his 'racing' to the highway at night was Otis Walker. He was considered by all who knew anything about moonshine to be the best of the wheelmen. His car was lightning-fast and he, like many of his counterparts, ran on stock Goodyear tires. 'They work the best in tight spots,' he often said."[27]

On Labor Day 1950, stock car racing entered the realm of the legal with the running of the first "Indianapolis of the South," a 500-mile race held at a new track in Darlington, South Carolina, and sponsored by the National Association for Stock Car Auto Racing.[28] Most of the cars still used street tires.

Four years later, Goodyear showed up at Darlington with a newly designed high-speed tire and asked some of the drivers to test them. The tires did well enough for the company to proceed with plans for a new line.[29] Called Blue Streaks, the tires debuted in 1958 and quickly proved their worth, showing up on the winner and seven of the top 10 finishers at the 1959 Darlington race and on the winner and eight of 10 top finishers at Daytona.[30] Lee Petty drove all 500 miles of Daytona on one set of Blue Streaks.[31] Other top drivers such as Richard Petty, Foyt and Gurney were impressed.[32] During the 1962 NASCAR season, "Goodyear led all tire manufacturers in number of victories, percentage of finishers in the top 10, and number of drivers using its tires."[33]

Goodyear threw its support behind stock car racing at a fortuitous time. By 1960, NASCAR had become the world's largest racing group, with some 1,500 officially sanctioned races run before 12 million fans each year, and more than $2 million in prize money awarded.[34] Still on top with

Stock car legend Lee Petty, father of legend Richard Petty, began testing tires for Goodyear in 1957. He won the Grand National (now Winston Cup) championship on Goodyears.

Indy cars, Firestone tried to stomp out Goodyear's fire, and "[w]hat had begun as a stock tire affair in NASCAR ... rapidly evolved into one of the most bitter battles in the annals of motor sports. Both companies were spending literally millions of dollars on tire design and compounding. They came up with new carcass designs, new compounds and new tread patterns. Week after week. And they worked on various combinations of these factors. All in all, there were dozens of types of tires at each tire test."[35]

And each type of tire received a grueling workout, recalled Don "Big Daddy" Garlits, a 17-time World Champion (NHRA, AHRA, IHRA) winner. "It was not unusual for us to make 25 runs at a test session. Hard on the car, but Goodyear would buy the engines. They would buy everything. Rent the tracks, have their own insurance, their own controls. I remember one test where I received nearly $50,000 for doing it because we were there so long."[36]

With so much riding on the tires, there was a certain amount of corporate espionage. Tires mysteriously disappeared from storage garages at both companies. "Fans" at racing events spent the entire day with binoculars sighted on the pits, watching every movement of the tire engineers. Decoy tires were produced and left lying around the garage in spots where they could be easily taken.[37]

Then Goodyear borrowed its own technology. The Double Eagle passenger car tire with Lifeguard Safety Shield — the "tire within a tire" that reduced the impact of blowouts — was a hot-selling product, and engineer Joe Hawkes fine-tuned the principle to work on tires traveling at high speeds.[38] Drivers Richard Petty and Darel Dieringer were hired to test them at Daytona by driving over metal spikes at race speeds:

> *"Petty's right front outer tire blew the first time he hit the sharp object on the back straightaway — at about 170 miles an hour. The car bobbled slightly as it entered Turn Three, but he gathered it skillfully up and came roaring into the pits.*
>
> *'Okay, boys, you've made a believer out of me,' Richard said. 'Let's do it again.'"*[39]

When NASCAR ruled that all tires on the speedways must be equipped with the inner liners, Goodyear passed on its lifesaving technology to Firestone, but Goodyear had already earned a lot of loyal converts. In the quarter-century following its entrance into stock car racing, Goodyear tires appeared on 17 of the 25 NASCAR champions.[40]

Breaking Records

With the almost instant success of its stock car program, Goodyear became involved in highly publicized attempts to set land-speed records during the early 1960s. The first American to attack Englishman John Cobb's one-mile record of 396 miles per hour was a 30-year-old Californian with more dreams than money. In 1959, Mickey Thompson persuaded Pontiac to supply him with four super-horsepower engines and built the *Challenger I* around them; Thompson's idea was to run all four engines simultaneously, one engine for each wheel.[41]

At the time, Dunlop was the leader in land-speed tires, which it built at maximum size for increased force. Thompson wanted a small tire, no larger than 30 inches in diameter, and Goodyear engineers agreed to supply them.[42] On August 30, 1959, at Bonneville Salt Flats, Utah, before a small crowd of family, friends, representatives from his sponsors, and the reporters who would present his attempts to the nation, Thompson set a new American land-speed record of 330.5 miles per hour by smashing the old mark of 266.8.[43] On October 7, he tried again to top Cobb's world record but nearly died when an oxygen tube broke, leaking fumes into his breathing mask. He did set world records at five kilometers, five miles, 10 kilometers and 10 miles.[44] He used the same set of Goodyear tires for every race attempt.[45]

Thompson was nothing if not determined. In a Mexican Road Race in 1954, he crashed to avoid hitting an old woman and, after officials

Mickey Thompson settles into *Challenger I* before his 1959 attempt at breaking the world land-speed record at the Bonneville Salt Flats in Utah.

TOM GREEN bested Mickey Thompson's mark a few months later when his jet-powered *Wingfoot Express* rocketed to 413.2 miles per hour. Eleven days later, Craig Breedlove, in *Spirit of America*, clocked in at 468 miles per hour, and on October 15 he became the first man to drive in excess of 500 mph, averaging 526.28 on the Bonneville Flats course. The record then fell to Art Arfon, standing at 576.553 before Breedlove returned in November 1964. The first man to drive 500 miles per hour became the first to top 600, by just .601 miles per hour.[1]

Every one of these records was accomplished on Goodyear tires.[2]

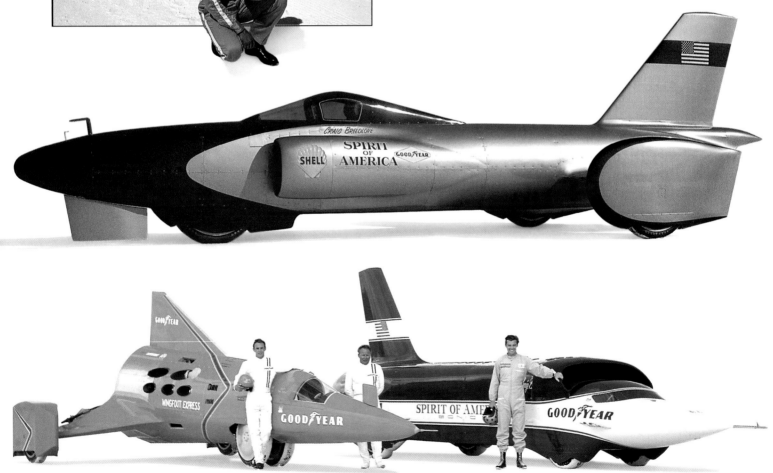

reported him dead, hitchhiked two days into Mexico City to call his wife, who fainted upon hearing his voice. Thompson's father was already on his way to Mexico to claim his son's body, which he discovered battered but fully alive.[46]

Thus, Thompson went back to the salt flats. The one-mile record was calculated by averaging the speeds of two runs which had to be completed within a period of one hour. Thompson used a new set of the treadless bias-belted tires, which Goodyear engineers had tested at more than 500 miles per hour.[47] He felt confident on the basis of his previous attempt, telling reporters:

"Before I started ... I had two major concerns — the engine and the tires. If the engines couldn't supply the power to go 400 miles per hour, or the tires would not hold up at that grueling speed, I was destined to be just another 'also-ran.' Now I know I've got the equip-

ment. The engines delivered more than enough speed and the tires held up beautifully."[48]

On September 6, 1960, Thompson achieved part of his goal by racing the fastest mile ever recorded by a man driving an automobile, 406.6 mph.[49] After stopping the car with a parachute, Thompson was exhilarated. But on the second run, necessary for the record, the car broke a transmission shaft. Although Thompson never set the official mark, Goodyear advertisements emphasized the remarkable posted speed, and three years later, the record came home to the company. In the Goodyear-equipped *Spirit of America*, Craig Breedlove averaged a speed of 407.45 miles per hour.[50]

Although Goodyear seemed to emerge nearly overnight as a leader in auto racing, from inside the pits it seemed an arduous process. Until 1967 the big prize, the

A.J. FOYT

Born: Jan. 16, 1935
First four-time winner of
Indy 500 (1977, 1967, 1964, 1961)
Winner of 1972 Daytona 500
Winner of 24 Hours of Le Mans in 1967.

N A 1997 interview, Anthony Joseph Foyt (universally known as A.J.) pointed to his ankle, wrist, arm and other parts of his body, recounting the various injuries he had suffered during his many years as a race car driver. The first injury occurred when a rambunctious 11-year-old Foyt burned his hands trying to put out the engine fire in his father's midget car, which the boy had taken out (unbeknownst to the elder Foyt) to race around his yard as three of his friends clapped and cheered. As bad as his hands hurt, the yard fared worse from the Ford V-8, as he recounted in his immodestly-titled book, *A.J. My Life As America's Greatest Race Car Driver.*[1] "The whole damn yard was torn up. The swing set was knocked over, and one corner of the house

— the one closest to the shop — was all chopped up. I had gotten a little close to it a few times. Still, it was my best corner. ..."[2]

"The next morning Daddy said very little. In fact, what he said was about the last thing I expected: 'I guess you're going to be a race driver, A.J. Well, you gotta promise me one thing: Always drive good equipment. If you're not gonna drive the best race cars in the best shape, then don't even bother. And, oh yeah, stay the hell out of the yard with the midget.'"[3]

Indy 500, remained out of reach, and Leo Mehl remembered the frustration:

"In terms of years, it went pretty quick but, you know, we didn't win the race until '67, and it seemed at the time like a very, very long time. ...

In 1966, Goodyear tires returned to the Indy Speedway for the first time since 1919, but it took four years of intense work and tire testing before a Goodyear driver took the title. This picture shows tire testing in 1966.

It was advice Foyt took to heart. In spite of all the bone-crunching, engine-blazing accidents, Foyt stayed in the game. He would eventually team up with Goodyear and win Goodyear's first Indy 500 race since 1919. "There had been problems in the early days. Tires chunked under full fuel loads and tires got slippery and there were crashes when tires blew, but Goodyear stayed right there, and they corrected the problems."[4] In 1997, Foyt summed up his years as a Goodyear driver: "Hell, I've been with Goodyear for such a long time, I feel like a part of Goodyear."[5]

That was a tough four years. We learned a lot. We won a lot of races but ... in '64 the tire we took to Indianapolis was too hard. In '65 it was too soft. In '66, all the cars crashed. Foyt, Gurney, everybody crashed. ... Every year seemed like 100 years at the time, because the pressure was tremendous internally."[51]

Mehl said Goodyear's executives were also impatient for the big win, and had set the Indy championship as a corporate goal. A total team effort evolved between the corporation, the racing department and the drivers.

"We were calling headquarters from Indianapolis at the end of the day saying we needed to change this or that, and everybody would work all night. We would get our tires around 3 p.m. the next day, flown down by a plane, to run them in practice. Management kept asking us, 'What's the problem? Do you need more people? Do you need more money? More equipment? What is it?'"[52]

The year 1964 marked the first time in more than four decades that Goodyear tires were shipped to the Indy track, although none were

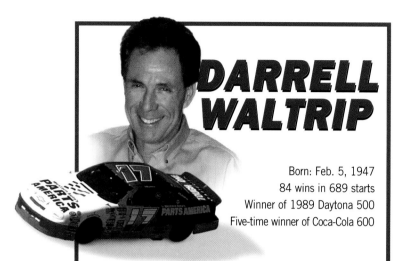

DARRELL WALTRIP

Born: Feb. 5, 1947
84 wins in 689 starts
Winner of 1989 Daytona 500
Five-time winner of Coca-Cola 600

D ARRELL WALTRIP'S relationship with Goodyear began in the early seventies when he was racing Bush Grand National cars in the Southeast, using M & H Racemaster and Firestone tires. Bobby Allison was racing with Goodyear T-16s. "Every week he beat me. I asked why, and was told he simply had better tires." Waltrip spoke with Leo Mehl, who supplied him with T-16s. Waltrip has been with Goodyear ever since — except during the fierce but brief Hoosier-Goodyear Tire War. The war began in 1988 and 1989. After five-year hiatus, Hoosier returned in 1994. By the end of the racing season, Goodyear was the unmistakable winner. Waltrip briefly switched from Goodyear to Hoosier, a decision he clearly regretted in a 1997 interview: "There's a story behind that, which I can't get into. But I didn't do it all on my own."[6] His relationship with Leo Mehl and Goodyear continued, however, and Waltrip soon returned to the Goodyear family.

"I ran on those other tires in maybe six or seven races. I realized I was going to get killed unless I got out of that deal. In racing, you start out with relationships that turn into friendships, and Leo and I had left the door open. I had told him that I hoped he understood why I was doing this, and 'if this doesn't work out I don't want to be out on a limb with the saw running.' The next year I went back to Goodyear and to Leo. I just love the man."[7]

used in the qualification rounds. The next year, Goodyear tires were installed on 12 of the 33 qualifiers, but the top Goodyear-shod finishers were eighth and ninth.[53] The following year, a Goodyear car finished fourth.

In 1967, A.J. Foyt became the first Goodyear driver since Howdy Wilcox in 1919 to win the Indy 500.[54] Foyt had traditionally raced on Firestone tires. However, there came a day when Firestone wouldn't give Foyt the same specialty tires they gave to driver Smokey Yunick. In his wonderfully anecdotal book, *A.J. My Life As America's Greatest Race Car Driver*, Foyt described how his relationship with Goodyear began:

"The thing that really did it was when they gave Smokey Yunick a special tire, because the roadster he built was lighter, they said. Mine was just as light, and they wouldn't give me the special tires. I didn't believe them. I felt it was because Smokey's cars were big in NASCAR and Firestone was battling like hell with Goodyear down there in the Southern stock-car circuit, so they were just playing favorites. Goodyear had just gotten started in racing and they had a pretty good stock-car tire, so they were starting to bother Firestone, who had reigned since year one.

"Well, I figured if they wanted to screw around with tradition, then I could, too. There wasn't anything in the rules that said you had to run on Firestone tires; it was just expected.

"I called Goodyear.

"Goodyear brought a supply of their Stock Car Special tires. They were wider than Firestone's, and lower. And slower. It would have made me feel real good if they had come down there and just blown everybody away with the wide tires, but they had been developed for a 3,800-pound stock car and for the high banks of the NASCAR tracks. Indy was a whole other ball game. ...

"I felt personally responsible for bringing Goodyear to the Speedway, and then they came down there and didn't do so well, so I made up my mind right there and then that if they would make arrangements to rent the Indy track after that year's 500, I would come and test the tires. I not only had the experience; I now had a cause. And having a cause is something that has always made things happen for me."[55]

The pit crew knows exactly where to position themselves when a driver comes into the pit. Here, Dale Jarrett gets split-second service at the 1997 Daytona 500. (Photo by Karine Rodengen.)

A similar story was told by Benny Parsons, who was inducted into the 1994 Motorsports Hall of Fame with 21 Winston Cup victories. In 1968, Parsons was running a race in Daytona on another tire. After losing two rear tires in the same race, someone finally told him to talk to Goodyear.

"Those tires just came apart. I got home and everyone was telling me that I should talk to the Goodyear people. I wrestled with that because I really didn't know them. I had no connection with them. I called anyway and said that I needed to develop some sort of relationship, and I needed to know what tires to run on different racetracks. They welcomed me with open arms. The month of February 1968 was the only time I ever ran on anything besides Goodyear."[56]

Other branches of motorsports likewise became enamored with Goodyear for its tires and its commitment to safety. In 1969, Dave Marcis began racing in NASCAR, the same year he switched from Firestone to Goodyear tires. "I'm a pretty big believer in Goodyear because they always worked hard to make sure we had a safe tire; they never brought in a tire that wasn't safe just to beat the competition," Marcis said in a 1997 interview.

"The most recent example that stands out is the Hoosier/Goodyear tire war. Both brought their tires to Charlotte, and neither one was a safe tire. Leo [Mehl] withdrew the Goodyear tire and pretty much let the other company have it. I went to Leo and said, 'Hey, I need a tire to run here in Charlotte.' He says, 'I really don't have anything to bring you other than the Daytona tires because NASCAR requires that if you bring it for one, you need to bring enough to service the field if others decide to go to it.' So I said, that's fine, I'll run on the Daytona tire. He was concerned, and asked if I thought I could get qualified using that tire. I told him I was willing to try because I wasn't going to run on the other one."

"Well, Leo brought in the Daytonas, and I did qualify. Meanwhile, the other tires were blowing out every 46 laps, and putting people up in the walls, wrecking cars. I was running, on average,

Starting in 1997, NASCAR agreed to use Goodyear tires exclusively for three years. (Photo by Kyle Newton.)

67 laps in Charlotte before I was having to make a pit stop. We were running in eighth position at the time, and the race was going to be mine because everyone else was making so many pit stops until one of the other cars wrecked me up into the wall. But before the day was over, others went to putting Goodyears on."[57]

Mehl's development team had learned enough to end Firestone's domination.

By 1975, Goodyear tires were the only brand in the race. In 1974, Firestone announced it was pulling out of Formula 1, and USAC racing, two years after it pulled out of NASCAR. For the ensuing 21 years, Goodyear had Indy to itself.[58] In 1995, Bridgestone/Firestone reentered IndyCar competition with strong showings at Indianapolis in 1995 and wins in four of the first five races in 1996.[59] But Goodyear's dominance has proven difficult to crack; an *Akron Beacon*

Journal report described the look at the Indianapolis track in 1996:

"A Goodyear 'No. 1 in Racing' sign hangs over the track's main exit. Goodyear occupies the prime suite overlooking the pits near the starting line. Its garage is attached to the main pit building.
"Firestone, on the other hand, doesn't have a suite. Its makeshift offices at the track have been planted near the back of the garage area and consist of tents hooked onto the back of a truck rig."[60]

In NASCAR racing, Goodyear's leadership was cemented with the 1997 pact that named the company as the exclusive supplier of the stock-car circuit. The three-year agreement blocks Bridgestone/Firestone from supplying tires. But with plans to enter Formula 1 racing in 1997. Bridgestone/Firestone is intent on erasing Goodyear's claim of being "Number 1 in tires," but the latter company has benefitted from the past 20 years of unchallenged leadership and continuous technological advances.[61]

After Richie Ginther won the 1965 Mexican Grand Prix on Goodyear tires, the company took a string of world championships, starting in 1966 with Jack Brabham, and in 1967 with Denny Hulme in a Brabham car, designed specifically to use Goodyear tires. By the mid-1980s, Goodyear had the monopoly in international Formula 1 competition, reaching a worldwide audience in excess of 500 million people.[62]

In 1983, all racing tire engineering and manufacturing was consolidated in the new $125 million World Technical Center, located in the renovated Plant 2 near company headquarters in Akron.[63] The year Goodyear entered racing for the second time, company sales stood at just under $1.5 billion. In 1995, the figure exceeded $13 billion.[64] While the entire measure of growth cannot be attributed to one area, Goodyear's affair with

Sir Jack Brabham in 1966, the year he won his second Formula 1 championship, which he accomplished on Goodyear tires.

auto racing has built a positive corporate image and kept it in the public eye.

The relationships between Goodyear, race drivers and ultimately the public have been built on mutual trust. As the drivers become legends, the tires upon which they build their reputations also become legends. In this way, Goodyear anchored itself in Formula 1 racing through its relationship with Sir Jack Brabham, whose name had been virtually synonymous with Grand Prix motor racing for years. In 1967, Brabham was knighted by the Queen of England for his services to motorsports. Australian-born Brabham, a triple world champion, has been the only

DON "THE SNAKE" PRUDHOMME

Born: April 6, 1941
Won seven U.S. Nationals titles
Total career victories at Springnationals,
Southern and California Nationals: 46

DON PRUDHOMME began testing Goodyear tires in the late 1960s. Echoing the sentiment of many race drivers, Prudhomme said he appreciated the way Goodyear kept a level playing field by supplying the same tire to every race driver. "They never had a tire for one competitor that was better than the other,"[10] he said in a 1997 interview.

Just as important, having Goodyear on your team often meant more than just having someone change your tires, he recalled. Prudhomme said he remembers when his engine "went away" (or "blew up," depending on your dialect) during the 1969 U.S. Nationals.

"I blew the engine going into the finals, and in those days we didn't have fancy rig trailers. Then it started to pour down rain. We went to the Goodyear tent where their employees were. They came out and helped me change my motor. Got all muddy doing it, but I wound up winning the race."[11]

Formula 1 driver to win a world title in a car of his own construction. Derek Bell, who himself won a slew of awards during his 31 years in racing, recalled how he was introduced to Goodyear tires through Brabham's car. "When I started to move upward [in Formula racing], I saw that Brabham's racing team always ran on Goodyears. If you used a Brabham-developed car, you were better off putting Goodyear tires on it because the car had been developed around that tire."[65] Bell added that he never forgot how Goodyear "supported Formula 1 for all these years when all the other manufacturers would come and go."[66]

In a 1997 interview, Brabham said he always enjoyed testing tires for Goodyear, because "they were always able to come up with something new. They always had several compounds to go and try, a fantastic amount of effort put in there by the company to make sure we had the best we could possibly have."[67]

Of course, there is an element of risk for the company, as there is for the drivers, for failures loom large and sometimes tragic. The "melancholy statistics" of Formula 1 competition, for instance, show that in the mid-eighties "the average driver will have an accident every two to three races; once every 11 races he will have a major accident involving physical injury. Of all the drivers who have won grands prix in the last 30 years, fewer than half are still alive."[68]

Jeff Gordon, the youngest Winston Cup Series champion in NASCAR history, said testing tires is particularly tough because both the endurance of the tires and the driver are tested. "You never get out of the car," he said.[69] Extensive testing has led to more than a few hairy moments, remembered Bobby Rahal, winner of the 1986 Indy 500. Rahal recalled that in 1984 he was testing radials at the Indy track when the right rear tire blew out "just as I was going into a turn. Boy, did I hit the wall," he said, laughing.

Above: The Modern F1, or Formula 1 logo.

Below: Formula 1 racing at Monza, Italy, in 1992. As in NASCAR, Goodyear tires have continued to dominate the motorsport.

"Fortunately, it was not to any detriment to my own person, but the Goodyear people were pretty upset."[70] Mario Andretti also remembered how the radial tire tests were different from anything he'd done before. "The nature of the beast is different. The setup of the car was totally different. You don't follow the heat pattern when you take the temperature of the tire like you usually do. You have to read the tire visibly, even more so than temperature-wise."[71]

Robert Dyson, winner of the 24 Hours of Daytona in 1997, recalled how his car weaved back and forth while testing a new kind of radial in 1985. "We were the first to start with a very low profile, and a real soft, pliant sidewall. In point of fact, it didn't work. It was too pliant. Down a straightaway, the car tended to wander, swaying back and forth."[72]

Regardless of the risks, drivers look forward to testing, particularly with Goodyear, said Al Unser, Jr., a two-time Indy 500 winner. Sometimes drivers would go to a test when they weren't even involved.

"We would go to Indianapolis on a Goodyear tire test, and basically sit there waiting for one of their test guys to blow an engine or have some type of problem with the car. And we would cross our fingers, hoping that Goodyear would come to you and say, 'Hey, are you guys doing anything? Want to run some tires?' The slogan always has been, 'If you want to go fast, go test for Goodyear. You'll go fast!'"[73]

Jeff Gordon and Rick Mears both commented that testing tires often gives a racing team an edge on several levels. Mears, a four-time Indy 500 champion, said testing was an important part of his learning curve when he first got into racing. "Roger Penske [when Mears was part of Team Penske] knew I needed lap time, and he was able to work me into the test pro-

gram. That was a big plus for me in my learning. And I came to enjoy the engineering aspect."[74] Gordon agreed:

"It's great experience for the team and driver to help develop a tire. You hope that the way you develop a tire is the way that the tire is gonna be built, and maybe it will be built around the type of driving style you have. Plus you get more track experience and track time without it actually counting against you as one of your tests with NASCAR."[75]

But just as importantly, new and better racing tires are sometimes adapted for use on the road, explained Stuart Grant, who was appointed general manager of Racing Worldwide for Goodyear in March 1996. Grant arrived at Goodyear in 1972, helped develop the "slick" tire used in stock car racing, and worked on the test tires that broke the 200-mile-hour barrier at the Indianapolis Motor Speedway.

"Now, where that's headed is hard to imagine, isn't it? But we try to be on the leading edge of mold shape development, material breakthroughs, specialty polymers, construction materials, that type of thing. That's really a lot of our role in terms of advancement of

Above: Stu Grant was named general manager of Racing Worldwide for Goodyear in 1996.

Left: Formula 1 tires, designed to run in the rain.

Above: Testing tires is important to drivers like Bobby Rahal, pictured here at the 1997 CART season opener. (Photo by Karine Rodengen.)

Below: An illustration of an Eagle GSC. Racing links Goodyear's tires to the drama and celebrity of motorsports.

technology. Some of the features that are incorporated in the truck tires and aircraft tires that make them attain their goals are proven on the race track because of the heat and durability you see in a stock car. Maybe there are some great materials we can learn about in a stock car race and apply them to an aircraft tire because of the loads and speeds. Obviously, you have the high performance tie-in because of what we learn about cornering and tread wear and things that apply to our Eagle high performance tires."[76]

Those advances could be seen in 1994, when Goodyear introduced the Eagle F1 High Performance tire, the latest in a line of high performance Eagles introduced since 1980 as a complement to the prestigious Eagle passenger tires.[77] According to Leo Mehl, Goodyear changed the name of its racing tires from Blue Streaks to Eagles to "create a conduit through which the consumer can better associate our motorsports activities with our street activities."[78] Jim Barnett, who retired from Goodyear as vice president of Original Equipment Sales, said a lot of people wanted to call the performance tires "Wingfoot." But Goodyear already had a tire called the Wingfoot GT. The Eagle name didn't have a tremendous amount of support, he added.

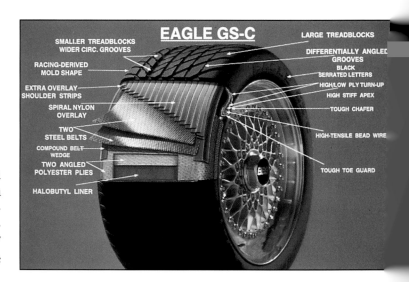

"I had a big meeting with about 20 people, and I said, 'We're gonna select a name this afternoon, and there are gonna be people who leave here with some bruised feelings, but hey, we're gonna lock step, we're gonna select a name, and then we're gonna spend our energy and time marketing it. So after the meeting is over, and we said, 'Eagle,' some people muttered, 'Augh.'"[79]

Barnett said he then spoke privately with Leo Mehl. " I said, 'Leo, there's one more thing. I want you to rename Goodyear's race tire Eagle. Who the hell knows a blue streak?' I said."[80]

In spite of the risks, reported *Newsweek*, racing has become "a natural expression of our modern preoccupations with speed, with sophisticated machinery, with competition for its own sake, with national rivalries, risk, money, glamour, and technical progress."[81] It is "a sport of dreams and fantasies. We know we can't run a four-minute mile or leap 10 meters into the air, but we can dream that we are at the wheel of a car going flat out."[82]

Goodyear has poured millions of dollars into furthering that dream, and into making it a safer reality for those behind the wheel. The payoff comes in victories both on and off the track. As one Ohioan who insisted his new Chevrolet Beretta come equipped with Goodyear Eagles said, "It's only natural to want to emulate your heroes — and that includes their tires . ... I was raised knowing Goodyear was a winner. I want their tires on my car."[83]

The link forged between Goodyear and winning race drivers is one consumers admire, especially if they know that their tires withstood the test of the track.

1982 — Robert Mercer becomes chairman and CEO after Chuck Pilliod steps down.

1986 — Sir James Goldsmith attempts hostile takeover of Goodyear and "loses," walking away with $94 million for his efforts.

1990 — Suffering from myriad ills, Goodyear posts its first loss since 1932, losing its number one position worldwide to Michelin.

1983 — Goodyear's directors unanimously approved the acquisition of Celeron Corporation, an oil and gas company.

1989 — Tom Barrett succeeds Mercer as chairman and CEO.

SECTION ❧ SEVEN

1991 — Tom Barrett steps down after modernizing and streamlining Goodyear's facilities.

1996 — Gault retires, Samir Gibara steps in as chairman and CEO with a mission to make Goodyear number one in the world again.

991 — Stan Gault comes in as chairman nd CEO, re-energizing Goodyear and stimuting a remarkable turnaround.

1992 — The Aquatred's revolutionary design makes it a hit with consumers and critics.

1997 — Goodyear settles with striking workers, leading the industry with a six-year pact that will carry it into the 21st Century.

Chairman Robert Mercer speaking at the victory rally. Mercer organized an executive SWAT team to fight off the takeover attempt.

CHAPTER FIFTEEN

YOU CAN'T SHOOT A BLIMP AND GET AWAY WITH IT

1980–1984

"Goodyear is under siege and our communities and citizens are caught in the crossfire. A major part of Goodyear's stock is now in the hands of a raider and the arbitrageurs or speculators who follow such activity with all the ethics and morals of a shark."

— *Washington Post, 1986*[1]

IN 1980, GOODYEAR STOOD as the lone domestic tire company to post a profit from the previous year's figures: sales swelled more than $100 million to reach a record level of $8.44 billion, and profits exceeded $230 million.[3] In 1981, the company claimed another industry first when it posted sales of $9.15 billion.[4] After spending considerable resources on new plants, Goodyear was able to pay down its debt during the first two years of the 1980s, from 47.8 percent of total debt and equity in 1979 down to 33.1 percent in 1982.[5]

Goodyear emerged from the seventies a leaner, more efficient company. Outdated plants in Los Angeles and Scotland had been closed, along with the Lee tire factory in Conshohocken, Pennsylvania. Plants in Louisiana and Mount Pleasant, West Virginia, were sold, as was Geneva Wheel, a producer of small wheels and axles for industrial equipment.[6] Managers were asked again and again to "squeeze every inch of fat" they could find. Expense budgets were scrutinized and questioned. "Efficiency and austerity were key words throughout the worldwide organization."[7]

Advertising was one area in which expenses were not cut. Goodyear remained the industry's biggest advertiser, with slogans such as "Out Front and Pulling Away" and "Out Front World-Wide." The popular "Put the Blimp Behind You" campaign combined a message of quality and reliability with humor, picturing motorists — a honeymooning couple, a young family and a group of nuns — who glance back to find a friendly blimp following their cars.[8] The company received a global public relations boost in July 1981, when the *Europa* assisted in the three-day television coverage of Lady Diana Spencer's wedding to Prince Charles. The British Parliament gave permission for *Europa*'s night sign to flash "Loyal Greetings" over London on the wedding night.[9]

Altering the Functioning Silo Concept

Another changing of the guard took place in 1981. Robert E. Mercer, who had been elected president in 1978, took over as chief operating officer and vice chairman when John Gerstenmaier retired.[10] Mercer had been with Goodyear since 1947, having served as president and CEO of the Kelly-Springfield division from 1973 until 1976, when he was elected vice president of tire marketing.

The Goodyear faithful comprised workers, ex-workers, their families of all generations, and the local media.

This blue and gold Goodyear flag was raised over the Lawton factory, the first to be dubbed a "World Class Competitor" for its competitiveness in productivity, quality, uniformity, product cost and value.

In 1981, four key executive vice presidencies were established in order to "strengthen the corporation's organizational structure in accordance with the growing complexity and requirements of our business at home and abroad," as Chuck Pilliod stated.[11] Filling the posts were Tom Barrett, corporate manufacturing and related services; J. Robert Hicks, finance and planning; Jacques R. Sardas, North American operations; and Ib Thomsen (also GIC president), international operations.[12] The realignment heightened the role of the corporate president, to whom the presidents of North American Operations and GIC would now report. Previously, they had reported directly to the chairman. The change was made to provide a better balance between multinational operations.[13]

During the transition from one decade to the next, Goodyear changed not only the faces with-

in management but its entire organizational structure. The industry shakeup caused by the radial tire, stiffer international competition and national strikes prompted managers to reexamine the way they did business, questioning old styles of management-worker relations and the relationships between divisions. With the success of the Lawton plant — and later the Gadsden factory, which implemented the Lawton plan — Goodyear believed it had hit on a new model of corporate efficiency. The company began the switch from a "functional silo" structure, long the standard for rubber companies and American industry in general, to a total systems approach, which eliminated barriers between divisions and departments and emphasized teamwork.[14]

Called the "silo" because employees focused attention on a single aspect of the organization rather than the corporation as a whole, the old system had been top-heavy, with six or more layers of management and little cooperation between separate functions. In fact, the vertical structure hindered communication by giving departments differentiated goals or quotas that tended to continue the status quo rather than provide a means for departments to work together in developing long-term solutions to problems.

With the help of Harvard's Richard E. Walton, Goodyear developed a horizontal structure built around the production business center, a nucleus for an integrated approach to quality control, problem-solving, and maintenance. Within each factory, several production centers were formed along departmental lines and operated on a "buyer-seller concept," with individual plants "creating and owning their own implementation processes."[15] Because individual workers were made responsible for the total quality output, they were encouraged to learn managerial skills, offer suggestions, and investigate relationships between jobs and departments. Employees were responsible to both the production center and their departments and were evaluated by their functional manager and by the production business center manager. Symbolic of the team approach, the production business center was physically located in the middle of the factory area it served, and members worked near each other to foster communication.

Dennis Dick, vice president and general manager of the Chemical Division, said the change has meant that more work was accomplished by fewer people.

"I can work my group as a team because I can coordinate my marketing, my sales and my research and development much better. We've improved our balance sheet that way and improved our service to our customers. ... A lot of the staff organizations are gone because when you have those individual functions, you have to have an organization to bridge across them or work between them. We just don't get into turf issues over boundaries."[16]

Brainstorming Sessions

The emphasis on long-range planning reflected by the total quality system was paralleled in Goodyear's executive ranks. Despite the increasing threat of foreign competition in 1980, Goodyear, Firestone and Goodrich still controlled 75 percent of the domestic tire market. Ten years later, three companies would control three-quarters of the market, but Goodyear was the only one of the original Big Three — and the only United States company — still in the contest. Its survival depended heavily on a commitment to long-range planning made in the early 1980s.[17]

Goodyear's forecasting had traditionally been conducted along a 12-month business cycle, but in 1982 a New Products Development Group was formed to encourage innovative products that would retain the company's industry leadership into the 1990s.[18] A subgroup of New Products was told to concentrate on what competitors would be doing in the coming years. "Using a technique pioneered in the 1970s by Royal Dutch Shell, Goodyear marketers, engineers, and others held meetings to come up with various scenarios of the tire industry's future. Wild ideas were encouraged rather than ridiculed, and several of the presentations evolved into business strategies."[19] The

forecasters were split into two teams, with one tracking Bridgestone and one following Michelin. They delivered presentations on their findings as if they were actual employees making reports to their bosses. The Michelin team even found a Goodyear staffer with a French accent to present its findings.[20]

The group agreed that within five years, struggling Firestone would merge with a foreign company, giving the buyer a huge chunk of the United States market and strengthening Firestone's ability to compete. With sharp foresight, the group picked Bridgestone as the most likely buyer and decided the best response would be to open a technical center in Asia to compete with the Japanese corporation directly.[21] In 1983, Goodyear bought land in Japan, but the shakeup of the following few years held off the development of the center for nearly a decade. Still, when the forecasted Firestone-Bridgestone merger became fact in 1988, Goodyear was poised to respond. Three years later, the company opened a new-product and testing facility in Tokyo, smoothing the way for Goodyear to get its tires on the cars of Japanese companies such as Toyota and Nissan.[22]

Another prediction made in the early eighties was that the 1990s customer would want an innovative, all-season, high-performance tire, and Goodyear designers got to work. A decade later the Aquatred was introduced, selling 2 million units in its first year.[23]

Bob Mercer, as president of Goodyear (left) and Chairman Chuck Pilliod in 1983.

On December 31, 1982, Chuck Pilliod relinquished his position as chairman to Robert Mercer, who was then succeeded as president by Tom Barrett.[24] Mercer took over at a time when the American auto industry was threatened by increasing consumer acceptance of Japanese imports. While Pilliod's task as chairman had been to "firm up the base business — tires, industrial products and aerospace — before considering moving into new fields," Mercer sought to decrease Goodyear's reliance on tire sales. He promoted Dennis Rich, GIC's European finance director, to director of corporate business strategy and analysis, and told him to locate and secure the best routes for diversification.[25]

Meanwhile, Goodyear's top tire during this period was the Tiempo, an all-season, low-profile elliptical tire which had debuted in 1978, and

the all-season Arriva, first advertised during the 1980 Winter Olympics at Lake Placid, New York.[26] The 23 minutes of commercial time devoted to the Arriva during the Olympics reached an estimated 60 million households.[27] Chuck Pilliod recalled that he and a few other executives came up with the all-season concept during a brainstorming session one day.

"We were sitting around a table talking about coming up with a low-cost, high-quality tire to compete with Japanese imports. Why not make it an all-season tire so people could get away from having to put winter tires on every year and storing the others in the garage? That was one of the best introductions we had."[28]

Celeron Corporation

On February 8, 1983, Goodyear's directors unanimously approved the acquisition of Celeron Corporation, an oil and gas company based in Lafayette, Louisiana.[29] As a wholly owned subsidiary and Goodyear's single largest non-tire venture, Celeron would continue its onshore explorations and production in 14 states. With Celeron, Goodyear became the 35th largest company in the United States, and Mercer believed it could lead in four major areas: tires, general products, aerospace, and technology and energy.[30] Eventually, Mercer hoped Celeron could provide 25 percent of Goodyear's income and relieve its heavy reliance on the auto industry.[31] During the next few years, Goodyear pumped $1 billion into building Celeron's crude

Above: The Tiempo radial, shown above during a rain test, and the Arriva All-Season radials, left, were Goodyear's top selling tires.

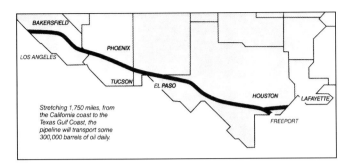

Stretching 1,750 miles, from the California coast to the Texas Gulf Coast, the pipeline will transport some 300,000 barrels of oil daily.

oil pipeline from Texas to California.[32] In 1982, Celeron earned $65 million in profit on revenues of $942.8 million, but by 1986 an oil glut would weaken the value of the pipeline.[33] For the first nine months of that year, despite an increase in sales, Goodyear's net income fell 27 percent, burdened by a $110.8 million after-tax write-down for gas and oil reserves.[34] Furthermore, to purchase $822 million of Celeron stock, Goodyear had issued common stock, a move that diluted its earnings.[35] "It was a real anchor on us at that stage," noted George Hargreaves, who took over the pipeline as president and CEO in 1991 and has since retired. "It was dragging down the corporation by about $2 a share."[36]

The company began to tighten its belt in a number of areas, but particularly in the field of research and development. In the past, Goodyear scientists and engineers had experimented freely, even if they did not have a specific goal or application in mind. This allowed for a wide range of discoveries, many of which Goodyear was able to license. In 1964, for example, Dr. Nissim Calderon stumbled upon olefin metathesis, a chemical reaction important in a diverse array of industries ranging from plastic to perfumes.[37] The reaction would find use in more than 300 patented applications in the petroleum, rubber and chemical industries, but Goodyear was not a particularly big user of the process. In 1986, chemists were instructed to focus on discoveries that would lead to new

Above: An illustration of the proposed path for the All-America pipeline, which Goodyear obtained through its acquisition of Celeron.

Below: An example of Goodyear's diversification plan, the pipeline was meant to decrease the company's reliance on the erratic automobile industry.

and better core products. The task of realigning the department fell to Calderon.

"When I became vice president of research, I was called into Tom Barrett's office. He said, 'Nissim, I'm going to ask you to do something that is going to be painful, but I think you can do it. I want you to reorient the whole research organization into core business.' When I took over the research organization we were doing bioengineering. We thought we would get into biotechnology,

doing research into non-tire related things such as foams and urethanes. He said we would have to find a way to redo everything."[38]

On September 13, 1986, Goodyear Aerospace returned to its own beginnings. After 50 years of being closed to the public, the doors of the giant Airdock were opened for the kickoff campaign of the United Way, and an energized crowd of more than 300,000 people celebrated a promising future inside one of the city's historical landmarks.[39] In attendance were representatives of the U.S. Navy, which was deciding on a $193 million contract that

Right: The airship *America* urges support for the United Way during the kickoff event.

Below: Chairman Mercer admitted to feeling emotional when the 12-ton doors of the Airdock opened to let in crowds for the kickoff of the United Way ceremonies.

could put 600 people back to work inside the Airdock building blimps.[40] The order eventually went to a British company, but on this clear September day, the *Akron Beacon Journal* commented: "The sun seemed to be shining on Akron as it had few times in recent history."[41]

Little did the newspaper — or Goodyear itself — know that within six days the sun would soon cloud over when a man named James Goldsmith bought 66,000 shares of Goodyear stock.[42] Goodyear — and Akron — were about to get a lesson in the economics of the 1980s.

Above: Attendees of the planned "Save Goodyear" turned the rally into a victory celebration when it was announced that Goldsmith was giving up his hostile takeover attempt.

The Corporate Raider

In the Oliver Stone movie *Wall Street*, Michael Douglas immortalized the atmosphere of high finance during the mid-eighties with his pronouncement that "Greed is good." Between March 1985 and December 1987, there were 105 hostile takeover battles in the United States involving at least $100 million each — a rate of nearly one per week.[43]

On October 7, 1986, Goodyear stock zoomed to a 15-year high.[44] None of the optimists who had filled the Airdock on that September day yet knew that around the same time, Sir James Goldsmith, a British-French financier who had amassed an estimated $1 billion, had met with two representatives of Merrill Lynch to discuss becoming partners in a hostile takeover attempt.[45] The three men had decided on a target: Goodyear, an 88-year old company with 133,000 employees in 28 countries and, in the estimation of Goldsmith, a complacent attitude toward its shareholders. Merrill Lynch was "so determined to make its reputation in the takeover market that they were prepared to participate in the deal by investing more than  $1.9 billion of their own resources," wrote Geoffrey Wansell in the magazine *Business Month.*[46] Goldsmith would finance the rest with $2.6 billion in bank credit and $230 million of his own and other investors' monies.[47] To avoid detection, Goldsmith gathered shares slowly, limiting his individual purchases to small blocks and letting arbitrageurs — speculators who gobble up rising stock amid takeover rumors — send the price higher.

By early October, Wall Street knew something was up; on September 25, one Merrill Lynch broker had sold 1.7 million shares to another Merrill Lynch broker who claimed he was representing Goodyear. When Goodyear stock liaison Mark Blitstein was told, he contacted CFO Oren Shaffer. The alarm was sounded.

On October 17, Goodyear stock became the most active on Wall Street. Bob Mercer called an emergency meeting in his office on Mahogany Row, the fifth-floor suite of executive offices at Goodyear headquarters.[48] The company also hired the high-powered investment firms Goldman, Sachs, & Company, and Drexel,

Retiring Congressman John Seiberling, grandson of Frank Seiberling, thanks supporters for their help in foiling Goldsmith's plans.

Burnham, Lambert, whose representative was Martin Siegel, a specialist in mergers and acquisitions.[49] Siegel brought in Joe Flom, a New York attorney known as an influential "takeover artist."[50] Mercer established a "war room" on the seventh floor and assembled an executive SWAT team with one purpose: determine the raider's identity. By October 24 — when 4.1 million shares

traded at a 15-year high of $44 per share — the team had identified Goldsmith.[51]

With such deep ties to a single industry and its representative company, Akron residents would have bridled at any outside attempt to control Goodyear. But the biography of this particular outsider supplied the city, the company and the media with the details needed to demonize the raider and transform a financial battle into an ideological struggle between perceived good and evil. Born with a silver spoon in his mouth big enough to irk the gritty Akron work ethic, Goldsmith had built his fortune by buying companies, splitting them into pieces, and selling off the parts without regard to the negative impact on communities or workers. At age seven, he is said to have informed his parents that he didn't need to learn to read and write, since one day he would be rich enough to hire people to read and write for him.[52] At 16, he quit school and supported himself by gambling.

Married three times and the father of six, he flaunted his affairs, living openly in one country with his wife and in another with a mistress; he had once vacationed with both families simultaneously, ensconcing them on different ends of the island of Sardinia and boating between.[53] In a 1997 interview, Mercer remembered his reaction when he heard that Goldsmith felt Goodyear was overdiversified. "Here's a guy that's got a wife and two mistresses, and he's accusing me of overdiversification. You know, the world has gone crazy."[54]

Already incredibly wealthy, Goldsmith had dismantled his own grocery empire and used the capital to buy and sell American companies. To dodge taxes, he spread his conglomerate from the Cayman Islands to Liechtenstein. One of the attorneys of the firm representing him in the Goodyear deal had served as director of administration of Richard Nixon's scandalous 1972 reelection campaign.

To top it off, Goldsmith was rumored to suffer a superstitious fear of the very product he was seeking to control: rubber. Geoffrey Wansell, a London journalist who wrote a biography of Goldsmith, told a *Beacon Journal* reporter that Goldsmith wouldn't allow pencils with rubber erasers into his office.[55] These tidbits were disseminated by the local media, both amusing and enraging Akronites.

The rumored takeover sent company stock soaring. When it topped $45 per share, many Akronites, including Goodyear employees, were unable to resist selling. That is, until details of Goldsmith's background surfaced, at which time community members clung to their shares with whitened knuckles. Goldsmith "found himself the subject of the most sustained and personal attack he had ever encountered in the United States."[56]

Women wearing sandwich boards urging Akronites to buy and hold Goodyear stock strode the streets of Akron. A high school class in nearby Cuyahoga Falls planned a stock-buying drive and drew unflattering cartoons of Goldsmith. Radio stations WKDD and WSLR cooperated with the University of Akron in a petition campaign to alert state and national elected officials. Yellow signs began popping up in the rear windows of automobiles all over the area — modeled after the popular "Baby on Board" signs, these read, "Sir James in Trunk." After the *Beacon Journal* reported Goldsmith's alleged fear of rubber and published his home address, Akronites sent him rubber bands by the thousands.[57]

Meanwhile, Bob Mercer's SWAT team informed him of the company's three options: Buy back Goldsmith's stock at an exorbitant "greenmail" price; push the stock price too high for him by quickly selling off subsidiaries, trimming operations and taking on debt; or find a "white knight" who would take over the company but do it in a less hostile fashion.[58] To Mercer, none of the options were very palatable. This "new and not very pretty world," as Mercer called it, was not entirely new to him.[59] In 1984, he had watched two competitors stave off raids. B.F. Goodrich had paid Carl Icahn $7 million in greenmail profits, and Uniroyal had liquidated because of another of Icahn's threats.[60]

On October 27, Mercer traveled to New York to meet Goldsmith face to face. The contrast between the two men was tremendous. After 40 years with Goodyear and 39 with one wife, Mercer practically had apple pie on his breath. Only the sixth chairman in Goodyear's 88-year history, Mercer was a Yale-educated father of five, and

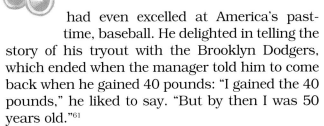

had even excelled at America's pasttime, baseball. He delighted in telling the story of his tryout with the Brooklyn Dodgers, which ended when the manager told him to come back when he gained 40 pounds: "I gained the 40 pounds," he liked to say. "But by then I was 50 years old."[61]

Arriving at Goldsmith's townhouse, Mercer entered the lavish surroundings, filled with statues and paintings of gorgeous, nude women. At the top of the staircase stood Sir James. Over lunch, the two men began to discuss the future of the company. When offered a glass of wine, Mercer demurred by saying he never drank before noon.

"Would you like water?" asked Goldsmith, and Mercer said yes. "Fizzy or otherwise?"

"Otherwise," Mercer said.[62]

During the ensuing discussion, Mercer grew angry at what he perceived to be Goldsmith's lack of industry knowledge. Goldsmith reiterated his

Above: Exposing his ignorance, Goldsmith chided Goodyear for its involvement in "areas where it knew nothing," notably the area of aerospace, unaware that Goodyear had been in the industry since 1911.

opinion that Goodyear was wasting reserves by becoming involved in areas it knew nothing about. When Mercer asked for an example, Goldsmith pointed to the Aerospace segment.

"My God," Mercer said, "We've been in aerospace since 1911!"

Goldsmith looked surprised. "You have?"[63]

Mercer said Goldsmith had staged the whole meeting with a fabulous lunch (of which he ate very little). Goldsmith sat so that Mercer faced a large painting of a nude woman. Mercer said the thought flew through his mind to say, "Gee, your mother's attractive."

"This guy was not going to catch me looking at that picture. He said he hoped we could remain friends, adding: 'I have a job for you on the board.' I said, 'Jimmy, I already have a job on the board. That's not an offer. I am concerned about my company and its employees.' He said, 'You've got to quit running that place as an institution and start running it as a business.' ... I told him that it was an institution, one that made more money in the rubber business than any other company. 'We're very paternalistic, that's why our employees love working there. It's not my job to see how many employees we can get rid of.'"[64]

The next day, Goldsmith filed with the Securities and Exchange Commission, announcing his intention to buy Goodyear and sell off all non-tire divisions. The SEC report showed Goldsmith to be the owner of 12.5 million shares, or nearly 11.5 percent of the company.[65]

Akron Mobilizes for War

Goldsmith was viewed as an evil outsider, but Merrill Lynch was seen as a traitor. On November 12, the Akron Police Department pulled more than $270,000 in insurance money from Merrill Lynch.[66] Other clients also withdrew funds, including $70,000 in union money for the UAW Local 856.[67] John Hagerman, president of Ohio Machine & Mold, a small supplier to Goodyear, sent a letter to Merrill Lynch president Daniel Tully, stating, "Your total lack of sensitivity to the company, their employees, and the many communities in this county is appalling. Your shameless greed leaves me with no alternative but to withdraw all of my funds from Merrill Lynch." Hagerman articulated the prevailing sentiment in the community when he told a local reporter that Merrill Lynch was hiding behind a "banner that says, 'We believe in a free enterprise system.' Well, I don't buy that. I think there's some moral ethics that should prevail."[68]

The next meeting between Goldsmith and Mercer, attended by attorneys for both sides and other representatives, differed from the first. It was held at the small Goodyear apartment near the United Nations, and Mercer served Diet Coke.[69] Goldsmith said he was prepared to make a tender offer of $49 per share for the 88.5 percent of Goodyear stock he didn't own, but when Mercer warned he would have a "fight on his hands," the financier agreed to wait two weeks to allow Goodyear to pursue a restructuring plan.[70]

Suddenly the company's fate turned on its ability to boost its stock price above the $49 mark, which it planned to do by "repurchasing as many as 20 million of its common shares, or 18.4 percent of the 106.8 million shares outstanding, and by selling as many as three major units."[71] Celeron and Motor Wheel were put on the auction block. On November 6, thousands of Goodyear Aerospace workers gathered again in the Airdock. This time they listened to an emotional GAC president, Robert Clark, tell them they were up for sale.

Akron mayor and Congressman-elect Tom Sawyer, an ardent Goodyear booster, helped rouse opposition to the hostile takeover attempt.

Above: Mercer thanking individuals who helped resist the raid before speaking to the crowd at the victory rally.

Below: An offshore Celeron drilling platform, searching for oil under the sea.

By mid-November, Goodyear lobbyists had three anti-takeover proposals before the Ohio legislature and Sir James became a victim of bad timing.[72] Akron Mayor Tom Sawyer had recently been elected to replace a retiring Congressman, but until January, the Akron district was still led by Representative John Seiberling, who had spent 17 years as a corporate lawyer for Goodyear and a good part of his childhood listening to his grandfather Frank Seiberling talk about the company's early days.

During the two-week period granted by Goldsmith, the news of Ivan Boesky's insider trading scandal broke, inflaming public and political contempt for corporate raiders. The indignant Ohio legislature agreed to review a total of five anti-takeover bills.[73] Mayor and Congressman-elect Sawyer regaled the press about the harm done by hostile takeovers. Saying a takeover would benefit only Goldsmith and a group of short-term investors, Sawyer told the *Washington Post*,

"Goodyear is under siege and our communities and citizens are caught in the crossfire. A major part of Goodyear's stock is now in the hands of a raider and the arbitrageurs or speculators who follow such activity with all the ethics and morals of a shark."[74]

Persuading fellow committee members to return from vacation, John Seiberling scheduled a special meeting of the House Subcommittee on Monopolies and Commercial Law for November 18.[75] Busloads of Goodyear workers and retirees wearing blue company caps drove to Washington to watch Mercer and Goldsmith square off in testimony. The proceedings were televised by C-Span.[76] In Akron and in plants across the country, workers huddled around radios to listen.[77]

Testifying first, Goldsmith evoked the revered Paul Litchfield, repeating his directive that the job of Goodyear was to build "better tires, cheaper and sell them harder." A company's commitment is to its shareholders, he said, and Goodyear executives had let them down. Goodyear had lost sight of its mission and strayed into areas where it didn't belong. He wanted to pull it back in line.[78]

Later, Congressman John Seiberling admitted to reporters that he could feel his blood pressure rising.[79] Sixty-one years and six months earlier, financiers had wrested control of his grandfather's company during a time of financial crisis. Seiberling recounted his feelings in the *Beacon Journal* :

"I was brought up knowing that investment bankers were evil men because of the Dillon, Read episode in which they squeezed [Frank Seiberling] out of Goodyear and took over control of the company. I was brought up on a tradition to have a low opinion of Wall Street and bankers, investment bankers. So, while I don't still have the generic view that they're all bad, I think it goes back to my early roots. The feeling of antagonism to bankers trying to take control of busi-

Losing Goodyear Aerospace was perhaps one of the most painful outcomes of the Goldsmith raid. GAC had become involved in the space shuttle program, building flexible quarters for the shuttle crew.

nesses is a very deep-seated feeling — not only in my personal life but in many, many people."[80]

After Goldsmith finished speaking, Seiberling took the floor. "I have just one question," he said. "Who the hell are you?"[81]

Akron cheered.

At a private lunch that day at Washington's famous Hay-Adams Hotel, Goldsmith told Mercer that because of political and public relations pressure, he was planning to make his tender offer immediately. When Mercer asked if he could be bought out, Goldsmith said his mind was open, and they agreed to consult their advisors and discuss the matter further the next day. Goldsmith was unavailable that evening. As chairman of a banquet marking the 10th anniversary of the Ethics and Public Policy Center, a conservative think tank, he was having dinner with President Reagan.[82]

At 2 a.m. on Thursday, November 20, a deal was reached. Goodyear acquired all of the shares held by Goldsmith's General Oriental (Bermuda I) Limited Partnership and General Oriental (Delaware I) Limited Partnership at $49.50 per

share — although the stock had dropped to $42.50 — and the selling parties agreed not to acquire Goodyear stock for five years.[83] The company also announced a tender offer for 40 million shares at $50 per, cash authorized.[84]

The restructuring program would require wide-ranging expense-reduction measures, the implementation of an early retirement program, and the selling of Motor Wheel, Celeron and Aerospace.[85] In a letter dated November 21 and sent to individual GAC employees, Mercer wrote, "While we at Goodyear will miss you greatly, and I personally find it very difficult to see corporate life ahead without Goodyear Aerospace, all of us take great comfort in knowing you will still remain as both friend and neighbor."[86]

The Aftermath

The legacy of the Goodyear battle, and similar ones involving such companies as Gillette, Boeing and Greyhound, was a lingering public belief that "it seemed clearly wrong that long-established local companies could be taken over, broken up, or forced to lay off employees, because of little-understood, far-off financial manipulations."[87] During the takeover craze of the eighties, "the rest of America compared the news of lavish spending on Wall Street with often more dismal news nearby — local plants closed, workers laid off, wage cuts for union employees, and farmers and miners out of work. Skilled men and women lost their jobs, and often had to settle for low-paying work or face the upheaval of moving in search of employment. States lost tax revenues and corporate support for civic activities."[88] After several states passed anti-takeover laws, the Supreme Court ruled in April 1987 that states could set up corporate statutes to make takeovers more difficult.[89]

During one of their meetings, Mercer had warned Goldsmith, "You can't shoot down a blimp and get away with it."[90] Although he didn't get the blimp, Goldsmith did walk away with a profit of $94 million for the abandoned takeover. The loser won; the winner lost. At a victory rally on November 22,

Tom Barrett took over Goodyear when it was still reeling from the raid.

Mercer sounded less than triumphant, using words like "painful" and "walking wounded." He acknowledged that there would be further personnel cuts. The following week, Goodyear announced that at least 680 jobs would be lost in Akron.[91] In a 1997 interview, Mercer acknowledged that the whole mess was a "lose-lose situation," because not even Goldsmith got what he wanted: to sell off 40 percent of the company. "We ran him off, but sold off 19 percent of the company to do it."[92]

Jim Boyazis, vice president and secretary, an assistant to Pilliod prior to the takeover attempt, worked closely with every chairman since Russell DeYoung and has been in a good position to observe how Goodyear changed over the years. He said the aborted raid "completely changed everything in this company."[93] The divestiture of Goodyear Aerospace was particularly painful. "The people at Aerospace who were my friends were devastated. As much as they were family, they were going on the block. ... We were committed to sell the non-tire assets."[94]

As distressful as these moves were, the episode helped prepare Goodyear for the future. The company learned how to balance its commitment to its workers with the harsh realities of an increasingly global market, explained Richard Adante, vice president of materials management.

"Much has been written and said about the things that occurred subsequent to the Goldsmith takeover attempt. As bad as some of those things were, I saw a change in the direction of the company, in the culture and in the people. And, quite frankly, it was a positive change. It woke up a lot of people to the things we had taken for granted, which we no longer could take for granted, such as our competitive position in the world. As a result, Goodyear had become a much more focused company, more driven and more responsive to the marketplace."[95]

But before Goodyear could focus on the future, it had to deal with the present, one that left the company hurt and in debt.

In keeping with Goodyear's retirement policy, Mercer, 65, retired as chairman in March 1989, giving way to Tom Barrett, who took over as CEO in January of the same year.[96] Born in Topeka, Kansas, Barrett had joined the company in 1953, after graduating from Kansas State University and serving a few years in the military. He started out as a chemical engineer in the Topeka facility, spent many years in Europe, and became president of the company in 1982.

In the final months of his chairmanship, Mercer campaigned against what he called "terrorists in three-piece suits."[97] Just days after Goldsmith had agreed to walk away, Mercer mused that maybe Goodyear could restructure by raiding someone else. "That's how dumb this thing is,'" he said. "And we can do it. But that's not our culture. That's not the way we operate. That's not what we're in business for. People think the bottom line is everything. Well, I wish that were so. But we've got some social consciousness that is involved around here. If that's taking away from the shareholder, then we've been taking it away from the shareholder for 88 years."[98]

Chairman Samir Gibara (left) and former chairman Stan Gault. Gault revitalized Goodyear, and Gibara is positioning it for the 21st century.

CHAPTER SIXTEEN

A GLOBAL TURNAROUND

1987–1997

*"I was convinced that [Goodyear was] capable of a far greater perfor-
mance. If I didn't believe that, do you think that at 65 and a half years
of age I would stick my neck in that noose?"*

— Stanley Gault, 1996[1]

I N A GLOBAL CORPORATION, the effects
of a raid reverberate literally around the
world. In 1987, Aerospace — including
the giant Airdock — was sold to Loral for
$588 million. The Rome base for the
Europa was sold and the airship,
launched in celebration of Goodyear's
75th anniversary, was retired. Motor
Wheel was purchased by its management. Plants in New Toronto, Canada and
Windsor, Vermont, as well as the Kelly-
Springfield factory in Cumberland, Maryland,
were closed.[2] The Arizona holdings, including
Goodyear Farms, Litchfield Park and the five-star
resort, the Wigwam, a favored meeting and golfing
place for Goodyear executives, went to SunCor
Development Corporation. In Akron, 700 salaried
and hourly staff positions were cut.[3]

Ironically, Goldsmith left his mark on
Goodyear in much the way he had intended, for
the company was once again dependent on tires
for 74 percent of its sales revenues. Major business operations were divided into two business
units: Tires and General Products.[4] Goldsmith
also left the company with a bill of $3.6 billion,
indebtedness at 66 percent of capital, and deep
psychological scars.[5]

Although saddled with debt, Goodyear continued to move forward, reorganizing itself and embark-
ing on new overseas ventures. The company split its
aviation products business from Aerospace and

established a new department for aircraft tires
and brake overhaul units, producing cus-
tomized tires for the Navy's A-12 attack
bomber and the McDonnell-Douglas MD-
11 jet. In 1989, this new department
developed the first asymmetrical aircraft
tire tread for the Air Force's F-15 fighter.[6]

That same year, Goodyear was permitted to reveal what had been a closely
guarded secret for almost a decade: it had
manufactured the tires for America's
famous Stealth fighter, the F-117. Only four
people in Goodyear had known what the tires were
for, including Joe Gingo, currently vice president of
the Asia region. Gingo was on special assignment
to Goodyear Aerospace from 1986 to 1987.
"Technically, it was not that much of a challenge to
build the tire because the F-117 is not that heavy of
a plane. It isn't exceptionally fast either."[7]

Partnering with Pacific Dunlop Ltd. in 1987,
Goodyear formed South Pacific Tyre Ltd., with
manufacturing and retailing operations in
Australia, New Zealand, and Papua, New Guinea.

The company also announced plans to
build a new headquarters and tire-testing
facility for Kelly-Springfield in Cumberland,

Popular Science awarded the Aquatred its "Best of What's New"
medal in 1992.

The *Stars and Stripes,* based out of Pompano Beach, Florida, flying over the Napanee plant, Ontario, Canada.

Maryland.[8] Having come a long way from the bitter patent squabble between Edwin Kelly and Frank Seiberling in the 1890s, the Kelly-Springfield division, the largest private brand tire producer in the country, celebrated a century of tire manufacturing in 1995.[9] Purchased by Goodyear in 1935, the subsidiary has continued to supply low-cost private and custom brands to such retailers as Wal-Mart and Sears, noted Kelly president and CEO Lee N. Fiedler. Over the years, Kelly-Springfield has dominated the growing private label market, supplying an average of 22 different brands at any given time.

"We're the leader not only in volume, but we are consistently ranked number one or two in every category. Where Goodyear may be looking to make a tire that makes a certain 1996 Cadillac ride smoother, we're looking to see that a guy can

affordably buy a low-cost, all-around good tire for an eight-year-old Cadillac to give him the traction and the mileage that he's looking for."[10]

In 1988, ground was broken for a state-of-the-art tire plant at Napanee, Ontario, Canada; phase two of a $132 million, 12,000-tires-per-day high expansion began at the Lawton plant; and the Industrial Products division celebrated its 75th anniversary by dedicating a $4.1 million joint venture V-belt plant and a $10 million expansion project in Taiwan.[11] The company also christened its new blimp *The Spirit of Akron* in tribute to the city that had given so much support to Goodyear during the Goldsmith raid.[12]

Falling from Number One

Tire sales continued at a healthy rate. As the dust settled, Goodyear remained the world's leader, with approximately 23 percent of the free world market. Michelin stood second at 13 percent and Bridgestone at 10 percent.[13] But, as *Forbes* noted, 1990 was "the year of the blowout for Goodyear Tire & Rubber Company."[14] Battered by price wars, a labor strike in Turkey, and a slumping Latin American economy, Goodyear's profits plummeted. Having earned just $27.9 million on sales of $5.6 billion in the first half of 1990, the company lost $14 million from operations in the third quarter and made just $14.7 million in the fourth.[15] In the midst of suffering its first annual loss since 1932, Goodyear lost its position as the world's largest tire company, held since 1926, when Michelin acquired Uniroyal-Goodrich.[16] With number three Bridgestone's acquisition of Firestone, Goodyear faced the prospect of slipping to third in world standings, and its market value slumped to only one-third of its late-1989 level.[17] Stock prices stood at a humbling $13 per share.[18]

Running at only 30 percent of capacity, the $1.6 billion California-to-Texas oil pipeline was an albatross. Responsible for losses of $2 per share, it was a demoralizing reminder of the company's failed diversification strategy.[19] The worst news of all was the $1 million per day the company was paying in interest on the debt it had accumulated to stave off Goldsmith.[20] "The takeover and the pipeline put a tremendous burden on us," said Tom Barrett, who was chairman and CEO at the time.[21] Wall Street analysts classified the Goodyear dividend, which had not been reduced in half a century, as "vulnerable."[22]

"All of a sudden you had three players," said Barrett. "Bridgestone, Michelin and Goodyear had 60 percent of the world market." The other companies had advantages that Goodyear did not share, he added. "Michelin could borrow money from its government at very low interest rates. And, of course, all the Japanese cared about was establishing market share. They came to the United States to establish market share, even if they had to lose money to do it."[23]

But crippled with debt and forbidden by domestic antitrust regulators to acquire other companies, Goodyear was unable to match the ambitious expansion plans of its competitors. In October 1990, the company announced another series of cost cuts, trimmed the workforce by an additional 3,000 people, limited capital spending to depreciation levels, and closed three plants,

including the 65-year-old New Bedford facility.[24] By 1991, the company was saving an estimated $250 million annually through consolidated operations, streamlined management structure, and reduced payroll.[25]

Barrett had made good progress modernizing facilities — the company spent $4 billion during the 1980s updating plants and equipment.[26] Although total employment was reduced from 133,000 in 1986 to 114,000 in 1988 and less than 100,000 in 1991, output per man hour climbed 51 percent in the same period.[27] "While all this was going on, we continued to upgrade our facilities," Barrett said in a 1997 interview. "Goodyear is the low-cost manufacturer. The technology from our R & D groups gave us the ability to develop products faster, and bring them to market quicker than our competition."[28]

Goodyear uses its diverse interests to recruit the company's future leaders and workers.

Stanley C. Gault

It wasn't enough. In June 1991, the company had lost money during three of the previous four quarters, and long-term debt had swelled from $250 million to $3.3 billion.[29] Goodyear needed a financial savior, and the board found one in its own backyard. On June 5, Tom Barrett resigned as chairman and CEO, and the board of directors chose the first chairman to come from outside company ranks since 1921. A member of the Goodyear board for two years, Stanley C. Gault had grown up in nearby Wooster, Ohio. In 1920, his father had helped found the Wooster Rubber Company, serving as the company's CEO before selling his interest in 1926. The company later became Rubbermaid, the company that Gault would transform from a little-known maker of dustpans to one of America's most admired companies.

Following service in the Army Air Corps, Gault graduated from the College of Wooster in 1948 and

joined General Electric the same year. He would remain with the company 31 years, rising to the rank of senior vice president. Over the years, he served as vice president and general manager of the Refrigerator Division, vice president and group executive of the Major Appliance Business Group, and senior vice president and sector executive of the Industrial Products and Components Sector.

In 1978, Gault was invited to serve on Rubbermaid's board. "You have to be careful what board you go on," he later noted with a chuckle. "You might end up running the company."[30] That happened to him at both Rubbermaid and Goodyear. From 1980 to 1991, Gault served as chairman and chief executive officer of Rubbermaid. During his tenure, the company topped the *Fortune* survey of America's most-admired companies several times. It was also the smallest company in the survey's top ten, and the only company to rank in the top ten every year the survey was conducted.[31]

By the time Goodyear came calling, Gault had already built a reputation as "one of the key industrialists of the 20th century."[32] In 1988, he had been one of six managers highlighted by *Business Week* as "The Best of Managers," and a 1989 *Industry Week* survey named him one of the nation's best CEOs. In 1990, he had been honored as Rubber Industry Executive of the Year.[33]

However, when Goodyear came calling, Gault turned down the offer three times. He had been retired from Rubbermaid for all of five weeks.

Gault's decision to come out of retirement was largely an emotional one — 43 years earlier, he had turned down a position on the Goodyear Squadron in favor of working for General Electric, where he felt he had more opportunity for advancement. As a GE salesman, he had visited Goodyear often.[34] In a 1994 interview, Gault revealed the deep feelings he had toward Goodyear.

"Goodyear has been very important for me because we are the last major American-owned tire company. And if Goodyear wasn't to make it,

Stanley Gault had already built his reputation as a "key industrialist" of the century when he was tapped to lead Goodyear back to glory.

it would mean that the tire industry in America would have been owned by companies outside of the United States. What a devastating condition that would represent. What a disgraceful, humiliating circumstance that would be. To have the great tire industry, which was founded in this country, all gone. That isn't wise socially, militarily, or economically."[35]

The $125 million Akron-based Technical Center, built in 1983, keeps Goodyear at the forefront of tire technology on both the racetrack and the road.

At age 65 and with no experience in the tire industry, Gault was a surprising choice to head Goodyear. Although he'd enjoyed great success in his 11 years heading Rubbermaid, Goodyear was 10 times that company's size. As *Financial World* pointed out when it named Gault its 1992 CEO of the Year, "everyone knew ... one of America's most celebrated managers was making the mistake of his career [by going to Goodyear]. ... The man who had transformed Rubbermaid during the 1980s from a sleepy spatula-maker into a $1.5 billion-in-sales consumer products powerhouse would destroy his reputation by presiding over the inevitable death of the ailing tire maker."[36]

Gault, though, recognized the company's strengths and its resilience. Propelling Goodyear back to the top of the industry would be his greatest challenge.

"The afternoon I came [to Goodyear] I said words to the effect that I know, by my own personal experience over the years, that Goodyear obviously has the best name in the industry. It has outstanding employees. It has a strong dealer organization and offers products of high quality. I was convinced that the company was capable of a far greater performance. If I didn't believe that, do you think that at 65 and a half years of age I would stick my neck in that noose?"[37]

The challenges were indeed formidable, Gault recalled. "At that point, we had a debt that had reached $3.7 billion, with high interest. We were paying more than a million dollars a day, and the company literally could not survive that. We were on the verge of violating our financial covenants made with the lenders — a very polite way for saying we were bordering on bankruptcy."[38]

In the nine short months between Goodyear's predicted demise and Gault's reign as CEO of the Year, the company's earnings soared from around 20 cents per share to $1.65 in the last quarter of 1991.[39] The stock price zoomed to $63 in March 1992.[40]

Gault's legacy at Goodyear was to turn a tire manufacturer into a marketing company. "All Goodyear people should be sales-oriented," he told the *Cleveland Plain Dealer* in late 1991.[41]

As chairman, Gault's longtime friend Tom Barrett had done well in streamlining the company's operations and improving production. The company's research and development teams were on the verge of introducing important new products, and Gault was able to capitalize on these improvements. However, Gault provided a much-needed change in spirit, noted an article in *Financial World.*

"Within months of Gault's hiring, the pall that had hung over Goodyear during his predeces-

sor's two-year tenure had lifted. Tom Barrett was a shy man whose sharp, technical mind helped engineer some new products that are now selling well. But Barrett lacked the charisma to jump-start the stalled industrial giant. Gault has charisma to burn."[42]

On his second full day as chairman and CEO, Gault had already called for a complete review of the company's costs, summoned senior executives for a battery of sunrise-to-sundown meetings, and started looking at what remaining non-tire assets might be sold.[43]

With characteristic style, he replaced the company limousines with family sedans and sold three of its five corporate jets.[44] He removed more than 25 light bulbs from the wall sconces and chandeliers in his office suite, for an estimated annual savings of $230. He brought bags of his own coffee filters into the office and paid for postage stamps for personal mail. He even made do with one secretary rather than two.[45]

To reflect an atmosphere of teamwork, he replaced the term "employee" with "Goodyear associate" and enlisted associates in cost-cutting measures. Press releases and memos were typed on both sides of sheets of paper, and more light bulbs were removed from the halls and offices at headquarters. He told vice presidents and janitors alike to call him Stan.[46]

To raise capital quickly, Gault embarked on a stock-selling campaign in late September 1991. He visited 13 cities around the world in as many days, making 39 presentations to major potential investors. The success of the venture reflected the financial community's enormous faith in Gault. He had planned to offer 10 million shares at $43 per share, but despite Goodyear's shaky position, sold 12 million shares at $50 each, with the proceeds going straight to debt reduction.[47] In the last half of 1991, Goodyear reduced its debt by more than $1 billion.[48]

Jim Boyazis, vice president and secretary, said he doubts whether anyone other than Gault could

have inspired so much faith. "When he said that Goodyear stock was going to be up to $50 a share by the end of the year, people believed him. ... He was another perfect guy when we needed one."[49]

The Aquatred: Getting a Firm Grip

Fond of saying he wanted to put the "Go" back in Goodyear, Gault accelerated the timetable for the release of new products that had been developed under Barrett's tenure. Three months after he took the helm, he oversaw the launch of four new products simultaneously. On September 30, he stood on the deck of the aircraft carrier USS *Intrepid*, moored at a Manhattan pier, to unveil the four tires before a flurry of flashbulbs: the Invicta GFE, a "green" tire promising 4 percent fuel savings; an all-purpose Wrangler for pickups and vans; a new line

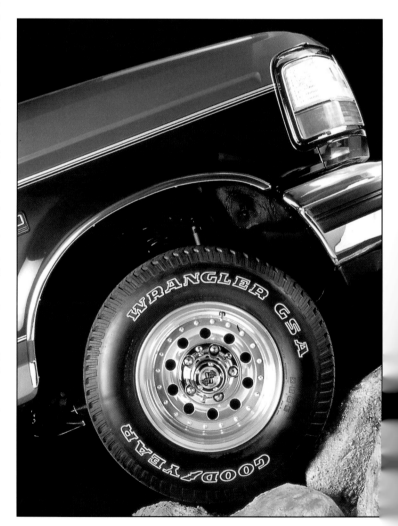

The Wrangler family of truck tires gave Goodyear much-needed success, at a time when the company was struggling financially.

Above: Goodyear's turnaround is often attributed to Stan Gault's flair for marketing. The hugely successful Aquatred, for example, was unveiled aboard the carrier USS *Intrepid*.

Right: The tread design isn't pretty, but its importance is unquestioned. The tread was adapted from the tire to the shoe sole, giving a firmer footing to athletes, walkers, boaters and even road crews.

tire division, said, "Around here we called it the baby's butt, and you don't want to put an ugly tire on the market."[52]

Beginning with a blitz of ads during the 1992 Winter Olympics, Goodyear marketed the Aquatred's safety advantages in television commercials depicting harrowing skids, and the tire became the company's most successful product of the nineties.[53] In the next two years, the tire sold more than 2 million units and won more than a dozen major awards, including Japan's prestigious "Good Product Design Award."[54]

Gault said the Aquatred and its descendants helped build momentum and esprit de corps in Goodyear because no one outside the organization thought it would sell. But "we put the muscle behind it, and that led us into the development of a whole family of them."[55] Gault said few men write letters expressing their delight in a tire's handling — and women never do. But people credited the tire for saving their lives when they skidded on slick pavement. Letters praising the Aquatred rained upon Goodyear.

of Eagle for the high-performance market; and the crowning glory, the all-season Aquatred, so named for the center indentation that channeled water from the sides of the tire, increasing traction 10 to 20 percent on wet roads and thereby reducing the risk of hydroplaning.[50] The Aquatred had languished in Goodyear labs for nearly a decade because it was thought to be too ugly and expensive to capture consumer confidence.[51] As John Fiedler, executive vice president of the North American

Turning the Company Around

In 1991, Hoyt M. Wells became president and chief operating officer. Wells was a longtime Goodyearite who had joined the company in 1951 shortly after graduating from the University of Nebraska with a master's degree in mechanical engineering. He started out as an engineer in the company's Lincoln, Nebraska, power transmission product plant and steadily moved up the company's ranks. In 1972, he was named vice president of general products for Goodyear Canada, Inc., in Toronto; in 1980 he became a corporate vice president; and in 1987 he was elected executive vice president and named president of General Products.

With Gault as CEO and chairman and Hoyt Wells as COO and president, Goodyear's fortunes quickly improved. In 1991, Goodyear reversed its downward slide, showing profits of $96 million on $10.9 billion in sales. By 1994, sales climbed to a record $12.3 billion, earnings to $567 million.[56]

The two men cut the company's debt by more than half and trimmed costs by more than $350 million per year, in the process raising operating margins from 6 percent of sales before Gault's arrival to 10 percent in 1994.[57]

The combination of Gault and Wells was the right mix at the right time, noted Robert Hehir, who retired as environmental health and safety vice president in 1996. "Gault stimulated the workforce. But he was fortunate to have Hoyt as his president. There wasn't anything that Hoyt couldn't do; he was a financial person, a chemist, mechanical engineer and a better tire person than anyone else. This was the most outstanding and complete manager/leader combination I've ever worked for."[58]

In 1993, earnings increased approximately 25 percent to a record $3.25 a share before accounting charges, on sales of $11.6 billion.[59] "If you'd bought 100 shares of Goodyear stock for $1,350 (split-adjusted) when Gault took charge," *Forbes* reported in February 1994, "You'd have close to $4,800 worth today."[60] In a 1996 interview, Wells modestly commented that "it was just a matter of discipline and getting organized."[61]

Hoyt Wells was named president and Chief Operating Officer in 1991. The combination of Wells and Gault was considered the right mix at the right time. In 1994, Wells was named vice chairman. He retired in 1995.

Sales in Latin America, which had been hurting the company, likewise turned around. Mike Roney, president and director of Goodyear Brazil, said production had mushroomed from just 12,000 tires a day in 1983 to more than 30,000 a day by 1997, making the subsidiary the second largest in the Goodyear family.[62] John Polhemus, in charge of Brazil from 1991 to 1995, when he returned to the United States to become vice president of Latin America, said Brazil has always been important to Goodyear; most of the executives in the International Division had worked in the country at one time or another. He noted that Latin America in general "has probably one of the finest distribution networks in the world. We have predominantly exclusive dealers, loyal family businesses that have been with us for years and years."[63]

In the United States, Gault's most controversial act as chairman came in 1992 when Goodyear antagonized dealers by selling tires through new distribution channels — its brand name tires were carried by Sears, and the Kelly-Springfield line went into Wal-Mart, Kmart and Discount Tire, a Scottsdale, Arizona, retailer known for low prices.[64] As Gault explained, his reluctance to alienate dealers was offset by the need to be a player in the burgeoning discount market. "Sears alone was replacing 1.8 million Goodyear tires a year."[65]

"The option of selling through Sears had been discussed for years. But when we determined that nearly two million worn-out Goodyear tires were *being replaced annually at Sears Auto Centers with another brand of tire, there was no question about the action we should take. As a result of these moves, the number of Goodyear and Kelly tire selling locations has increased by more than 3,100 — or 35 percent — since 1991."*[66]

Gault stepped down as CEO on January 1, 1996. Six months later, on June 30, 1996, Gault retired as chairman with his reputation enhanced.

In 1995, Goodyear added Penske to its distribution chain when Penske took over 860 Kmart service outlets and decided to deal exclusively in Goodyear tires.

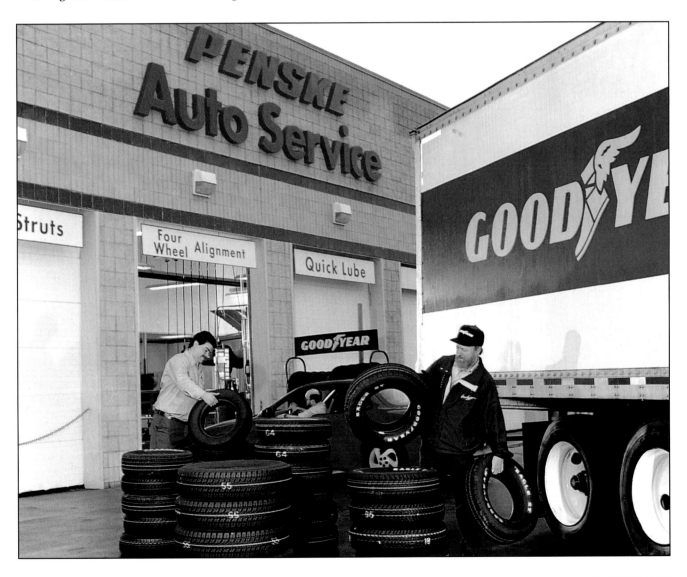

He has been called a "miracle worker," a "marketing guru," and "the man who came down from the mountains with all the tablets."[67] Goodyear was the leader in domestic sales but only third globally, behind Michelin and Bridgestone. But the company was revitalized. "While the turnaround at Goodyear has been much quicker and much stronger than many thought possible," Gault wrote in 1992, "it has come as no surprise to me."[68]

The Mission into the 21st Century

Replacing Gault as Goodyear's chairman was Samir F. Gibara, who shared with his predecessor a natural charm that may help "continue the dynamic turnaround set in motion by Gault."[69] The choice of Egyptian-born Gibara reflected the continuing importance of Goodyear's global operations, which in 1995 accounted for 45 percent of revenue and 56 percent of operating income.[70]

With a bachelor's degree from Cairo University and a master's degree from Harvard, Gibara is fluent in English, French and Arabic, and spent years with Goodyear International in France and Morocco. He has served as advisor to the International Trade Center in Brussels, economic advisor to the Moroccan government's delegation to the United States, and vice president and board member of the American Chamber of Commerce in France.[71]

Gibara joined Goodyear in 1964 as a management trainee in France. He became manager of Goodyear's Paris office in 1966, and served as comptroller for Goodyear in France from 1967 to 1970. After many years in Europe, he became a corporate officer in 1992 when he was elected vice president of strategic planning and business development, and given additional responsibility as acting vice president of finance. In 1994, he became executive vice president, with responsibility for the company's North American tire operations. In 1995, he became president and chief operating officer of Goodyear, and chairman in 1996.

Gibara's experience in developing dealer programs throughout the world, as well as successfully battling Michelin on its own ground in France in the mid to late seventies, helped prepare him to lead Goodyear back to global tire dominance.

Gibara's background was unique for another reason. In 1981, he left Goodyear to work for International Harvester, returning to Goodyear in 1983 to head up operations in France. "I must say that was a very rare case for Goodyear, for someone to leave and then come back," he said. "At management levels, the company usually never took anyone back." But he received a call requesting that he return. He moved back to France to once again take the reins of the operation there.[72]

In 1989, Gibara became president and CEO of Goodyear Canada, where he was given a new set of challenges: "In France and Morocco, my mission was to grow the companies. In Canada,

Samir Gibara is on a mission to make Goodyear number one again in tires worldwide.

I had to do what is now called reengineering; back then it was called downsizing. It wasn't pleasant at all. The company had grown too fast and didn't watch the cost side as much as it should have."[73] Through his varied experiences at Goodyear, Gibara developed a deep appreciation of the importance of healthy but careful growth. This feeling was shared by Gault, the chairman at the time, who had assured him that the "next chairman will believe in strategic planning or else he won't be the next chairman."[74]

Gibara said his first reactions after becoming chairman were pride and pleasure. "That lasts about two days," he noted. "Then what you really realize is the sense of responsibility you have, big responsibility, and that far overwhelms your initial reactions."[75]

To return Goodyear to its position as world leader, Gibara established a strategy to purchase small tire companies, with a particular focus on companies in developing nations. In 1995, for instance, Goodyear began manufacturing in China; expanded its facilities in Indonesia, Brazil, Malaysia and Thailand; and acquired the leading Polish passenger tire manufacturer, TC Debica, making Goodyear the first tire company with a manufacturing presence in the world's four high-growth areas: Central Europe, India, China and Latin America.[76] Sales offices were also established in Beijing, Budapest, Moscow, Prague and Warsaw.[77] In 1994, Goodyear also acquired a 60 percent interest in a $20 million joint venture with Qingdao Gold Lion Hose Company, the largest producer of auto hose in China.[78]

The opening of offices in China highlighted the growing importance of the Asian market for American business overall. Joe Gingo, vice president of the Asia region, said Goodyear's growth outside Japan is phenomenal. "I don't count Japan because the country is developed like us.

With the exception of Japan, we are talking 5.5 percent up to 9 or 10 percent a year. I mean, 5.5 percent is the smallest growth we're experiencing."[79] By contrast, the North American market is growing by 2 percent a year and Western Europe by 1 to 2 percent. "There is always something happening. I am always dealing in an acquisition or a joint venture."[80]

Goodyear has established agreements with Sumitomo Rubber Industries Ltd., in Japan, and had purchased Sime Darby Pilipinas Inc. in the Philippines, Goodyear's second plant in the Manila area. Under the Sumitomo agreement, Goodyear will supply tires for Sumitomo subsidiaries Dunlop Tire Corporation and The OHTSU Tire & Rubber Co. Ltd. in North America, while Sumitomo will supply tires for Nippon Goodyear, in Japan.

The Sumitomo agreement accomplishes two goals: it avoids creating over-capacity in the industry, which could occur if Goodyear built another plant, and it reduces exposure of both companies to future economic cycles in the U.S. and Japan.

Returning to South Africa in January 1997, Goodyear purchased 60 percent interest in Contred, the tire and engineered products subsidiary of Consol, Ltd. The $121 million transaction included a factory in Cape Province (which Goodyear had sold to Contred in 1989), a major chain of 195 retail stores and South Africa's largest retreading operation, with 41 plants.

In its second major move in Eastern Europe, Goodyear announced two joint ventures with the Sava Group in Kranj, Slovenia in May 1997. The Sava Group comprises several companies involved in the production of wide variety of products. Goodyear has taken a 60 percent inter-

A Goodyear worker in China inspects a Goodyear tire for quality.

est in Sava's tire business — composed mostly of car and truck tires — and a 75 percent interest in its engineered products line.

Not all of the acquisitions occurred overseas. The 1996 purchase of Belt Concepts of America Inc., in Spring Hope, North Carolina, made Goodyear the world's leader in the conveyor belt industry. The acquisition provides a complete line of lightweight belts to authorized distributors. Goodyear was already the world leader in the heavy-duty belt industry.

By mid-1997 these and other global acquisitions and agreements had resulted in more than $1 billion in sales.[81]

The global strategy is part of a larger initiative, which Gibara has called "The Mission Into the 21st Century." The goal is to make Goodyear number one again worldwide by learning to succeed in the global economy. "Becoming the biggest is a byproduct of being the best," Gibara noted in a recent interview.[82] With more than 90,000 people working in 31 countries,[83] the company is learning what it means to be global, noted Jessie Williams, vice president of human resource policy, employment practices and systems. Williams, who joined Goodyear in 1962 as a management trainee, said the company wants to "think global and act local." We fully realize and accept the fact that we are in a global competitive struggle. I can say without hesitation that my last 10 years have been tougher than the first 24 years put together, because of global competition."[84]

Thinking and acting globally means allowing regional managers to respond to their region's needs, while maintaining a global perspective to better meet those needs, commented Randy Browning, director of Global Export Operations.

"Global perspective means, 'How can we use global resources to better serve our customers?' The regions, Europe, Latin America, Asia, etc., are closer to the customer's needs, but we need to coordinate some functions with Akron. Keep the regional thing because it works well, but make sure the regions work together where they can."[85]

Called the total quality program, this method strives to make quality universal and uniform, so that challenges can be tackled in a unified way.

Workers are taught to look at the quality aspect from the customer's point of view, and to approach problems as teams. Michael Burns, vice president of Human Resources, said officers toured manufacturing centers around the world to develop a training program to inoculate Goodyear's culture with the team concept.

"The whole process of the culture change in the company is not achieved with one initiative. It's the total way of thinking about business, what I call 'connect the dots,' understanding how all the pieces support the behavior change. We want an honest culture, very direct and business-oriented, but also one that says not only what's in it for the business, but what's in it for the people? What are we asking them to give, and what do they get for that? Our goal is always to be number one, and should be. That's our history; that's our passion."[86]

The total quality concept extends to research into new styles and ways to improve performance and durability. Dr. Richard Steichen, vice president of Worldwide Tire Technology, discussed how far tires have come and where they are likely to go.

"Just looking over your shoulder, you can see that there's been substantial improvement over the last 20 to 30 years: you expected your tires to last 15,000 to 20,000 miles; now 60,000 miles is not unexpected. Changes that are occurring right now include tire sizes. Sixteen-inch tires used to be pretty uncommon, but now you're seeing vehicles at the Detroit Auto Show with 20-inch rims on the tires. It's almost beginning to look like a carriage wheel now with the big rim and the little rubber."[87]

As research continues, Steichen said, the life and dependability of tires will get even better. For example, the extended mobility tire — or run-flat, as some call it — is already on two commercial vehicles, the Plymouth Prowler and the Chevrolet Corvette. Even after losing air, the tire maintains its shape without the internal pressure. That improvement may lead to the need for pressure sensors in the tire itself, Steichen added, in which computer chips send messages back to the car concerning tire pressure and temperature.[88]

"We're in an information age here, and when you think about it, we're getting more feedback and information on just about everything we do. The readouts you get on cars in terms of mileage and projected mileage and the condition of your brakes and so forth and so on. Sensors in tires is something that we're working on building. Particularly when you get into truck tires, you want to be able to probe the tire to determine whether or not it's been abused or run overloaded before retreading."[89]

Goodyear continues to lead the domestic market, led by the success of the Aquatred line, now expanded into tires for pickups and vans. In 1996, Goodyear launched the Infinitred, the first passenger tire with a manufacturer's lifetime treadwear guarantee.[90] Even an albatross has turned swan: beginning in 1994, the Celeron pipeline, its named changed to the All America pipeline, turned a profit and, true to Bob Mercer's predictions, is bolstering company cash flow.[91]

Having committed more than $600 million in capital expenditures in both 1995 and 1996, Goodyear is looking to the future with the same innovative, confident spirit that has served it for nearly a century. On May 8, the company successfully

negotiated Goodyear's first master contract with the United Steelworkers Union, which absorbed the Akron-based United Rubber Workers International in 1995. The six-year contract was hammered out after more than 12,000 Goodyear workers went on strike that lasted from April 20, 1997 to May 12. The pact is twice the usual length for the industry, and has made Goodyear the industry trend-setter once again in labor relations.

Samir Gibara said Goodyear is ready to once again take the mantle as the world's leader in its industry.

"For 70 years, this company was the leader in the industry, by far head and shoulders above the rest. Then we lost all that in the last 10 years. But we are regaining that sense of pride that says we can win. Stan Gault has done some of that. Because of the circumstances, his mission was to turn this company around. Now what this company needs to do is go to the next level, go to world leadership, regain its position as the undisputed leader in the tire industry worldwide."[92]

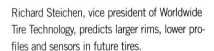

Richard Steichen, vice president of Worldwide Tire Technology, predicts larger rims, lower profiles and sensors in future tires.

NOTES TO SOURCES

Chapter One

1. *American Phrenological Journal,* December 1856, p. 125.
2. Maurice O'Reilly, *The Goodyear Story,* (The Benjamin Company, Elmsford, New York, 1983), p. 8.
3. *Ibid.,* p. 9.
4. *Historical Highlights,* The Goodyear Tire & Rubber Company. Goodyear archives.
5. Charles Spencer Hart, "Injun Rubber Man," *The Elks Magazine,* May 1935, p. 11.
6. *Boston Sunday Globe,* September 7, 1969, p. B59, (Multiple sources).
7. Hugh Allen, *Charles Goodyear: An Intimate Biographical Sketch,* The Goodyear Tire & Rubber Company, 1939, p. 4.
8. *Ibid.,* p. 3.
9. *Ibid.,* p. 4.
10. *Ibid.,* p. 5.
11. *Ibid.*
12. *Woburn Daily Times,* September 17, 1969, p. 24D.
13. *Ibid.*
14. W.A. Gibbons, *The Rubber Industry, 1839-1939,* p. 1200.
15. *The Hartford Daily Times,* April 19, 1930. Archival fragment.
16. *National Geographic,* July 1916. Reprint.
17. Hart, p. 12.
18. Memorandum on Charles Goodyear, The Goodyear Tire & Rubber Company. Goodyear archives.
19. Allen, p. 6.
20. James A. McLaughlin, *Charles Goodyear of Woburn, Massachusetts,* pamphlet produced and published by Walter Wilcox and The Tanners National Bank, Woburn, Massachusettes, 1932, p. 3.
21. R.W. Lunn, "Charles Goodyear 1800-1860." Centenary of Rubber Vulcanization," Reprint from *Industrial and Engineering Chemistry,* Vol. 31, October 1939, p. 192.
22. Allen, p. 5.
23. *Ibid.,* p. 3.
24. Memo on Charles Goodyear, The Goodyear Tire & Rubber Company. Undated, Goodyear archives.
25. McLaughlin, p. 8.
26. R.W. Lunn, p. 192.
27. Allen, p. 6.
28. *Ibid.,* p. 7.
29. *Ibid.,* pp. 7-8.
30. Charles Goodyear, *Gum-Elastic,* Vol. 1, 1855, pp. 188-189.
31. "Rubber & Plastics News," *The Rubber Industry's Forthnightly Newsletter,* April 24, 1972, p. 17.
32. Allen, p. 8.
33. *Ibid.,* p. 3.
34. *Woburn Daily Times,* September 17, 1969, p. 240.
35. *Ibid.,* p. 240.
36. "Rubber & Plastics News," April 24, 1972, p. 17.
37. *Harper's Weekly,* April 4, 1957.
38. *American Phrenological Journal,* December 1856, p. 125.
39. *Ibid,* p. 9.
40. *Ibid.*
41. *Ibid.*
42. *Boston Sunday Globe,* September 7, 1969.
43. Allen, p. 9.
44. *Ibid.,* 12.
45. *Ibid.*
46. *Ibid.,* p. 14.
47. Charles Goodyear, *Gum-Elastic,* p. 71.
48. *The New Haven Register,* May 8, 1977.

Chapter Two

1. Frank Seiberling speech, transcript, p. 3.
2. *The Seiberling: A Publication By and For Employees of the Seiberling Rubber Company,* August 1955.
3. Hugh Allen, *The House of Goodyear,* (The Superior Printing & Lithograph Company, Akron, Ohio, 1936), p. 4.
4. W.D. Shilts, *The First Ten Years,* unpublished manuscript, p. 19.
5. Frank Seiberling speech given to "SSS Men of Goodyear," undated transcript. Goodyear archives.
6. Maurice O'Reilly, *The Goodyear Story,* (The Benjamin Company, Elmsford, New York, 1983), p. 8.
7. Frank Seiberling speech, undated transcript, p. 2.
8. *Ibid.,* p. 3.
9. Paul Campbell, "The Campbell Review," unpublished, manuscript, pp. 11-12.
10. W.D. Shilts, *The First Ten Years,* p. 2.
11. Seiberling speech, p. 3.
12. *Ibid.*
13. O'Reilly, p. 13.
14. O'Reilly, p. 12.
15. Campbell, p. 13.
16. *Ibid.*
17. *A History of the Goodyear Tire & Rubber Company,* published by The Goodyear Tire & Rubber Company, 1977, p. 2.
18. Campbell, p. 14.
19. Company memo from E.J. Thomas, undated.
20. Campbell p. 13.
21. *Historical Highlights,* The Goodyear Tire & Rubber Company. Goodyear archives.
22. O'Reilly, 13.
23. *Historical Highlights.*
24. Campbell p. 18.
25. *Ibid.*
26. O'Reilly, p. 14.
27. Seiberling speech, pp. 5-6.
28. O'Reilly, p. 14.
29. Seiberling speech, p. 6.
30. *Ibid.,* p. 7.
31. *Ibid.,* pp. 7-8.
32. O'Reilly, p. 14.
33. *Ibid.*
34. *Ibid.*
35. Seiberling speech, p. 12.
36. *Ibid.*
37. O'Reilly, p. 15.
38. *Historical Highlights.*
39. *Ibid.*
40. O'Reilly p. 15.
41. *Ibid.*
42. Allen, p. 11.
43. Shilts, p. 25.
44. *The Seiberling: A Publication By and For Employees of Seiberling Rubber Company,* company newsletter, August 1955.
45. Campbell, p. 16.
46. O'Reilly, pp. 15-16.
47. *Ibid.,* p. 17.
48. P.W. Litchfield, *Goodyear's Homecoming, 30th Anniversary Program and General Data,* October 15-18, 1928.
49. Allen, p. 15.
50. Shilts, p. 31.
51. *Ibid.,* p. 31.
52. *Ibid.,* 32.
53. *Ibid.*
54. *Ibid.,* p. 34.
55. *Ibid.,* p. 36.
56. Campbell, p. 20.

Chapter Three

1. Papers of Irene Harrison, p. 47. Goodyear archives.
2. *Historical Highlights,* The Goodyear Tire & Rubber Company. Goodyear archives.
3. *Ibid.*
4. W.D. Shilts, *The First Ten Years.* Unpublished manuscript, p. 40.
5. John Bell Rae, *The American Automobile Industry,* (G.K. Hall & Company, Boston, Massachusetts, 1984), p. 1.
6. *Ibid.,* 5-6.
7. *Ibid.,* 12.
8. Ralph Epstein, *The Automobile Industry: Its Economic and Commercial Development,* (The Arno Press, New York, New York, 1978), p. 95. First published in 1928.
9. Philip Hillyer Smith, *Wheels Within Wheels,* (Funk & Wagnall, New York, New York, 1970), pp. 25-26.
10. *Ibid.*

11. *Ibid.*, p. 10.
12. *The New York Times*, January 26, 1908.
13. Jeffrey L. Rodengen, *The Legend of Nucor*, (Write Stuff Enterprises, Fort Lauderdale, Florida, 1997), p. 14.
14. Rae, p. 9.
15. Smith, pp. 34-35.
16. *Ibid.*, p. 8.
17. Rae, p. 24.
18. *Ibid.*, p. 180.
19. Epstein, p. 20.
20. *Ibid.*, p. 19.
21. Hugh Allen, *The House of Goodyear*, (The Superior Printing and Lithography Company, Akron, Ohio, 1936), p. 14.
22. *Ibid.*, p. 16.
23. Shilts, p. 44.
24. *Ibid.*
25. Rae, p. 180.
26. Maurice O'Reilly, *The Goodyear Story*, The Benjamin Company, (Elmsford, New York, 1983), p. 19.
27. Allen, p. 17.
28. O'Reilly, p. 19.
29. Papers of Irene Harrison, p. 47. Goodyear archives.
30. Allen, pp. 13-14.
31. *Ibid.*, p. 14.
32. O'Reilly, p. 19.
33. *Ibid.*
34. *Historical Highlights.*
35. O'Reilly, p. 19.
36. *Ibid.*, p. 20.
37. Allen, p. 18.
38. Frank Seiberling speech given to "SSS Men of Goodyear," undated transcript. Goodyear archives.
39. Shilts, p. 47.
40. Frank Seiberling, "Buying or Selling—Which Counts Most?" *System: The Magazine of Business*, August 1920, p. 220.
41. Rae, p. 180.
42. *Ibid.*, p. 31.
43. *Ibid.*, p. 32.
44. Smith, p. 40.
45. O'Reilly, p. 21.
46. Shilts, p. 48.
47. *Ibid.*
48. "The Story of Goodyear," *The Goodyear News: A Magazine for Goodyear Dealers*, December 1926, p. 23.
49. Shilts, p. 48.
50. *The New York Times*, February 17, 1909.
51. *Ibid.*, February 14, 1909.
52. *Ibid.*, February 17, 1909.
53. *Ibid.*, June 1, 1913.
54. Shilts, p. 50.
55. O'Reilly, p. 20.
56. Allen, p. 19.
57. *Historical Highlights.*
58. Shilts, p. 59.
59. O'Reilly, p. 21.
60. *Historical Highlights.*
61. Shilts, p. 62-63.
62. *The New York Times*, February 7, 1909.
63. Shilts, p. 64.

64. *The New York Times*, February 7, 1909.
65. Allen, p. 22.
66. Shilts, p. 64.
67. *Historical Highlights.*
68. Shilts, 64.
69. *The New York Times*, January 15, 1911.
70. *Historical Highlights.*
71. *The New York Times*, August 9, 1913.
72. *Historical Highlights.*
73. *Ibid.*
74. *Ibid.*
75. Allen, p. 27.
76. O'Reilly, p. 26.
77. "The Story of Goodyear," p. 7.
78. Allen, p. 28.
79. O'Reilly, p. 26.
80. *Wingfoot Clan*, June 1, 1912.
81. *The New York Times*, April 9, 1916.
82. *Historical Highlights.*
83. Shilts, pp. 69-71.
84. *Historical Highlights.*
85. O'Reilly, p. 31.
86. Frank Seiberling, "Address to the Stockholders of the Goodyear Tire & Rubber Company," Akron, Ohio, December 3, 1917. Transcript, p. 7.
87. *Historical Highlights.*
88. *Ibid.*
89. 1928 Annual Report, p. 17; *Historical Highlights.*

Chapter Four

1. *Wingfoot Clan*, May 13, 1921.
2. *Ibid.*, December 19, 1917, p. 7.
3. *Historical Highlights.*
4. *The New York Times*, September 19, 1918.
5. *Los Angeles Examiner*, April 27, 1919.
6. *Goodyear: A Family Newspaper*, September 1919.
7. *Historical Highlights*, The Goodyear Tire & Rubber Company. Goodyear archives.
8. P.W. Litchfield, *Thirty Years of GY 1898-1928: A Statement to the Stockholders of The Goodyear Tire & Rubber Company*, p. 4. Goodyear archives.
9. Hugh Allen, *The House of Goodyear*, (The Superior Printing and Lithography Company, Akron, Ohio, 1936), p. 30.
10. W.D. Shilts, *The First Ten Years*, unpublished manuscript, p. 16.
11. *Ibid.*
12. Maurice O'Reilly, *The Goodyear Story*, (The Benjamin Company, Elmsford, New York, 1983), p. 38.
13. G.M., Stadelman, "Facts About Goodyear," undated information pamphlet.
14. Shilts, p. 20.
15. Clyde Schetter, *A History of Goodyear (Second Ten Years)*. Unpublished manuscript, p. 132r.
16. Schetter, p. 132r.
17. P.W. Litchfield, *Industrial Voyage*, (The Country Life Press, Garden City, New York, 1954), pp. 135-136.
18. O'Reilly, p. 39.

19. *Ibid.*
20. Shilts, p. 19.
21. *Ibid.*
22. O'Reilly, p. 40.
23. *Ibid.*
24. Schetter, p. 17.
25. P.W. Litchfield, p. 155.
26. Jack Walsh, "The Romance of Rubber," *Detroit Saturday Night* magazine, November 14,1936.
27. *A Wonder Book of Rubber*, The B.F. Goodrich Rubber Company, 1917, p. 24.
28. Litchfield, p. 157.
29. Schetter, p. 135.
30. Frank Seiberling letter to stockholders, December 3, 1917, p. 3.
31. Schetter, p. 136.
32. Litchfield, p. 157.
33. *Ibid.*, p. 158.
34. Schetter, p. 136.
35. Litchfield, p. 158.
36. Schetter, p. 138.
37. *Ibid.*
38. "The Story of the Tire," pamphlet published by The Goodyear Tire & Rubber Company, 1948, pp. 9-12.
39. The Story of the Tire, p. 9.
40. *Ibid.*, p. 9.
41. Frank Seiberling, *System: The Magazine of Business*, August 1920, p. 321.
42. Litchfield, p. 159.
43. Frank Seiberling, "Address to the Stockholders of The Goodyear Tire & Rubber Company," December 3, 1917.
44. Litchfield, p. 160; Seiberling address, p. 3.
45. Schetter, p. 141.
46. Litchfield, p. 161.
47. Seiberling address, p. 5.
48. Schetter, pp. 142-143.
49. Shilts, p. 3.
50. O'Reilly, p. 41.
51. Shilts, p. 23.
52. Litchfield, p. 177; Schetter, p. 155.
53. Litchfield, p. 177.
54. *The New York Times*, February 13, 1917.
55. Seiberling address, p. 11; Schetter, p. 152.
56. Seiberling address, p. 11.
57. Litchfield, p. 177.
58. Schetter, p. 155.
59. *The New York Times*, May 31, 1917.
60. Schetter, p. 156.
61. *Ibid.*
62. *The New York Times*, May 31, 1917.
63. *Ibid.*
64. Schetter, p. 151.
65. *Historical Highlights*, The Goodyear Tire & Rubber Company. Goodyear archives.
66. Schetter, p. 156.
67. *Ibid.*, p. 157.
68. Litchfield, p. 178.
69. Schetter, pp. 157, 159.
70. O'Reilly, p. 44.
71. George Tindall, David Shi, *America*, W.W. Norton & Company, Inc., New York, NY, 1989, p. 637.
72. Shilts, p. 40.

73. *Ibid.*
74. O'Reilly, p. 44.
75. Shilts, p. 40.
76. *Ibid.*, p. 25.
77. O'Reilly, p. 44.
78. Shilts, p. 42.
79. *Ibid.*, p. 41.
80. *Ibid.*, pp. 161-62.
81. *Ibid.*, p. 161.
82. Schetter, p. 162.
83. *Ibid.*, p. 169.
84. *Ibid.*, p. 165.
85. *Ibid.*, p. 169.
86. *Ibid.*
87. *Financial World*, September 15, 1919, p. 15.
88. O'Reilly, p. 46.
89. *Ibid.*
90. *The New York Times*, December 7, 1919.
91. Shilts, p. 63.
92. *Ibid.*, p. 13.
93. *Ibid.*, p. 54.
94. *The New York Times*, December 19, 1917.
95. Schetter, p. 179.
96. Letter to stockholders, October 4, 1919. Goodyear archives.
97. O'Reilly, p. 47.
98. *Goodyear: A Family Newspaper*, October 1919.
99. O'Reilly, p. 47.
100. *Ibid.*
101. Letter to stockholders, May 27, 1920. Goodyear archives.
102. Schetter, p. 184.
103. Letter to stockholders, May 27, 1920.
104. *Econostat*, July 22, 1933.
105. Schetter, p. 184.
106. *Ibid.*, p. 187a.
107. *Ibid.*
108. Litchfield, p. 194.
109. *Ibid.*, pp. 194-95.
110. *Ibid.*, p. 195.
111. Schetter, p. 190a.
112. Litchfield, p. 195.
113. Schetter, p. 191.
114. O'Reilly, p. 51.
115. *Ibid.*, p. 49.
116. *Ibid.*, p. 51.
117. Shilts, p. 92.
118. *Ibid.*, p. 93.
119. *Ibid.*
120. O'Reilly, p. 52.
121. Schetter, p. 193a.
122. *Ibid.*
123. Schetter, p. 195.
124. *Wingfoot Clan*, May 13, 1921.
125. O'Reilly, p. 49.
126. *Ibid.*, p. 52.
127. *Ibid.*
128. *The Seiberling: A Publication By and For the Employees of The Seiberling Rubber Company*, company newsletter, August, 1955.

Chapter Five

1. Litchfield, P.W. *Industrial Voyage*. (The Country Life Press, Garden City, New York, 1954), p. 200.
2. *Ibid.*, p. 197.
3. Maurice O'Reilly, *The Goodyear Story*. (The Benjamin Company, Elmsford, New York, 1983), p. 54.
4. Litchfield, p. 207.
5. W.D. Shilts, Unpublished manuscript, May 13, 1921 to December 31, 1927. Goodyear archives, pp. 2-3.
6. W.D. Shilts, "Officers as Elected by Board of Directors," p. 1. Goodyear archives,
7. Litchfield, p. 200.
8. O'Reilly, p. 53.
9. Litchfield, p. 206.
10. Shilts, unpublished manuscript, p. 7.
11. *Ibid.*, p. 5.
12. *Ibid.*, p. 4.
13. O'Reilly, p. 53.
14. Litchfield, p, 200.
15. *Ibid.*, p. 201.
16. Litchfield, p. 202-203.
17. Shilts, p. 12.
18. *Ibid.*, p. 5.
19. *Ibid.*, p. 10.
20. Clyde Schetter, *History of Goodyear: 1898-1967*, unpublished manuscript, p. 238. Goodyear archives.
21. Shilts, p. 13.
22. Litchfield, p. 201.
23. Schetter, p. 242.
24. Litchfield, p. 208.
25. *Ibid.*, p. 182.
26. Schetter, p. 231.
27. Litchfield, p. 208.
28. O'Reilly, p. 32.
29. Litchfield, p. 183.
30. P.W. Litchfield, *The Industrial Republic*, (The Corday & Gross Co., Cleveland, Ohio, 1946), pp. 52-53.
31. Litchfield, *Industrial Voyage*, pp. 184-185.
32. *Ibid.*, p. 227.
33. *Ibid.*
34. *Ibid.*
35. Litchfield, *Industrial Voyage*, pp. 202, 201.
36. *Ibid.*, p. 204.
37. *Ibid.*, p. 205.
38. *Ibid.*
39. O'Reilly, p. 54.
40. Shilts, p. 18.
41. *Ibid.*, p. 18.
42. Schetter, 244.
43. *Ibid.*, p. 245.
44. *Ibid.*, p. 212.
45. *Ibid.*
46. 1928 Annual Report, p. 17.
47. Litchfield, pp. 208, 211.
48. *Ibid.*, p. 210.
49. Shilts, p. 35.
50. *Historical Highlights*, The Goodyear Tire & Rubber Company. Goodyear archives.
51. Shilts, p. 57.
52. Hugh Allen, *The House of Goodyear*, (The Superior Printing & Litho. Co., Akron, Ohio, 1936), p. 74.
53. *Ibid.*, p. 75.
54. Shilts, p. 56.
55. Schetter, p. 259..
56. Allen, p. 76.
57. *The New York Times*, June 4, 1925.
58. Allen, p. 76.
59. *The New York Times*, June 4, 1925.
60. Stadelman, p. 52.
61. P.W. Litchfield, *Thirty Years of Goodyear, 1898-1928: A Statement to the Stockholders of The Goodyear Tire & Rubber Company*, p. 5.
62. Schetter, p. 272.
63. *Ibid.*
64. Litchfield, p. 212.
65. *Ibid.*
66. O'Reilly, p. 55.
67. *Ibid.*
68. *Ibid.*
69. *Ibid.*
70. Shilts, p. 31.
71. *Ibid.*, p. 32.
72. *Ibid.*
73. Schetter, p. 253.
74. Litchfield, p. 221.
75. *Ibid.*
76. O'Reilly, p. 55; Litchfield, p. 222.
77. O'Reilly, p. 55.
78. Litchfield, p. 222.
79. *Ibid.*

Chapter Five Sidebar

1. P.W. Litchfield, *The Industrial Republic*, (The Corday & Gross Co., Cleveland, Ohio, 1946), p. 2.
2. Litchfield, *Industrial Voyage*, p. 212.
3. *Ibid.*, p. 211.
4. P.W. Litchfield, *The Industrial Republic*, (The Corday & Gross Co., Cleveland, Ohio, 1946), pp. 13-14.
5. *Ibid.*, pp. 35-36.
6. Litchfield, *Industrial Voyage*, p. 182.
7. Litchfield, *Industrial Republic*, pp. 36-37.
8. Anonymous, "Rubber Slavery in Akron," *The Industrial Pioneer: An Illustrated Labor Magazine*, August 1925, p. 4.
9. *Ibid.*, p. 5.
10. *Ibid.*

Chapter Six

1. P.W. Litchfield, *Industrial Voyage*, (The Country Life Press, Garden City, New York, 1954), pp. 247-248.
2. Sarah M. Evans, *Born for Liberty*, (The Free Press, A Division of MacMillan, New York, New York, 1989), p. 198.
3. *Wingfoot Clan*, April 13, 1932, p. 3.
4. Maurice O'Reilly, *The Goodyear Story*, (The Benjamin Company, Elmsford, New York, 1983), p. 60.
5. *Historical Highlights*, The Goodyear Tire & Rubber Company. Goodyear archives.
6. 1930 Annual Report, p. 12.
7. O'Reilly, 60.
8. Clyde Schetter, *History of Goodyear, 1898-1967*, unpublished manuscript, Goodyear archives, p. 306.

9. Seiberling letter to Isaac Harter, June 29, 1909.
10. *Industrial Voyage*, p. 137.
11. *Ibid.*, pp. 138-139.
12. Goodyear Airship Operations Enterprise. Company release. Undated.
13. Seiberling letter to O.E. Olin, July 8, 1912.
14. *Wingfoot Clan*, July 15, 1912, p. 1.
15. Litchfield, p. 139.
16. Goodyear Airships Enterprise. Undated company release.
17. Schetter, p. 264.
18. *Ibid.*, p. 215.
19. *Ibid.*, pp. 215-216.
20. *Ibid.*, p. 218.
21. *Ibid.*, p. 217.
22. *Ibid.*, p.218.
23. *Ibid.*, p. 219A.
24. *Ibid.*, p. 270.
25. O'Reilly, p. 66.
26. *Aerial Ambassadors*, company booklet, September 1984.
27. Hugh Allen, *The House of Goodyear*, The Superior Printing & Litho, Co., 1936, p. 391.
28. Dr. Arl Arnstein, "Why Airships?" *U.S. Air Service Magazine*, December 1932, p. 8.
29. C.L. Merrell, "The Blimps Carry On," *Southern Flight*, November 1937, p. 10.
30. Allen, p. 394.
31. O'Reilly, p. 66.
32. Goodyear memo, February 20, 1930.
33. Goodyear Airship Operations Enterprise. Company release. Undated.
34. *Aerial Ambassadors*, brochure published by The Goodyear Tire & Rubber Company, September 1984.
35. Goodyear Airship Operations Enterprise, company release.
36. Hugh Allen, "World War Zeppelins," *Our Navy*, November 1939, p. 18.
37. O'Reilly, p. 60.
38. *Ibid.*, p. 61.
39. *Ibid.*
40. "1-¹/₂ Million Cubic Foot Zeppelin Airship," Goodyear-Zeppelin Corporation Proposal, April 1924.
41. *Ibid.*
42. Schetter, p. 268a.
43. City of Akron-Summit County-Akron Chamber of Commerce Agreement with the Goodyear-Zeppelin Corporation October 22, 1928.
44. Schetter, p. 302.
45. *Ibid.*
46. *Ibid*, p. 307.
47. *Ibid.*
48. *Ibid.*
49. *Wingfoot Clan*, May 27, 1931, p. 5.
50. *Wingfoot Clan*, August 31, 1931, p. 1.
51. *Wingfoot Clan*, September 23, 1931, p. 1.
52. O'Reilly, p. 62.
53. *Ibid.*
54. J.C. Hunsaker, "Transoceanic Air Travel," Presented at the National Aeronautic Meeting of the Society of

Automotive Engineers at New York, May 6-7, 1930, p. 3.
55. Hunsaker, p. 2.
56. *Daily Mirror*, November 12, 1935. Archival fragment.
57. Dr. Karl Arnstein, "Transoceanic Airships." *Aviation*, June 1936. Reprint.
58. Litchfield, p. 246.
59. *Ibid*, 246-247.
60. O'Reilly, p. 63.
61. *America Must Be First In the Air*. Booklet published by The Goodyear-Zeppelin Corporation.
62. Litchfield, p. 245.
63. *Ibid*, 247-248.
64. O'Reilly, p. 64.
65. *Ibid.*
66. "Airship Investigation: Report of Colonel Henry Breckinridge," Counsel for the Joint Committee to Investigate Dirigible Disasters, 73rd Congress, 1933, p. 21.
67. Report of the Federal Aviation Commission January 1935.
68. O'Reilly, p. 64-65.
69. Litchfield, p. 249.
70. Statement made to the Federal Aviation Commission by Dr. Hugo Eckener of the Luftschiffbau Zeppelin, Friedrichshafen, Germany, at a Hearing October 29, 1934.
71. Litchfield, p. 249.

Chapter Six Sidebar

1. Clyde Schetter, *A History of Goodyear, 1898-1967*, unpublished manuscript, p. 912.
2. Maurice O'Reilly, *The Goodyear Story*, (The Benjamin Company, Elmsford, New York, 1983), p. 139.
3. *Ibid.*, p. 140.
4. *Ibid.*
5 Schetter, p. 951.
6. *The New York Times*, November 6, 1966.
7. Schetter, p. 951.
8. O'Reilly, p. 143.
9. Tom Riley, interviewed by the author, January 17, 1997. Transcript, pp. 10-11.
10. *Ibid.*
11. Schetter, p. 950
12. *Ibid.*
13. Jerry Jenkins, interviewed by the author on board the *Stars & Stripes*. Transcript, pp. 4-5.
14. *Ibid.*, pp. 4-5.

Chapter Seven

1. James Barnett, interviewed by the author, September 18, 1996. Transcript, p. 15.
2. Hugh Allen, *The House of Goodyear*, (The Superior Printing & Litho. Company, Akron, Ohio, 1936), p. 344.
3. Allen, p. 344.
4. *Wingfoot Clan*, July 29, 1936, p. 1.
5. Daniel Nelson, *American Rubber Workers and Organized Labor, 1900-*

1941, (Princeton University Press, Princeton, New Jersey, 1988), p. 112.
6. Nelson, p, 112.
7. P.W. Litchfield, *Industrial Voyage*,(The Country Life Press, Garden City, New York, 1954), p. 255.
8. Maurice O'Reilly, *The Goodyear Story*, (The Benjamin Company, Elmsford, New York, 1983), p. 67.
9. Nelson, p. 113.
10. *Cleveland Plain Dealer*, February 26, 1936, p. 2.
11. O'Reilly, p. 71.
12. Nelson, p. 115.
13. *Wingfoot Clan*, September 14, 1932.
14. Clyde Schetter, *History of Goodyear, 1898-1967*, unpublished manuscript. Goodyear archives, p. 357.
15. *Ibid.*, p. 360.
16. *Ibid.*, pp. 368, 371.
17. O'Reilly, p. 76.
18. *Ibid.*
19. Schetter, pp.362-363.
20. O'Reilly, p. 67.
21. Schetter, p. 365.
22. Allen, 350.
23. *Cleveland Plain Dealer*, April 8, 1936, p. 13;CPD July 20, 1936, p. 7.
24. *Cleveland Plain Dealer*, July 20, 1936, p. 7.
25. Schetter, p. 390.
26. Allen, p. 352.
27. *Cleveland Plain Dealer*, March 6, 1936, p. 14.
28. *Cleveland Plain Dealer*, March 3, 1936, p. 8.
29. Schetter, p. 391.
30. *Ibid.*
31. *Wingfoot Clan*, July 22, 1936.
32. O'Reilly, p. 70.
33. *Historical Highlights*, The Goodyear Tire & Rubber Company. Goodyear archives.
34. Nelson, p. 117, 118.
35. *Ibid.*, pp. 118, 121.
36. Harold S. Roberts, *The Rubber Workers: Labor Organization and Collective Bargaining in the Rubber Industry*, (Harper Brothers, New York, New York, 1944), p. 205.
37. Nelson, p. 131.
38. *Ibid.*, p. 149.
39. *Wingfoot Clan*, September 12, 1934, p. 1.
40. Nelson, p. 149.
41. *Ibid.*
42. *Akron Beacon Journal*, March 11, 1935, p. 1.
43. Nelson, p. 154.
44. *Ibid.*, p. 159.
45. *Cleveland Plain Dealer*, January 7, 1936, p. 9.
46. Nelson, p. 176.
47. *Cleveland Plain Dealer*, January 7, 1936, p. 9.
48. *Cleveland Plain Dealer*, February 1, 1936, p. 1.
49. *Cleveland Plain Dealer*, February 5, 1936, p. 20.
50. *Cleveland Plain Dealer*, February 15, 1936, p. 5.
51. Nelson, p. 184.
52. *Cleveland Plain Dealer*, February 15, 1936, p. 1.
53. *Cleveland Plain Dealer*, February 18, 1936, p. 1.

54. *Cleveland Plain Dealer*, February 20, 1936, p. 5.
55. *Cleveland Plain Dealer*, February 18, 1936, p. 1.
56. *Cleveland Plain Dealer*, February 26, 1936, p. 2.
57. *Akron Beacon Journal*, June 25, 1934; *Cleveland Plain Dealer*, February 26, 1936, p. 6.
58. *Cleveland Plain Dealer*, February 25, 1936, p. 1.
59. *Cleveland Plain Dealer*, March 1, 1936, p. 18.
60. *Cleveland Plain Dealer*, February 22, 1936, p. 9.
61. *Cleveland Plain Dealer*, February 27, 1936, p. 1.
62. *Cleveland Plain Dealer*, March 1, 1936, p. 1.
63. *Cleveland Plain Dealer*, March 2, 1936, p. 1; Nelson, p. 194.
64. *Akron Beacon Journal*, March 3, 1936, p. 1.
65. *Cleveland Plain Dealer*, March 5, 1936, p. 1.
66. Nelson, p. 196.
67. *Cleveland Plain Dealer*, March 16, 1936, p. 6.
68. *Akron Beacon Journal*, March 16-18, 1936; ATP, March 17-20, 1936.
69. *Cleveland Plain Dealer*, March 16, 1936, p. 6.
70. James Barnett, interviewed by the author, September 18, 1996. Transcript, p. 15.
71. Nelson, p. 202.
72. *Cleveland Plain Dealer*, March 22, 1936, p. 5.
73. *Cleveland Plain Dealer*, February 20, 1936, p. 7.
74. *Cleveland Plain Dealer*, May 7, 1936, p. 1.
75. *Cleveland Plain Dealer*, May 25, 1936, p. 1.
76. *Wingfoot Clan*, May 6, 1936, p. 3.
77. *Cleveland Plain Dealer*, March 22, 1936, p. 5.
78. *Wingfoot Clan*, March 26, 1936.
79. O'Reilly, p. 75.
80. *Ibid.*, p. 76.
81. *Ibid.*, p.76.

Chapter Eight

1. G. Stocking, and M.W. Watkins, *Cartels in Action*, (The Twentieth Century Fund, New York, New York, 1946), p. 56.
2. *Wingfoot Clan*, April 9, 1939, p. 1.
3. *Wingfoot Clan*, March 8, 1939, p. 1.
4. Clyde Schetter, *A History of Goodyear, 1898-1967*, unpublished manuscript, p. 408.
5. *Ibid.*, p. 409.
6. *Wingfoot Clan*, August 14, 1940, p. 1.
7. P.W. Litchfield, *Industrial Voyage*,(The Country Life Press, Garden City, New York, 1954), p. 284.
8. *Ibid.*, p. 136.
9. *Wingfoot Clan*, August 14, 1940, p. 1.
10. *Wingfoot Clan*, August 14, 1949, p. 1.
11. Charles Phillips, Jr., *Competition in the Synthetic Rubber Industry*, (University of North Carolina Press, Chapel Hill, North Carolina, 1963), p. 18.
12. *Ibid.*, p. 18.
13. *Ibid.*
14. *Ibid.*

15. *Ibid.*, p. 20.
16. Schetter, p. 355.
17. Maurice O'Reilly, *The Goodyear Story*, (The Benjamin Company, Elmsford, New York, 1983), p. 79.
18. *Ibid.*
19. Schetter, p. 384.
20. *Wingfoot Clan*, November 10, 1937, p. 2.
21. *Ibid.*
22. Phillips, pp. 23-24.
23. O'Reilly, p. 89.
24. *Ibid.*
25. *Historical Highlights*, The Goodyear Tire & Rubber Company. Goodyear archives.
26. Stocking and Watkins, p. 56.
27. *Ibid.*, p. 41.
28. *Ibid.*
29. *Ibid*, p. 42.
30. *Ibid.*
31. Synthetic Rubber Plants and Facilities: Second Supplementary and Final Report of the War Assets Administration to the Congress, June 18, 1946. Washington, D.C., p. 4.
32. *Ibid.*
33. O'Reilly, p. 89.
34. Litchfield, pp. 292-293.
35. Phillips, p. 4.
36. O'Reilly, p. 83.
37. *Ibid.*

Chapter Eight Sidebar: Basketball

1. *Akron Beacon Journal*, June 30, 1996, D8.
2. *Ibid.*
3. *Ibid.*
4. *Ibid.*
5. *Ibid.*

Chapter Eight Sidebar: LifeGuard Tire

1. Clyde Schetter, *History of Goodyear 1898-1967*, unpublished, Goodyear archives, p.386.
2. *Wingfoot Clan*, June 9, 1937, p. 1.

Chapter Nine

1. *Wingfoot Clan*, December 10, 1941, p. 1.
2. Maurice O'Reilly, *The Goodyear Story*, (The Benjamin Company, Elmsford, New York, 1983), 85.
3. Hugh Allen, *The House of Goodyear*, (The Corday & Gross Company, Cleveland, Ohio, 1949), pp. 602-603.
4. O'Reilly, p. 88.
5. Allen, pp. 608-609.
6. *Ibid.*, p. 610.
7. O'Reilly, p. 88.
8. Allen, p. 592.
9. *Wingfoot Clan*, September 20, 1939, p. 1.
10. *Ibid.*, July 17, 1940, p. 5.
11. *Ibid.*, October 9, 1940, p. 1.
12. Robert Leckie, *The Wars of America*, (Harper & Row, New York, New York, 1981), p. 708.

13. Leckie, p. 726.
14. *Ibid.*, p. 711.
15. *Wingfoot Clan*, January 29, 1941, p. 1.
16. *Wingfoot Clan*, December 10, 1941, p. 3.
17. *Ibid.*, p. 785.
18. *Ibid.*
19. *Ibid.*, p. 761.
20. Clyde Schetter, *History of Goodyear, 1898-1967*, unpublished manuscript, Goodyear archives, pp. 433-434.
21. O'Reilly, p. 87.
22. *Wingfoot Clan*, November 12, 1941, p. 1.
23. *Ibid.*, p. 1.
24. Schetter, p. 454.
25. *Wingfoot Clan*, July 30, 1941, p. 1.
26. *Ibid.*
27. Allen, p. 624.
28. *Ibid.*, p. 625,
29. Schetter, p. 434.
30. *Ibid.*, p. 436.
31. Allen, p. 534.
32. Schetter, p. 437.
33. O'Reilly, p. 86.
34. Allen, p. 543.
35. *Ibid.*, p. 538-44.
36. Schetter, p. 436.
37. *Wingfoot Clan*, December 10, 1941, p. 1.
38. P.W. Litchfield, (*Industrial Voyage*, The Country Life Press, Garden City, New York, 1954), p. 290.
39. Charles F. Phillips, Jr., *Competition in the Synthetic Rubber Industry*, (University of North Carolina Press, Chapel Hill, North Carolina, 1963), p. 252.
40. Hugh Allen, *Goodyear Aircraft*, (Corday & Gross Company, Cleveland, Ohio, 1947), p. 24.
41. Schetter, p. 474.
42. *Wingfoot Clan*, December 24, 1941, p. 3.
43. *Ibid.*
44. Allen, *Goodyear Aircraft*, p. 417.
45. Schetter, p. 498.
46. Allen, *House of Goodyear*, p. 417.
47. *Ibid.*, p. 418.
48. *Ibid.*, p. 7.
49. Schetter, p. 438.
50. Allen, *Goodyear Aircraft*, p. 157.
51. *Ibid.* p. 23.
52. Schetter, p. 494.
53. Allen, *Goodyear Aircraft*, p. 24.
54. *Ibid.*, p. 24.
55. Allen, *House of Goodyear*, p. 416.
56. Allen, *Goodyear Aircraft*, p. 49.
57. *Ibid.*
58. Schetter, p. 456.
59. *Ibid.*
60. Allen, *House of Goodyear*, p. 511.
61. O'Reilly, p. 91.
62. *Ibid.*
63. Allen, *House of Goodyear*, p. 511.
64. Allen, *Goodyear Aircraft*, p. 30.
65. *Ibid.*, pp. 111-112.
66. *Ibid.*, p. 127.
67. *Ibid.*, p. 159.
68. *Ibid.*, p. 31.
69. Leckie, pp. 825-826.

70. O'Reilly, pp. 90, 93.
71. *Ibid.*, p. 92.
72. *Ibid.*
73. Leckie, p. 761,
74. O'Reilly, p. 92; Schetter, p. 470.
75. Allen, *Goodyear Aircraft*, p. 84.
76. Allen, *Goodyear Aircraft*, p. 83; O'Reilly, p. 93.
77. Allen, *Goodyear Aircraft*, p. 101.
78. *Ibid.*, p. 107.
79. *Ibid.*, p. 107-108.
80. *Ibid.*
81. O'Reilly, p. 94.
82. *Ibid.*
83. *Ibid.*
84. Allen, *The House of Goodyear*, p. 450.
85. *Ibid.*
86. *Ibid.*
87. *Ibid.*
88. O'Reilly, p. 96.
89. *Ibid.*, p. 97.
90. Allen, *The House of Goodyear*, p. 631-632; *Historical Highlights.*
91. *Historical Highlights.*
92. Allen, *House of Goodyear*, p. 632.
93. Schetter, pp. 459-460.
94. *Ibid.*, p. 476.
95. Allen, *Goodyear Aircraft*, p. 151.

Chapter Ten

1. *Wingfoot Clan*, September 25, 1946, p. 1.
2. 1945 Annual Report, p. 6.
3. Clyde Schetter, *History of Goodyear: 1898-1967*, unpublished. Goodyear archives, p. 552; Maurice O'Reilly, *The Goodyear Story*, (The Benjamin Company, Elmsford, New York, 1983), p. 98.
4. *Wingfoot Clan*, February 9, 1946, p. 1.
5. O'Reilly, p. 106.
6. Hugh Allen, *The House of Goodyear*, (The Corday & Gross Company, Cleveland, Ohio, 1949), p. 669.
7. *Wingfoot Clan*, August 7, 1946.
8. *Wingfoot Clan*, January 2, 1946, p. 2; O'Reilly, p. 101.
9. 1948 Annual Report, p. 36.
10. *Wingfoot Clan*, November 15, 1949, p. 6.
11. 1945 Annual Report, p. 14.
12. *Wingfoot Clan*, March 27, 1946, p. 1.
13. 1945 Annual Report, p. 7.
14. *Wingfoot Clan*, March 10, 1948, p. 1.
15. O'Reilly, p. 98.
16. *Ibid.*, p. 99.
17. *Historical Highlights.*
18. *Wingfoot Clan*, May 29, 1946, p. 1.
19. *Ibid.*
20. *Ibid.*
21. *Wingfoot Clan*, July 24, 1946, p. 1.
22. *Wingfoot Clan*, September 25, 1946, p. 1.
23. *Ibid.*
24. Allen, p. 635.
25. 1945 Annual Report pp. 6-7.
26. *Ibid.*, p. 6.
27. Allen, p. 660.
28. *Ibid.*
29. Schetter, p. 571.

30. *Ibid.*, p. 572.
31. *Ibid.*, p. 573.
32. *Ibid.*, p. 572.
33. O'Reilly, p. 99.
34. *Wingfoot Clan*, January 8, 1947, p. 1,
35. Schetter, p. 576.
36. *Wingfoot Clan*, August 13, 1947, p. 1.
37. Allen, p. 639.
38. *Wingfoot Clan*, August 13, 1947, p. 1.
39. Allen, p. 642.
40. *Wingfoot Clan*, January 23, 1946, p. 1.
41. 1946 Annual Report, p. 29.
42. Allen, pp. 663-665.
43. *Ibid.*, p. 667.
44. *Ibid.*, p. 666.
45. 1946 Annual Report, p. 23.
46. Allen, p. 667.
47. *Ibid.*, p. 655.
48. *Ibid.*
49. *Ibid.*, pp. 655-666.
50. 1946 Annual Report, p. 36.
51. Allen, p. 658.
52. 1947 Annual Report, p. 39.
53. 1948 Annual Report, p. 23.
54. *Ibid.*, p. 29.
55. *Ibid.*, 28-29.
56. *Ibid.*, p. 27.
57. Allen, p. 637.
58. *Ibid.*, p. 638.
59. 1947 Annual Report, p. 5.
60. 1950 Annual Report, p. 18.
61. *Ibid.*
62. O'Reilly, p. 107.
63. *Ibid.*
64. O'Reilly, 107; 1950 Annual Report, p. 7.
65. 1950 Annual Report, p. 18.
66. *Ibid.*
67. O'Reilly, p. 108.
68. James Barnett, interviewed by the author, September 18, 1996. Transcript, p. 5.
69. 1950 Annual Report, p. 19.
70. Schetter, p. 588.
71. *Historical Highlights*, The Goodyear Tire & Rubber Company. Goodyear archives.
72. O'Reilly, p. 106.
73. *Historical Highlights.*
74. O'Reilly, p. 119.
75. 1950 Annual Report, pp. 2, 5.

Chapter Eleven

1. Maurice O'Reilly, *The Goodyear Story*, (The Benjamin Company, Elmsford, New York, 1983), p. 116.
2. Clyde Schetter, *History of Goodyear: 1898-1967*, unpublished. Goodyear archives, p. 606.
3. 1951 Annual Report, p. 3.
4. *Wingfoot Clan*, February 27, 1952, p. 1.
5. *Historical Highlights*, The Goodyear Tire & Rubber Company. Goodyear archives.
6. Schetter, p. 597.
7. 1951 Annual Report, p. 3.
8. *Wingfoot Clan* January 3, 1951, p. 1.
9. *Ibid.*
10. *Ibid.*, February 22, 1954, p. 8.
11. 1955 Annual Report, p. 19.

12. *Wingfoot Clan*, February 27, 1952, p. 1.
13. O'Reilly, p. 115,
14. Charles F. Phillips, Jr. *Competition in the Synthetic Rubber Industry*, (The University of North Carolina Press, Chapel Hill, North Carolina, 1963), p. 158. Figures are cited from "Rubber and Motor Vehicle Facts, 1962," published by the Firestone Synthetic Rubber and Latex Company, p. 3.
15. O'Reilly, p. 116.
16. *Ibid.*, p. 115.
17. *Ibid.*, p. 115.
18. *Ibid.*, p. 101.
19. *Ibid.*, p. 115.
20. *The New York Times*, August 13, 1952, p. 1.
21. *Ibid.*
22. O'Reilly, p. 112.
23. *Wingfoot Clan*, September 24, 1952, p. 3.
24. *Ibid.*, p. 1.
25. O'Reilly, p. 113.
26. Schetter, p. 620.
27. *The New York Times*, August 13, 1952, p. 19.
28. O'Reilly, p. 113.
29. *Ibid.*
30. *The New York Times*, August 17, 1952, p. 2.
31. O'Reilly, p. 113.
32. Schetter, p. 738.
33. *Wingfoot Clan*, August 20, 1952, p. 1.
34. 1955 Annual Report. p. 5, 21.
35. O'Reilly, p. 120.
36. 1958 Annual Report, p. 25.
37. O'Reilly, p. 113.
38. 1951 Annual Report, p. 1; Schetter, p. 608.
39. O'Reilly, p. 113.
40. *Ibid.*, p. 113.
41. Schetter, p. 608.
42. O'Reilly, p. 113.
43. 1956 Annual Report.
44. O'Reilly, p. 115.
45. 1958 Annual Report.
46. Scott Busby, interviewed by the author, January 16, 1997. Transcript, p. 10.
47. O'Reilly, p. 124.
48. *Ibid.*
49. *Wingfoot Clan*, January 16, 1952, p. 1.
50. Schetter, p. 673.
51. *Ibid.*, 671.
52. *Wingfoot Clan*, May 26, 1954, p. 3.
53. Schetter, p. 673.
54. *Ibid.*
55. O'Reilly, p. 118.
56. *Wingfoot Clan*, August 11, 1954, p. 1.
57. Schetter, p. 674.
58. Schetter, p. 674; *Wingfoot Clan*, August 11, 1954, p. 1.
59. *Wingfoot Clan*, August 11, 1954, p. 1.
60. *Wingfoot Clan*, October 6, 1954, p. 5.
61. *The New York Times*, September 11, 1954, p. 20; Schetter, p. 675.
62. O'Reilly, p. 118-119.
63. *Ibid.*, p. 108.
64. *Ibid.*
65. Schetter, p. 682.
66. O'Reilly, p. 109.
67. *The New York Times*, October 7, 1958, p. 51.
68. Schetter, p. 625.

69. *Ibid.*, p. 626.
70. O'Reilly, pp. 113-114.
71. *Ibid.*, p. 114.
72. *Wingfoot Clan*, March 24, 1954, p. 2.
73. 1954 Annual Report, p. 7.
74. Schetter, p. 796.
75. *Ibid.*, p. 703.
76. *Wingfoot Clan*, August 17, 1955, p. 1.
77. *Ibid.*
78. *Ibid.*
79. Schetter, p. 715.
80. *Ibid.*, p. 710.
81. *Ibid.*, p. 711.
82. *Ibid.*, p. 758.
83. *Wingfoot Clan*, October 9, 1957, p. 2.
84. O'Reilly, p. 120.
85. Schetter, p. 759.
86. *Akron Beacon Journal*, June 24, 1958, p. 1; O'Reilly, p. 120.
87. *Akron Beacon Journal*, June 24, 1958, p. 1.
88. *Ibid.*, p. 2.
89. *Ibid.*
90. *Ibid.*
91. *Ibid.*
92. *Wingfoot Clan*, June 11, 1958, p. 6.
93. O'Reilly, p. 129.
94. *Wingfoot Clan*, October 8, 1958, p. 2.
95. *Ibid.*
96. *Akron Beacon Journal*, October 7, 1958, p. 24.
97. P.W. Litchfield, *Industrial Voyage*, (Doubleday & Company, Garden City, New York, 1954), pp. 325-326.
98. *Akron Beacon Journal*, October 7, 1958, p. 24.

Chapter Twelve

1. Fred Steel, interviewed by the author, February 2, 1997. Transcript, pp. 28-29.
2. George Tindall, and David Shi, *America*, (W.W. Norton & Company, New York, New York, 1989), p. 864.
3. *The New York Times*, April 24, 1960, F3.
4. 1969 Annual Report, p. 3.
5. Maurice O'Reilly, *The Goodyear Story*, (The Benjamin Company, Elmsford, New York, 1983), p. 131.
6. Clyde Schetter, *History of Goodyear: 1898-1967*, unpublished. Goodyear archives, p. 800.
7. Steel interview, pp. 28-29.
8. *The New York Times*, August 11, 1968, p. 12.
9. O'Reilly, p. 130.
10. *The New York Times*, October 11, 1964, p. 3.
11. *Ibid.*
12. *The New York Times*, April 7, 1964, p. 43.
13. *The New York Times*, October 11, 1964, p. 3.
14. O'Reilly, p. 156.
15. *Ibid.*
16. *Ibid.*
17. Schetter, p. 901.
18. O'Reilly, p. 156.
19. Fred Kovac, *Tire Technology*, published by The Goodyear Tire & Rubber Company, 1978, p. 155.
20. 1960 Annual Report, p. 3; 1969 Annual Report, p. 3.
21. Bill Massey, interviewed by Karen Nitkin, January 20, 1997. Transcript, p. 9.

22. Schetter, p. 801.
23. Samir Gibara, interviewed by the author, September 19, 1996. Transcript, p. 8.
24. *Ibid.*
25. Sylvain Valensi, interviewed by the author, January 20, 1997. Transcript, p. 5.
26. O'Reilly, p. 144.
27. *Ibid.*
28. *Ibid.*
29. *Ibid.*, p. 145.
30. *Ibid.*, p. 146.
31. Schetter, p. 812.
32. O'Reilly, p. 147.
33. 1969 Annual Report, p. 6.
34. Schetter, p. 806.
35. O'Reilly, p. 147.
36. Schetter, p. 805-807.
37. George Tindall, and David Shi, *America*, (W.W. Norton & Company, New York, New York, 1989), p. 861.
38. Schetter, p. 807.
39. *Ibid.*
40. 1966 Annual Report, p. 4.
41. *The New York Times*, August 11, 1988, p. 12.
42. *Ibid.*
43. *Ibid.*
44. O'Reilly, 131; Schetter, p. 800.
45. *Ibid.*, p. 132.
46. *Ibid.*
47. Schetter, p. 801.
48. O'Reilly, p. 132-133.
49. Schetter, p. 801.
50. *Ibid.*
51. 1966 Annual Report, p. 4.
52. *Ibid.*
53. Schetter, p. 801.
54. 1963 Annual Report, p. 2.
55. Schetter, p. 913.
56. *Ibid.*, p. 913.
57. *Ibid.*, p. 916.
58. *Ibid.*, p. 918.
59. *The New York Times*, April 18, 1966, p. 43.
60. O'Reilly, p. 163.
61. *Ibid.*, p. 165.
62. *Ibid.*, pp. 164-166.
63. Walter Curtiss, interviewed by the author, January 16, 1997. Transcript, pp. 12-13.

Chapter Thirteen

1. Chuck Pilliod, interviewed by the author, September 17, 1996. Transcript, p. 11.
2. *The New York Times*, July 23, 1970, p. 39.
3. John J. Nevin, "The Bridgestone/Firestone Story," *California Management Review*, 1990, p. 116.
4. Maurice O'Reilly, *The Goodyear Story*, (The Benjamin Co., Elmsford, New York, 1983), p. 164.
5. Nevin, p. 115.
6. *Historical Highlights*, The Goodyear Tire & Rubber Company. Goodyear archives.
7. *Business Week*, March 28 1977, p. 43.
8. *Historical Highlights*,
9. *Ibid.*
10. O'Reilly, p. 170.

11. *Ibid*, pp. 170-171.
12. George Strickler, interviewed by the author, January 13, 1997. Transcript, pp. 11-12.
13. O'Reilly, p. 165.
14. *Ibid.*
15. *Ibid.*
16. *Ibid.*
17. *Ibid.*, p. 172.
18. *Ibid.*
19. *Ibid.*, p. 168.
20. *Ibid.*, pp. 166-167.
21. *Ibid.*, p. 166.
22. *Ibid.*, pp. 166-167.
23. *Historical Highlights.*
24. John Gerstenmaier, "Environmentalism—The Need For A Balanced Approach," *Akron Business and Economic Review*, October 1979, p. 14.
25. Gerstenmaier, p. 14.
26. *Ibid.*
27. James Whiteley, interviewed by the author, September 19, 1996. Transcript, p. 6.
28. Gerstenmaier, p. 14.
29. *Ibid.*
30. *Ibid.*
31. Carol Birkland, "Scrap Tire Disposal," *Fleet Equipment*, 1993, p. 31.
32. *Ibid.*
33. *Ibid.*
34. Gerstenmaier, 14.
35. *Ibid.*, p. 15.
36. *Ibid.*, pp. 15-16.
37. *Historical Highlights.*
38. O'Reilly, p. 173.
39. *Ibid.*
40. *Ibid.*, p. 175.
41. *Ibid.*, 176.
42. *Historical Highlights.*
43. *The New York Times*, August 24, 1975, p. 1.
44. Robert Mercer, interviewed by the author, February 22, 1997. Transcript, p. 15.
45. *Historical Highlights.*
46. Paul Gibson, "Goodyear Vs. Michelin." *Forbes*, August 7, 1978, p. 63.
47. *Ibid.*, p. 62.
48. John Perduyn, interviewed by the author, September 17, 1996. Transcript, p. 2.
49. Modern Office Procedures, January 1974, p. 35.
50. "Can The Sun Still Shine In Akron When It's Raining In Detroit?" *Financial World*, July 1974, p. 19.
51. *Financial World*, July, 1974, p. 19.
52. Ron Shinn, "Through the Wringer at Goodyear," *The New York Times*, May 24, 1981, p. 6.
53. *Historical Highlights.*
54. Fred Kovac, interviewed by the author, September 17, 1996. Transcript, p. 15.
55. Gary Miller, interviewed by the author, January 14, 1997. Transcript, p. 20.
56. *Ibid.*
57. Shinn, p. 6.
58. Robert Ball, "The Michelin Man Rolls Into Akron's Backyard." *Fortune*, December 1974, p. 143.

59. *Ibid.*
60. *Financial World*, July 1974, p. 19.
61. Ball, p. 138.
62. *Ibid.*
63. *Ibid.* p. 186.
64. *Ibid.* p. 138.
65. *Ibid.* p. 186.
66. Gibson, 63.
67. Gene Culler, interviewed by the author, January 14, 1997. Transcript, p. 5.
68. *Ibid.*, p. 7.
69. Pilliod interview, p. 11.
70. *Historical Highlights*, The Goodyear Tire & Rubber Company. Goodyear archives.
71. O'Reilly, p. 180.
72. *Historical Highlights.*
73. Shinn, p. 6; Ball, p. 138.
74. Pilliod interview, p. 11.
75. O'Reilly, p. 186.
76. H. Clay Orme, interviewed by the author, January 14, 1997. Transcript, pp. 6-7.
77. O'Reilly, p. 186.
78. Nevin, p. 116.
79. *Historical Highlights.*
80. O'Reilly, p. 183.
81. *Cleveland Plain Dealer*, October 21, 1976, p. D5.
82. O'Reilly, p. 185.
83. *Ibid.*
84. *Ibid.*
85. Shinn, p. 1.
86. Nevin, p. 123.
87. *Cleveland Plain Dealer*, September 14, 1977, p. D5; and February 24, 1977, p. C2.
88. "The Rubber Union's Rift Deepens," *Business Week*, October 30, 1978, p. 147.
89. *Business Week*, October 30, 1978, p. 147.
90. "No Give On Either Side in Rubber Talks," *Business Week*, March 28, 1977, pp. 43-44.
91. *Ibid.*, p. 44.
92. O'Reilly, p. 194.
93. *Ibid.*
94. Kenneth Labich, "The King of Tire Is Discontented," *Fortune* magazine, May 28, 1984, p. 67.
95. *Ibid.*
96. William Sharp, interviewed by the author, September 18, 1996. Transcript, p. 7.
97. Sharp interview, p. 7.
98. O'Reilly, p. 194.
99. Shinn, p. 1.
100. *Ibid.*
101. "The Big Layoffs Are Yet To Come," *Business Week*, December 10, 1979.
102. *Cleveland Plain Dealer*, June 8, 1980, p. 2E.
103. *Cleveland Plain Dealer*, January 11, 1978, p. D5.
104. O'Reilly, p. 196.
105. *Historical Highlights.*
106. Shinn, p. 6.
107. *Ibid.*
108. *Ibid.*
109. *Ibid.*
110. *Ibid.*

Chapter Fourteen

1. Al Unser, Jr., interviewed by the author, February 28, 1997. Transcript, p. 2.
2. William Neely, *Tire Wars*, (Aztex Corporation, Tucson, Arizona, 1993), p. 20.
3. *Ibid.*
4. Hugh Allen, *The House of Goodyear*, (The Corday & Gross Company, Cleveland, Ohio, 1949), p. 24.
5. Neely, p. 19.
6. *Ibid.*
7. Allen, p. 24.
8. Neely, p. 21.
9. Allen, pp. 26-27.
10. *Ibid.*, p. 28.
11. Neely, p. 25.
12. *Ibid.*, pp. 26-27.
13. "Automobile Racing Season 1919: Dedicated to the Drivers of Goodyear," booklet produced by The Goodyear Tire & Rubber Company, reprint edition June 1994, p. 9.
14. "The Beaming Smile of Goodyear's Corporate Face: Leo Mehl Interview," *Motoring News*, November, 1984. Reprint, p. 2.
15. "Goodyear's History in Formula One," booklet produced by The Goodyear Tire & Rubber Company, 1982, p. 3.
16. "Automobile Racing 1919 Season: Dedicated to the Drivers of Goodyear," booklet produced by The Goodyear Tire & Rubber Company, Reprint edition June 1994, pp. 18-9.
17. Neely, p. 25.
18. Automobile Racing Season 1919: Dedicated to the Drivers of Goodyear, p. 20.
19. Neely, p. 29; "Automobile Racing Season 1919: Dedicated to the Drivers of Goodyear," p. 12.
20. Neely, p. 35.
21. Goodyear News Bureau, Goodyear Racing Backgrounder, 1987 Racing Press Kit, Goodyear archives, p. 2.
22. *Ibid.*
23. *Ibid.*
24. Maurice O'Reilly, *The Goodyear Story*, (The Benjamin Company, Elmsford, New York, 1983), pp. 135-136.
25. *Ibid.*, p. 136.
26. Neely, p. 37.
27. *Ibid.*, pp. 37-38.
28. *Ibid*, p. 45.
29. *Ibid*, pp. 49-50.
30. O'Reilly, p. 137.
31. Goodyear News Service, 1960 Press kit.
32. O'Reilly, p. 1137.
33. *Ibid*, p. 136.
34. Goodyear News Service, 1960 Press kit.
35. Neely, p. 80.
36. Don Garlits, interviewed by the author, March 20, 1997. Transcript, p.5.
37. Neely, p. 80.
38. *Ibid.*, p. 90.
39. *Ibid.*, p. 91.

40. O'Reilly, p. 207.
41 Neely, p. 53.
42. *Ibid.*, p. 54.
43. *Independent Press Telegram*, August 30, 1959, sent from Long Beach, California.
44. *New York Herald Tribune*, October 7, 1959.
45. *Goodyear Triangle*, October 13, 1959, p. 1.
46. Goodyear internal memo from Trog Keller to Robert Masson, October 19, 1960, Taken from a conversation with Mickey and Judy Thompson.
47. Goodyear news release, August 11, 1960.
48. Goodyear news release, September 18, 1960.
49. *Goodyear Triangle*, September 13, 1960, p. 1.
50. O'Reilly, p. 138.
51. Leo Mehl, interviewed by the author, September 19, 1996. Transcript, p. 6.
52. *Ibid.*
53. O'Reilly, p. 137.
54. *Ibid.*
55. A.J. Foyt, William Neely, *My Life As America's Greatest Race Car Driver*, (Times Books, 1983), pp. 125-126.
56. Benny Parsons, interviewed by the author, March 19, 1997. Transcript, p. 1.
57. Dave Marcis, interviewed by Bonnie Bratton, March 13, 1997. Transcript, pp. 1-2.
58. Neely, p. 133.
59. *Akron Beacon Journal*, May 26, 1996, pp. C1, C3.
60. *Ibid.*
61. *Ibid.*
62. *Newsweek*, March 21, 1983.
63. Neely, p. 153.
64. 1995 Annual Report, taken from The Goodyear Tire & Rubber Company website: URL www.Goodyear.com/ar 1995/index.html.
65. Derek Bell, interviewed by Bonnie Bratton, March 25, 1997. Transcript, p. 2.
66. *Ibid.*
67. Sir Jack Brabham, interviewed by the author, February 25, 1997. Transcript, p. 2.
68. *Newsweek* March 21, 1983. Reprint.
69. Jeff Gordon, interviewed by Bonnie Bratton, March 24, 1997. Transcript, p. 2.
70. Bobby Rahal, interviewed by Bonnie Bratton, March 24, 1997. Transcript, p. 3.
71. Mario Andretti, interviewed by the author, February 28, 1997. Transcript, p. 4.
72. Robert Dyson, interviewed by the author, February 24, 1997. Transcript, pp. 4-5.
73. Al Unser, Jr., interviewed by the author, February 28, 1997. Transcript, p. 2.
74. Rick Mears, interviewed by the author, February 28, 1997. Transcript, p. 3.
75. Gordon interview, transcript, p. 2.
76. Stu Grant, interviewed by the author, September 19, 1996. Transcript, p. 22.
77. 1995 Annual Report.
78. Neely, p. 150.
79. Jim Barnett, interviewed by the author. Transcript, p. 41.
80. *Ibid.*
81. *Newsweek*, March 21, 1983. Reprint.
82. *Ibid.*
83. *Akron Beacon Journal*, May 26, 1996, p. C3.

Chapter Fourteen Sidebar 1

1. A.J. Foyt, William Neely, *My Life As America's Greatest Race Car Driver*, (Times Books, 1983), pp. 16-17.
2. *Ibid.*
3. *Ibid.*
4. *Ibid.*
5. A.J. Foyt, interviewed by the author, March 25, 1997. Transcript, p. 3.
6. Darrell Waltrip, interviewed by the author, March 1997. Transcript, p. 7-8.
7. *Ibid.*
8. Leo Mehl, interviewed by the author, September 19, 1996. Transcript, p. 22.
9. Mario Andretti, interviewed by the author, February 28, 1997. Transcript, pp. 2-3.
10. Don Prudhomme, interviewed by Bonnie Bratton, March 1997. Transcript, pp. 3-4.
11. *Ibid.*

Chapter Fourteen Sidebar 2

1. Maurice O'Reilly, *The Goodyear Story*, (The Benjamin Company, Elmsford, New York, 1983), pp. 137-139.
2. *Ibid.*, pp. 138-139.

Chapter Fifteen

1. *Washington Post*, November 15, 1986, p. F2.
2. Robert Mercer, interviewed by the author, February 22, 1997. Transcript, p. 38.
3. Maurice O'Reilly, *The Goodyear Story*, (The Benjamin Company, Elmsford, New York, 1983), p. 203.
4. *Ibid.*, p. 204.
5. *Ibid.*
6. *Ibid.*, p. 203.
7. *Ibid.*, p. 204.
8. *Ibid.*, p. 205.
9. *Ibid.*
10. *Ibid.*, pp. 198, 208.
11. *Ibid.*, p. 208.
12. *Ibid.*
13. *Ibid.*, p. 209.
14. Jerry C. Butcher, and Phil S. Ensor, "A Tiremaker Retreads Its Corporate Structure." *Mechanical Engineering*, April 1988, p. 46.
15. Butcher and Ensor, p. 47.
16. Dennis Dick, interviewed by Alex Lieber, January 23, 1997. Transcript, p. 12.
17. "How Goodyear Forecast A Great Decade," *American Demographics*, March 1995, p. 39.
18. *Ibid.*
19. *Ibid.*
20. *Ibid.*
21. *Ibid.*
22. *Ibid.*
23. *Ibid.*
24. O'Reilly, p. 214.
25. *Ibid.*, p. 216.
26. *Ibid.*, p. 201.

27. *Ibid.*
28. Chuck Pilliod, interviewed by the author, September 17, 1996. Transcript, p. 16.
29. *Akron Beacon Journal*, November 30, 1986, p. B5.
30. Geoffrey Wansell, "Sir James Takes on Goodyear," *Business Month*, July 1987, p. 47.
31. *Akron Beacon Journal*, November 30, 1986, p. B5.
32. *Ibid.*, p. B3.
33. O'Reilly, p. 216.
34. *The New York Times*, November 4, 1986, p. D9.
35. *Ibid.*, p. D1.
36. George Hargreaves, interviewed by the author, January 20, 1997. p. 17.
37. Dr. Nissim Calderon, interviewed by the author, September 18, 1996. Transcript, p. 6.
38. Calderon interview, transcript, p. 12.
39. *Akron Beacon Journal*, November 30, 1986, B1.
40. *Ibid.*
41. *Ibid.*
42. *Ibid.*
43. *Personal Investor*, January 1988, p. 8.
44. *Akron Beacon Journal*, November 30, 1986, p. B3.
45. *Ibid.*, p. B1.
46. Geoffrey Wansell, "Sir James Takes on Goodyear." *Business Month*, July 1987, p. 47.
47. *Akron Beacon Journal*, November 30, 1986, p. B3.
48. *Ibid.*
49. *Ibid.*, p. B4.
50. *Ibid.*
51. *Ibid.*, pp. B4-B5.
52. *Ibid.*, p. B3.
53. *Ibid.*
54. Robert Mercer, interviewed by the author, February 22, 1997. Transcript, p. 38.
55. *Ibid.*, pp. B2-3.
56. Geoffrey Wansell, "Sir James Takes on Goodyear." *Business Month*, July 1987, p. 49.
57. *Akron Beacon Journal*, November 30, 1986, pp. B7.
58. *Ibid.*, p. B5.
59. *Ibid.*, p. B7.
60. *Ibid.*, p. B8.
61. *Ibid.*
62. *Ibid.*
63. *Ibid.*
64. Mercer interview, p. 42.
65. *Ibid.*
66. *Ibid.*, p. B7.
67. *Ibid.*, p. B6.
68. *Ibid.*
69. *Ibid.*
70. *The Wall Street Journal*, November 7, 1986; *Akron Beacon Journal*, November 30, 1986, p. B6.
71. *The Wall Street Journal*, November 7, 1986.
72. *Akron Beacon Journal*, November 30, 1986, B8.
73. *Ibid.*

74. *Washington Post*, November 15, 1986, p. F2.
75. Geoffrey Wansell, "Sir James Takes on Goodyear," *Business Month*, July 1987, p. 49.
76. *Ibid.*
77. *Akron Beacon Journal*, November 30, 1986, p. B8.
78. Testimony of Sir James Goldsmith as presented Tuesday, November 18, 1986, before the Monopolies and Commercial Law Subcommittee of the House Judiciary Committee. File of Jim Boyazis.
79. *Akron Beacon Journal*, November 30, 1986, B8.
80. *Ibid.*
81. *Ibid.*
82. *Ibid.*, B9.
83. Goodyear press release, November 20, 1986.
84. *Ibid.*
85. *Ibid.*
86. Letter from Robert Mercer, dated November 21, 1986. File of Jim Boyazis.
87. Randy Welch, "States Checkmate Corporate Raiders," *State Legislatures*, January 1988, p. 14.
88. *Ibid.*
89. *Ibid.*
90. *Akron Beacon Journal*, November 30, 1986, p. B8.
91. *Ibid.*, p. B9.
92. Mercer interview, transcript, p. 48.
93. Jim Boyazis, interviewed by the author, September 17, 1996. Transcript, p. 14.
94. *Ibid.*
95. Richard Adante, interviewed by the author, January 14, 1997. Transcript, p. 17.
96. *Historical Highlights*, The Goodyear Tire & Rubber Company. Goodyear archives.
97. "The Easy Wit and Iron Will of Goodyear's Bob Mercer," *Business Week*, March 7, 1988, p. 28.
98. *Akron Beacon Journal*, November 39, 1986, p. B9.

Chapter Sixteen

1. Stanley Gault, interviewed by the author, September 18, 1996. Transcript, p. 15.
2. *Historical Highlights*, The Goodyear Tire & Rubber Company. Goodyear archives.
3. *Ibid.*
4. "Goodyear Feels the Heat," *Business Week*, March 7, 1988, p. 27.
5. *Ibid.*
6. *Historical Highlights*.
7. Joe Gingo, interviewed by the author, January 14, 1997. Transcript, p. 19
8. *Historical Highlights*.
9. *Ibid.*
10. Lee Fiedler, interviewed by the author, September 19, 1996. Transcript, p. 18.
11. *Historical Highlights*.
12. *Ibid.*
13. Testimony of Donald DeScenza, analyst with Nomura Securities, as presented November 18, 1986, before the Monopolies and

Commercial Law subcommittee of the House Judiciary Committee. File of Jim Boyazis.

14. *Forbes*, January 7, 1991, p. 40.
15. "How Well Can Goodyear Take the Bumps Ahead?" *Business Week*, October 15, 1990, p. 31.
16. *Forbes*, January 7, 1991, 40.
17. *Ibid.*
18. *Akron Beacon Journal*, June 9, 1991, A6.
19. "How Well Can Goodyear Take the Bumps Ahead?" p. 31.
20. "The Easy Wit and Iron Will of Goodyear's Bob Mercer," *Business Week*, March 7, 1988, p. 28.
21. Tom Barrett, interviewed by the author, March 18, 1997. Transcript, p. 22.
22. "How Well Can Goodyear Take the Bumps Ahead?" *Business Week*, October 15, 1990, p. 31.
23. Barrett interview, p. 12.
24. "How Well Can Goodyear Take the Bumps Ahead?" p. 31.
25. *Forbes*, January 7, 1991, p. 40.
26. *Fortune*, September 7, 1992, p. 71.
27. *Ibid.*
28. Barrett interview, p. 12.
29. *Akron Beacon Journal*, June 9, 1991, p. A6.
30. Gault interview, p. 4.
31. *Ibid.*, p. 3.
32. "Hometown Hero and Turnaround Champion." American Management Association August 1994, p. 8.
33. Stanley Gault biography, provided by Goodyear, July 1996.
34. *Cleveland Plain Dealer*, June 10, 1991, p. 6C.
35. "Hometown Hero and Turnaround Champion," *American Management Association*, August 1994, p. 10.
36. Nancy Hass, "CEO of the Year: Stanley Gault of Goodyear," *Financial World*, March 31, 1992, p. 26.
37. Gault interview, p. 15.
38. *Ibid.*, p. 16.
39. Hass, p. 26.
40. *Ibid.*
41. *Cleveland Plain Dealer*, December 38, 1991, p. 5F.
42. Hass, p. 27.
43. *The New York Times*, June 9, 1991, C1.
44. Peter Nulty, "The Bounce Is Back at Goodyear," *Fortune*, September 7, 1992, p. 71.
45. Nancy Hass, "CEO of the Year: Stanley Gault of Goodyear," p. 30.
46. Peter Nulty, "The Bounce Is Back at Goodyear," *Fortune*, September 7, 1992, p. 71.
47. Lloyd Stoyer, "Who Is Stan Gault? From Paperboy to CEO," *MTD*, March 1992, p. 29.
48. Stanley C. Gault, "Marketing in the Nineties," *A.N.A./The Advertiser*, Winter, 1992, p. 13.
49. Jim Boyazis, interviewed by the author, September 17, 1996. Transcript, p. 12.
50. "Goodyear May Be Getting Some Traction at Last," *Business Week*, October 7, 1991, p. 38.
51. Nulty, p. 70.
52. *Ibid.*, p. 72.
53. Gault, "Marketing in the Nineties," p. 18.
54. *Historical Highlights*.
55. Gault interview, pp. 20-21.
56. *Historical Highlights*.
57. Lubove, Seth. "The Last Bastion." *Forbes* February 14, 1994, p. 57.
58. Robert Hekis, interviewed by the author, January 13, 1997. Transcript, p. 20.
59. Seth Lubove, "The Last Bastion," *Forbes*, February 14, 1994, p. 57.
60. *Ibid.*
61. Hoyt Wells, interviewed by the author, September, 18, 1996. Transcript, p. 32.
62. Mike Roney, interviewed by Karen Nitkin, January 20, 1997. Transcript, p. 3.
63. John Polhemus, interviewed by the author, January 20, 1997. Transcript, p. 14.
64. "And Fix That Flat Before You Go, Stanley." *Business Week*, January 16, 1995, p. 35.
65. Gault interview, p. 17.
66. Gault, "Marketing In the Nineties," p. 17.
67. "And Fix That Flat Before You Go, Stanley." p. 35.
68. Gault, "Marketing In the Nineties," p. 12.
69. Gail Dutton, "Who Will Run the Company?" *Management Review*, August 1996, p. 22.
70. 1995 Annual Report.
71. Dutton, p. 22.
72. Samir Gibara, interviewed by the author, September 19, 1996. Transcript, p. 23.
73. *Ibid.*
74. *Ibid.*
75. *Ibid.*, p. 29.
76. *Business Week*, March 4, 1996; 1995 Annual Report.
77. 1995 Annual Report.
78. *Historical Highlights*.
79. Joe Gingo, interviewed by the author, January 14, 1997. Transcript, p. 32.
80. *Ibid.*
81. Goodyear press release, 1996-1997.
81. Gibara interview, transcript, pp. 30-31.
82. 1995 Annual Report.
83. Jesse Williams, interviewed by the author, September 18, 1996. Transcript, pp. 11-12.
84. Randy Browning, interviewed by the author, January 14, 1997. Transcript, pp. 14-15.
85. Michael Burns, interviewed by the author, January 14, 1997. Transcript, pp. 16-17.
86. Rich Steichen, interviewed by the author, January 20, 1997. Transcript, p. 10.
87. *Ibid.*
88. *Ibid.*
89. 1995 Annual Report.
90. *Ibid.*
91. Gibara interview, transcript, pp. 30-31.

INDEX